Animal Dignity

ALSO AVAILABLE FROM BLOOMSBURY

The History of Animals: A Philosophy, by Oxana Timofeeva
The Pornography of Meat: New and Updated Edition,
by Carol J. Adams
Ecofeminism: Feminist Intersections with Other Animals and the Earth, edited by Carol J. Adams and Lori Gruen
Animal Rights Law, by Raffael N. Fasel and Sean C. Butler
Why Climate Breakdown Matters, by Rupert Read

Animal Dignity

*Philosophical Reflections
on Non-Human Existence*

**Edited by
Melanie Challenger**

BLOOMSBURY ACADEMIC
LONDON • NEW YORK • OXFORD • NEW DELHI • SYDNEY

BLOOMSBURY ACADEMIC
Bloomsbury Publishing Plc
50 Bedford Square, London, WC1B 3DP, UK
1385 Broadway, New York, NY 10018, USA
29 Earlsfort Terrace, Dublin 2, Ireland

BLOOMSBURY, BLOOMSBURY ACADEMIC and the Diana logo are trademarks of Bloomsbury Publishing Plc

First published in Great Britain 2023

Copyright © Melanie Challenger and Contributors, 2023

Melanie Challenger has asserted her right under the Copyright, Designs and Patents Act, 1988, to be identified as Editor of this work.

The Florida Panther © 2021 Angela Manno, from her series *Sacred Icons of Threatened and Endangered Species*. www.angelamanno.com

For legal purposes the Acknowledgements on p. xviii constitute an extension of this copyright page.

Cover design: Ben Anslow
The Florida Panther © 2021 Angela Manno, from her series *Sacred Icons of Threatened and Endangered Species*. www.angelamanno.com

All rights reserved. No part of this publication may be reproduced or transmitted in any form or by any means, electronic or mechanical, including photocopying, recording, or any information storage or retrieval system, without prior permission in writing from the publishers.

Bloomsbury Publishing Plc does not have any control over, or responsibility for, any third-party websites referred to or in this book. All internet addresses given in this book were correct at the time of going to press. The author and publisher regret any inconvenience caused if addresses have changed or sites have ceased to exist, but can accept no responsibility for any such changes.

A catalogue record for this book is available from the British Library.

A catalog record for this book is available from the Library of Congress.

ISBN: HB: 978-1-3503-3166-2
PB: 978-1-3503-3167-9
ePDF: 978-1-3503-3169-3
eBook: 978-1-3503-3168-6

Typeset by RefineCatch Limited, Bungay, Suffolk

To find out more about our authors and books visit www.bloomsbury.com and sign up for our newsletters.

Contents

List of Illustrations ix
List of Contributors x
Foreword, Memories of Greybeard, *Dr. Jane Goodall, DBE* xiv
Acknowledgements xviii

Introduction

Prelude I: Frogs
   Simon Rich 3

Beginning with Dignity
   Melanie Challenger 5

Part One **Defining the Concept: *What is Dignity?***

Summary 23

Prelude II: 33,000 Birds
   Jonathan Safran Foer 25

1 A Place for Animals? Rethinking the History of Human Dignity
   Remy Debes 33

2 Philosophical Approaches to Dignity, and their Applicability to Non-Human Animals, *Suzy Killmister* 49

Part Two Approaches to Dignity: *What are the Grounds for Animal Dignity?*

Summary 63

Prelude III: Ways of Seeing an Octopus, *Sy Montgomery* 67

3 On Standing *Harriet Ritvo* 79

4 Wild Dignity *Lori Gruen* 83

5 Dignity in Dogs *Alexandra Horowitz* 91

6 The Heart of the Scorpion *Kathleen Dean Moore* 97

7 'An Old Joy': Ways of Attending to Dignity *Deborah Slicer* 107

8 Dignity in Their World *Danielle Celermajer* 115

Part Three Forms of Dignity: *Are There Separate Cultural Conceptions of Animal Dignity?*

Summary 125

Prelude IV: Lead Me into Thy Nest
Nelson Bukamba 129

9 Killing Dogs in Zambia: Prospects for *Ubuntu*
Julius Kapembwa 133

10 Let All Beings Be Happy: Dignity and *Prana*, the Vital Force in Indian Thought
Meera Baindur 145

11 Two-Eyed Seeing: Animal Dignity through Indigenous and Western Lenses
Cristina Eisenberg and Michael Paul Nelson 155

12 Dignity in Non-Humans: A Theological Perspective
Michael J. Reiss 165

Part Four Dignity in Practice: *What Work Can Animal Dignity Do?*

Summary 177

Prelude V: The Last Safe Habitat
Craig Santos Perez 179

13 Extending the Capabilities Approach to Non-Human Animals
Martha Nussbaum 181

14 Beyond Animal Welfare: Respecting Animal Dignity in Continental Law
Eva Bernet Kempers 191

15 Animal Dignity as More-Than-Welfarism
Visa A. J. Kurki 201

16 Dignity: A Concept for All Species
Lori Marino 209

17 Four Legs Good, Three Legs Bad?
The Aesthetics of Animal Dignity
Samantha Hurn 219

18 Looking Up to Animals and Other Beings:
What the Fishes Taught Us
Becca Franks, Christine Webb, Monica Gagliano, and Barbara Smuts 229

19 Dignity, Respect, and the Education of Biologists
David George Haskell 239

Afterthoughts

Prelude VI: Characteristics of Life
Camille T. Dungy 249

Ways Forward
Melanie Challenger 251

Index 267

Illustrations

The following images are reproduced with gratitude. We would like to extend our special thanks to the photojournalist, Jo-Anne McArthur, who provided many of the images. She is the founder of **We Animals Media**, which provides quality animal photojournalism in support of the wellbeing of non-human animals and offers many images licensed but Royalty Free. See https://weanimalsmedia.org/

1	David Greybeard.	xvi
2	Wild frog.	13
3	Chicken unable to stand.	26
4	Bear in zoo.	57
5	Duke.	68
6	Octopus.	72
7	Elephant, close up.	85
8	Dog.	93
9	Scorpion.	104
10	Guard bear.	111
11	Dany and Jimmy.	118
12	Wenka.	130
13	Bull in Varanasi, India.	146
14	Wolf up close.	158
15	Polar bear at Zoo.	171
16	Calf suckling concrete.	206
17	Orca.	213
18	Moon.	221
19	Koi fish swimming.	235
20	Turtle hearts.	242
21	Hawaiian tree snail.	250

Contributors

Meera Baindur is Associate Professor and Program Head of India Studies at the School of Liberal Arts and Sciences at RV University, Bangalore. She works at the intersection of Indian Intellectual Thought, Culture, and Environment.

Eva Bernet Kempers is a postdoc at the Animal & Law Chair of the University of Antwerp in Belgium and Junior Research Associate at the Cambridge Centre for Animal Rights Law. Her research focuses on the legal status of animals in continental law.

Nelson Bukamba is a wildlife veterinarian in Uganda with an interest in zoonoses prevention and wildlife conservation. He specializes in wild great ape behaviour, health management, and epidemiological research.

Danielle Celermajer is Professor of Sociology and Criminology at the University of Sydney, Deputy Director of the Sydney Environment Institute, Australia, and lead of the Multispecies Justice project. She is the author of *Summertime: Reflections on a Vanishing Future* (2021).

Melanie Challenger is a writer and broadcaster on environmental history, philosophy of science, and bioethics. She is a Vice President of the RSPCA and Deputy Co-Chair of the Nuffield Council on Bioethics. Her most recent book is *How to Be Animal: What it means to be human* (2021).

Remy Debes is Professor and Chair of Philosophy at the University of Memphis. He is the editor of *Dignity: A History* (2017) and Editor-in-Chief of *The Southern Journal of Philosophy*.

Camille T. Dungy is Distinguished Professor of English at Colorado State University. She is the author of several books, including *Trophic Cascade* (2017) and *Soil: The Story of a Black Mother's Garden* (2023).

Cristina Eisenberg is Associate Dean for Inclusive Excellence and Director of Tribal Initiatives at Oregon State University in the College of Forestry, where she is the director of the Indigenous Natural Resource Office and the Traditional Ecological Knowledge (TEK) Lab. She is of mixed Raramuri and Western Apache heritage.

Becca Franks is Assistant Professor of Environmental Studies at New York University, where she studies animal behaviour, aquatic animal welfare, quantitative methods, and human–animal relationships.

Monica Gagliano is Research Associate Professor in Evolutionary Ecology at the Biological Intelligence Lab, Southern Cross University, Australia.

Jane Goodall, DBE, is Founder of the Jane Goodall Institute and UN Messenger of Peace. She is a world-renowned ethologist and activist known for her ground-breaking studies of wild chimpanzees in Gombe Stream National Park, Tanzania.

Lori Gruen is the William Griffin Professor of Philosophy at Wesleyan University in CT where she coordinates Wesleyan Animal Studies. Her books include *Entangled Empathy* (2015), *Animal Crisis* (2022, with Alice Crary), and *Ethics and Animals* (2nd edn, 2021).

David George Haskell is William R. Kenan Jr. Professor of Biology at The University of the South. He is the author of the books *The Forest Unseen* (2012), *The Songs of Trees* (2017), and *Sounds Wild and Broken* (2022).

Alexandra Horowitz is a Senior Research Fellow and Director of the Dog Cognition Lab at Barnard College, USA, where she also teaches seminars in canine cognition and audio storytelling. She is the author of *Inside of a Dog: What Dogs See, Smell, and Know* (2009) and three other books, most recently *The Year of the Puppy: How Dogs Become Themselves* (2022).

Samantha Hurn is Associate Professor in Anthropology, Programme Director for the MA and PhD programmes in Anthrozoology, and Director of the Exeter Anthrozoology as Symbiotic Ethics (EASE) working group at the University of Exeter, UK.

Julius Kapembwa is a Lecturer in the Department of Philosophy and Applied Ethics at the University of Zambia. He researches on animal ethics, especially wild animals, and social ethics.

Suzy Killmister is a Senior Lecturer in the Philosophy Department at Monash University. Her core research interests are human rights, dignity, and autonomy, and her most recent book is *Contours of Dignity* (2020).

Visa A. J. Kurki is Associate Professor of Jurisprudence at the University of Helsinki. He works on animal law and personhood, and his work has been used in several animal rights trials in the United States.

Lori Marino is a neuroscientist and scholar-advocate for other animals. She is currently the President of the Whale Sanctuary Project and adjunct professor in Animal Studies at New York University.

Kathleen Dean Moore is the former Distinguished Professor of Environmental Philosophy at Oregon State University. The prize-winning author of a dozen books, she left academia to write about the moral urgency of action on the climate and extinction crises. Her most recent work is *Earth's Wild Music* (2021).

Sy Montgomery is the author of more than thirty books about animals, including bestsellers *The Good Good Pig* (2006), *The Soul of an Octopus* (2015), and the picture book, *Becoming a Good Creature* (2020).

Michael Paul Nelson is Professor of Environmental Ethics and Philosophy at Oregon State University. He is the author of more than 200 essays and articles in environmental ethics, and several books, most notably *Moral Ground: Ethical Action for a Planet in Peril* (2010, co-edited with Kathleen Dean Moore).

Martha Nussbaum is Ernst Freund Distinguished Service Professor of Law and Ethics at the University of Chicago. She is the author of numerous books, most recently *Justice for Animals: Our Collective Responsibility* (2023).

Craig Santos Perez is an Indigenous Pacific Islander from Guam. He is the author of six books of poetry and the co-editor of six anthologies.

Michael J. Reiss is Professor of Science Education at UCL, President of the International Society for Science and Religion, and a member of the Nuffield Council on Bioethics.

Simon Rich is an American humourist, screenwriter, and author. He is the author of the novel *What in God's Name* (2012) and the collections *Spoiled Brats* (2014) and *The World According to Simon Rich* (2016).

Harriet Ritvo is the Arthur J. Conner Professor of History Emeritus at the Massachusetts Institute of Technology, Cambridge, USA.

Jonathan Safran Foer is an internationally best-selling American novelist and nonfiction author. His nonfiction works include *Eating Animals* (2009) and *We are the Weather: Saving the Planet Begins at Breakfast* (2019).

Deborah Slicer is Professor Emerita with the University of Montana's Department of Philosophy. She has published on Animal Studies for over three decades.

Barbara Smuts is Professor Emerita, University of Michigan, and studies dog social relationships and how science needs to change to promote core values of animal well-being and preserve biodiversity more effectively.

Christine Webb is a Lecturer in the Department of Evolutionary Biology, Harvard University, Cambridge, USA. She is a primatologist whose latest work engages critically with the anthropocentric biases that affect the way we approach primatology, science, and our relationship with the natural world.

Foreword
Memories of Greybeard
Dr. Jane Goodall, DBE

When I think back to my early days in Gombe, and the chimpanzees I knew so well, one of them stands out – I named him David Greybeard. He was the first individual who began to lose his fear of me. And it was he who showed me, on that never to be forgotten day, that chimpanzees can use and make tools. Back then, in the early 1960s, science believed that this was unique to the human animal: We were defined as 'Man the Toolmaker'.

David was breaking off grass stems and carefully pushing them down into openings into a termite mound and picking off the insects who were clinging on with their jaws trying to defend their nest. And sometimes he picked a leafy twig and had to remove the leaves to create a suitable tool, the primitive beginnings of tool *making* – modifying a natural object to make it suitable for a specific purpose. It was David, too, from whom I learned that chimpanzees sometimes hunt and eat meat.

David Greybeard was special. Because he came to trust the strange white ape who had so suddenly appeared in the forest, he helped me to get closer to the other chimpanzees. Because he sat calmly as I approached a group, the others, who were clearly nervous, seemed ready to run, but it was as though they looked from me to David and back and realized I could not be so dangerous after all.

David was a leader. He was not the top ranking or alpha male of the community – that was his close friend Goliath. But because he was so calm and tolerant, youngsters and low-ranking individuals often ran to him for reassurance. And he nearly always calmed them by gently patting or embracing them. I often saw him walking through the forest followed by a trail of adolescent or other low-ranking individuals.

It wasn't until I got to university to do a PhD in ethology that I began to understand the reductionist attitude of science towards other-than-human animals. As I had never been to college, I had no idea that I should have given my 'subjects' numbers, not names. Or that I couldn't talk about their personalities, minds, or emotions as those were unique to the human animal. In fact, I was considered guilty of the sin of anthropomorphizing – attributing human characteristics to non-human animals. Fortunately, I had a wonderful teacher when I was a child who had taught me that in this respect the scientists were wrong – and that was my dog, Rusty. Anyone who has had a meaningful relationship with an animal knows that we are not the only beings with personalities, minds, and emotions. Nor are we the only sentient animals. The difference between us and other animals, as Charles Darwin pointed out, is one of degree, not kind.

I was shocked to find that I should not even give the chimpanzees the dignity of their (very obvious) sex – in my first scientific article, submitted to *Nature*, the editor struck out all references to 'he', 'she' and 'who' and substituted 'it' and 'which'. I was enraged – crossed out every 'it' and 'which' and underlined my original wording – which made it into print. It was my first victory.

Since that time, behaviours once thought unique to us have been observed in many species. It's as though the chimpanzees, who share 98.6 per cent of the composition of our DNA, broke down the barrier that science and many religions had created separating humans from all other animals. Now there have been ever more studies proving that the only fundamental difference is the explosive development of the human intellect and a language that enables us to teach about things not present, plan for a distant future and discuss problems to find solutions. Today there is research into culture, grief, depression, sense of humour, insight, imagination, empathy – and now dignity – in many different species.

The old superior and arrogant attitude towards animals that considers them as mere 'things' robs animals of their dignity. But it was never confined to science. Elephants in the wild seem, to me, the most dignified of creatures. Yet when they are trained to perform in a circus, to sit on a stool and do other degrading tricks, I feel they are robbed of that dignity. Male gorillas often appear dignified in the wild, as they sit calmly feeding, surrounded by their females and young. Yet I knew a gorilla in a very small, bare concrete cage, so crazed with boredom he was reduced to poking a straw into the urine that collected beyond his prison bars, then sucking it. Inventive, but hardly dignified. And I hate to even think about the billions of farm animals bred for food, crowded into tiny spaces with no respect for them as individuals, yet each one capable of feeling despair, fear, and pain.

This book presents scholarly opinions and examples that argue for the appropriateness of attributing the concept of dignity to non-human animals. It is a fascinating and timely contribution to our ever-expanding understanding of the true nature of the beings with whom we share – or should share – our planet.

But let me return once more to David Greybeard and to an incident, from those early days, that is still vivid in my mind. I was following him one day, as he wandered alone through the forest. I got tangled up

Figure 1 David Greybeard, credit Jane Goodall Institute / Hugo van Lawick.

when he moved through a patch of thorny undergrowth, and I thought I had lost him. But when I finally got through, there he was sitting – and looking back almost as though he was waiting for me. Perhaps he was. I sat down, near him, and saw the bright red fruit of an oil nut palm on the ground. I picked it up and held it towards him on the palm of my hand. He turned his face away. I inched my hand closer. He turned back and, looking directly into my eyes, reached out, took the nut, and dropped it. Then he very gently squeezed my fingers – which is how a chimpanzee may reassure a nervous subordinate.

In that moment we communicated using a gesture that may have existed in our common ancestor, some six million years ago. I understood he didn't want the nut but realized that I meant well. And I was reassured by that gentle pressure of his fingers. Then he lay and closed his eyes – and I sat there quietly amazed and deeply moved by an interaction that I shall never forget.

Acknowledgements

We would like to thank the following for permission to reprint or adapt excerpts of prior work:

'Frogs' is reproduced from *The World According to Simon Rich* (2016) by permission of Simon Rich/Serpent's Tale.

'33,000 birds' is an excerpt from *Eating Animals* (2009) by Jonathan Safran Foer, reprinted by permission of Little, Brown, an imprint of Hachette Book Group, Inc.

'Ways of Seeing an Octopus' by Sy Montgomery is an adaptation of her prior essay, 'Deep Intellect', which appeared in the Nov/Dec 2011 issue of *Orion Magazine*.

'Wild Dignity' by Lori Gruen is a reworking of material that is found in *Ethics and Animals: An Introduction* (2021) published by Cambridge University Press and 'Dignity, Captivity, and an Ethics of Sight' in *The Ethics of Captivity* (Gruen (ed), 2014) published by Oxford University Press.

'Dignity in Their World' by Danielle Celermajer includes some material reworked from *Summertime: Reflections on a Vanishing Future* (2021) published by Penguin Books Australia.

'The Last Safe Habitat' by Craig Santos Perez, in *Habitat Threshold*, Omnidawn Publishing, 2020. Used by permission of the author.

'Extending the Capabilities Approach to Non-Human Animals' by Martha Nussbaum is taken from a section of *Justice for Animals: Our Collective Responsibility* (2023), reproduced by permission of Simon & Schuster.

'Characteristics of Life' by Camille T. Dungy from *Trophic Cascade*, © 2017 Camille T. Dungy. Published by Wesleyan University Press, Middletown, CT. Used by permission.

Introduction

PRELUDE I
Frogs
Simon Rich

'Hey, can I ask you something? Why do human children dissect us?'
'It's part of their education. They cut open our bodies in school and write reports about their findings.'
'Huh. Well, I guess it could be worse, right? I mean, at least we're not dying in vain.'
'How do you figure?'
'Well, our deaths are furthering the spread of knowledge. It's a huge sacrifice we're making, but at least some good comes out of it.'
'Let me show you something.'
'What's this?'
'It's a frog-dissection report.'
'Who wrote it?'
'A fourteen-year-old human from New York City. Some kid named Simon.'
(Flipping through it.) 'This is it? This is the whole thing?'
'Uh-huh.'
'Geez. It doesn't look like he put a lot of time into this.'
'Look at the diagram on the last page.'
'Oh, my God . . . it's so crude. It's almost as if he wasn't even looking down at the paper while he was drawing it. Like he was watching TV or something.'

---

* 'Frogs' is reproduced from *The World According to Simon Rich* (2016) by permission of Simon Rich/Serpent's Tale.

'Read the conclusion.'
'"In conclusion, frogs are a scientific wonder of biology." What does that even mean?'
'It doesn't mean anything.'
'Why are the margins so big?'
'He was trying to make it look as if he had written five pages, even though he had only written four.'
'He couldn't come up with one more page of observations about our dead bodies?'
'I guess not.'
'This paragraph looks like it was copied straight out of an encyclopaedia. I'd be shocked if he retained any of this information.'
'Did you see that he spelled "science" wrong in the heading?'
'Whoa . . . I missed that. That's incredible.'
'He didn't even bother to run it through spell-check.'
'Who did he dissect?'
'Harold.'
'Betsy's husband? Jesus. So, this is why Harold was killed. To produce this . . . "report."'
(Nods.) 'This is why his life was taken from him.'
(Long pause.)
'Well, at least it has a cover sheet.'
'Yeah. The plastic's a nice touch.'

Beginning with Dignity
Melanie Challenger

In the words of E. B. White, the author of beloved children's books, *Charlotte's Web* and *Stuart Little*, 'Humour can be dissected, as a frog can' (White and White, 1941). Laughter and comedy often puncture power, disrupting the status quo (Morreall, 1981: 55–70). But for humour to work, there must be sufficient shared meaning in the words and concepts for most people to get the joke.

Simon Rich's humorous sketch, which opens this book of philosophical reflections, turns on an idea of dignity we can all grasp. In the story, we have two frogs pondering the degradations that follow from the fact that they are classroom specimens, kept alive only until they will be used as dissection models. At first, their predicament doesn't seem so bad. They die nobly 'to further the spread of knowledge.' But this is swiftly undercut by recognition of the lacklustre reports handed in by the children. One child makes the margins bigger to pass off a slight effort. 'He didn't even bother to run it through spell-check,' one of the frogs notes wryly.

At one level, the humour derives from anthropomorphism. We all know frogs don't chat together about human inventions like 'spell-check'. Nor do they give one another names like 'Betsy' and 'Harold'. The absurdity of their endearing, humanlike quality carries with it just the faintest bite of human exceptionalism. We could argue that the joke is on the frogs because they're not smart enough to get the joke in the first place.

Yet Rich subverts this with his punchline. The gratitude the frogs express for the plastic sheeting covering the children's dissection reports – 'a nice touch' – is perfect pathos. It is a *pathetic* sentiment not because it exposes the baseness of the frogs but rather our own dereliction. The frog's thankfulness for a plastic document cover is only funny because we recognize the absolute indignity with which we treat many animals in our lives. And so, comedy allows us to reveal something of how the concept of dignity could relate to other animals.

That we can talk of animal dignity is controversial, even, for some, a laughable idea but that is the challenge set by this volume. Dignity as a modern concept belongs to moral philosophy and finds its place in practical branches of philosophy: ethics, particularly bioethics and medical ethics, and law and rights policy. But the concept is also extensively invoked across institutions where the potential for vulnerable relations exists, such as in hospitals or prisons.

And dignity has older and vernacular senses – as a rightful form of bearing or as, in a related sense, comportment, and, of course, high rank. Indeed, dignity as alignment with a rightful state of being was once *only* associated with social rank.

Today, in the moralized sense, this 'rightful state' has more to do with fundamental psychological and physical needs and with identity. By the commonest definition, dignity is the unconditional and universal moral status of a human being. And it has a normative function (by which ethicists mean: the reasons and standards by which people act or desist from acting). Normativity is important here. Dignity isn't *just* standing or worth or respect. It is a form of respect that matters to a moral agent as a guide, even an imperative, for how we ought to act. For some theorists, dignity is the basis of the fundamental human rights owed to each of us.

Yet definitions of human dignity have often sought not only to distinguish what is special about human beings within nature, but to *detach* humans from their animal origins. In his book *Human Dignity*, George Kateb writes that 'the dignity of the human species lies in its uniqueness in a world of species. I am what no one else is, while not existentially superior to anyone else; we human beings belong to a species that is what no other species is; it is the highest species on earth – so far' (Kateb, 2011: 17).

Or consider the words of African anthropologist and ethicist Divine Fuh. To be human is to have dignity as 'a respectable and respected social being, rather than just a brute biological organism' (Fuh, 2020: 86).

Such sentiments have a direct line of descent from the distinctions offered by luminaries such as Immanuel Kant. James Rachels put it succinctly, with a touch of humour. 'It is an old idea,' he writes, 'from ancient times, humans have considered themselves to be essentially different from all other creatures – and not just different but *better*. In fact, humans have traditionally thought themselves to be quite fabulous. Kant certainly did' (Rachels, 1986: 114). Rachels singles out Kant's 1779 Lecture on Ethics, in which the philosopher argues we can have no direct duties to other animals because they exist 'merely as means to an end. That end is man.' But Kant wasn't only concerned with how we diverge from other species. For Kant, our rational, self-willed moral gifts grounded our worth as a being 'with ends'. It was essential to Kant that we avoid reducing our status to physical acts that run too close to animality, such as sex or masturbation. As Suzanne Cataldi notes, for Kant 'to be undignified or without dignity is to fall to the level of the "beasts"' (Cataldi, 2002).

I will return to this crucial relationship between human dignity and our struggles with our animality later. For now, it is sufficient to note that human dignity discussions have not just sought to clarify our existential uniqueness; they have sought to base our status on what marks us out from other animals. But how, then, if dignity has always applied to humans and has come, in its formal uses, to justify and explain the *exclusive* moral status of humans, can it apply to non-human animals? That difficult question is the starting place for this book.

This volume is the first of its kind to take the idea of animal dignity as its primary subject. It builds on the work of philosophers who have already argued that animal dignity should be recognized in our world (e.g., Cataldi, 2002; Nussbaum, 2006; Gruen, 2011). As such, the contributions collected here present readers with the possibility that the concept of dignity can and should apply to other species. But that is not to say that such an application is straightforward or without potential rebuttal. Nor do the contents of the book determine that there is only one philosophical pathway to what we might reasonably call 'animal dignity'. Instead, while commonalities emerge, there are different proposals for the forms that animal dignity might take and different cultural conceptions. Further, as the title of the book makes plain, this is not a collection in which the claim of animal dignity is contested.

Nor is this an assortment of arguments that reason for or against the concept of dignity itself. There is excellent discourse on the topic elsewhere. Recently, Remy Debes published *Dignity: A History* (2017), which charts the intellectual genealogy of the older term and the circumstances through which the concept of dignity shifted into a catch-all idea for 'fundamental moral status belonging to all humans'. Debes's contribution to this volume offers an overview of this scholarship. He also lays down the gauntlet. For any successful claim to be made for animal dignity, we must first qualify the concept. What is dignity and what, specifically, is *animal* dignity?

One of the first challenges any scholar or thinker faces when making claims about dignity is the derided nature of the concept itself. In a May 2008 edition of *The New Republic*, Harvard psychologist Steven Pinker published an article entitled 'The Stupidity of Dignity.' Pinker was reacting to perceived trends within American bioethics, for which the concept of dignity had become, in his words, 'a rubric for expounding' an unexamined disquiet about biomedical and technological advances. While Pinker's broader point on the dangers of misunderstandings of science giving way to mistrust is a valid one, his essay also exposes one of the chief reasons that dignity has been treated with scepticism by some philosophers. It is 'a squishy, subjective notion' (Pinker, 2008).

And Pinker is not the first to say as much. Bioethicist Ruth Macklin wrote an editorial in the *British Medical Journal* five years prior to Pinker's essay with the provocative title 'Dignity Is a Useless Concept' (Macklin, 2003). Both received considerable pushback. Still, as Pinker later noted, Macklin's argument had practical ramifications. The US President's Council acknowledged the exigency of clarifying the term.

So, we must begin with the concept itself. Is 'dignity' a useful and reasonable concept or is it a vague stand-in for some other concept, like autonomy? Both Pinker and Macklin see dignity as a means of smuggling religious bioconservatism into scientific policy. To resist this move, Macklin argued that dignity is conceptually inadequate. Her point was that the principle of autonomy already did the work that dignity might do, specifically within medical ethics. Similar suggestions have been made elsewhere (e.g., Bayertz, 1996; Zuolo, 2016; Kirchhoffer, 2020). By appealing to personal autonomy, an individual might be safeguarded against the kinds of violations associated with dignity.

But is this true? Despite criticisms that dignity is 'hopelessly amorphous, incurably theological or just plain incoherent,' Charles Foster has argued that 'sometimes nothing but dignity will do.' He goes on: 'It is wrong to use the head of a dead person as a football. . . . The wrongness can only properly be described in the language of dignity' (Foster, 2012). Suzanne Cataldi makes a similar point. 'Dignity,' she writes, 'is an intuitive response that exposes a range of morally objectionable relations. Freedom and dignity are conceptually related but distinct ideas. When we say, "beyond freedom and dignity", we are not just saying "beyond freedom and freedom"' (Cataldi, 2002).

Another common charge against dignity is that it is relative – the term has undergone conceptual transformation and inconsistency over time. This seems a fair criticism, though one that can be levelled at scientific terms like 'species' as well as abstract philosophical ideas such as 'nature'. Conceptual relativity across time and culture is not necessarily a weakness but rather a consequence of cultural flexibility and of the refusal of some forms of human knowledge to conform to an immutable or absolute state.

A further charge is that dignity can admit as much harm as it seeks to prevent. This is another species of relativity, inasmuch as the harms often follow from assumptions that dignity can be misused by those who believe they have the monopoly on being dignified. There is a risk here. But it is a risk so commonplace as to render it meaningless as a sound rebuttal. If we were to seek to remove those terms and concepts that have the potential to be misused by nefarious actors, we would have a gravely impoverished conceptual stock.

Still, exact definitions of dignity are hard to come by. In the European Union Agency for Fundamental Rights, it is written that 'human dignity is inviolable.' This suggests that dignity is a 'thing,' a possession or a set of properties. Several philosophers have made claims as to what such a 'thing' as dignity might be, most often reducible to capacities such as rationality or moral autonomy. This reason-centred conception of dignity holds that the practical quality of human reason (i.e., that it guides conduct) is the basis of the special respect we are due.

There are also relational approaches that see dignity as an emergent property of certain kinds of interactions. Colin Bird has said that dignity is 'abroad', inasmuch as it manifests in our relations with one another, rather than as a discrete property of the world (Bird, 2013: 150). Dignity is certainly 'abroad' in more ways than Bird intended. The idea has moved powerfully across cultures, histories, and eras, and, unlike many other concepts within philosophy, is readily grasped at an intuitive level by publics. A quick internet search will reveal well over two hundred million pages featuring the term, as well as pop songs, dictionary definitions, Wikipedia pages, legal documents, constitutions, and so on. In a literature review, Kerri Holloway and Francesca Grandi found that 'every foundational UN document and other major international legal instrument, as well as many national constitutions and judicial texts, have enshrined the notion of human dignity' (Holloway and Grandi, 2018: 5). They count one hundred and fifty-two national constitutions that mention it. In *The Cambridge Handbook of Human Dignity*, edited by Marcus Düwell *et al.* (2014), there are discussions on dignity across the laws and constitutions of China, France, India, Japan, America, Germany, South America, and Africa. And so, dignity today feels intuitive. It is also pan-cultural.

Elsewhere, in less formal contexts, *The Collins Dictionary* notes that dignity is the 'qualities of being worthy of esteem,' whereas the top line of Wikipedia claims that dignity is 'a right to be valued and respected' for one's own sake. Other definitions suggest that dignity flows from within the individual that possesses self-respect. These diverse and much-used definition sites matter because they are the places that a member of the general populace or any non-philosopher (including a student or a politician or policymaker) might go first to look for clarity. We can sift the philosophical literature for its definitional antecedents, but it is equally, if not more, important to understand the way the term and its meanings are shifting and circulating among communities and cultures. How does the common sense understanding of dignity relate to a formal definition from within law or philosophy?

The idea of dignity seems to cluster around the ageing, dying or dead, for instance. There are funeral homes named 'Dignity,' and declarations on dignity from care homes and hospices. Yet the young and the employed also feature prominently. Universities, schools, and childcare facilities, as well as companies, offer commitments to treat their populations with dignity. Here dignity is invoked for those who may be rendered vulnerable by their relative powerlessness, whether through age, impairment or even death.

The fact is that dignity is a thoroughly 'domesticated' concept. However, by filtering through the minds of so many individuals and populations, dignity's meaning can seem elusive, unstable, and dynamic. This can frustrate those that wish to pin down a coherent, analysable concept and derive its normative functions in ethics and law. But there's something uncomfortable in a concept that has become so popular, part of common parlance, and yet is treated with such sniffiness by philosophers. Who gets to determine that dignity is 'useless' when it is so clearly *in use*?

Vulgarization is a problem that philosophy struggles with. In seeking rational argumentation – claims and counterclaims, premises, formal arguments – to qualify a principle upon which we ought to act, philosophers can lose sight of the fact that concepts sometimes appeal because they map intuitively to how people are *already* acting.

Dignity has entered people's lives in a far more habitual and intimate way than even common philosophical and legal norms like 'rights', which many argue are grounded in dignity. It is much more likely that people may speak casually about their dignity than about their rights. Though it is undoubtedly a concept of many (moving) descriptive and evaluative parts, dignity is reached for repeatedly to help us make sense of certain acute experiences that seem to share core aspects. It is for this reason that dignity remains a significant idea. It occupies a less abstract space within human discourse and psychology and is implicit in a range of contexts from research ethics to gold standards in medical practice.

Attempts to do away with dignity are both naïve and potentially counter-productive. That said, failing to clarify a term that has captured the imaginations of so many people around the world is a missed opportunity. Tom Wein, a fair development advocate who founded the 'Dignity Project', paraphrases Canadian political philosopher Philippe-Andre Rodriguez to remind us that 'dignity will be better able to do the work we want it to if its theoretical basis is properly established' (Wein 2020).

Sometimes so-called 'cluster' concepts arise because they give us a special word for something we intuit yet struggle to name. The modern notion of dignity sweeps up inside a single word the many forms it has taken as it has refracted across different spheres of human experience. Yet it is clearly doing useful work for us. Indeed, as Foster says, sometimes only 'dignity' will do. Nonetheless, if we are to make some headway in animal dignity, we must try and pin down the concept and, also, ask ourselves why we would seek to apply the concept to other species. So, what might it *do* for non-humans?

Dignity has the potential to matter to other species because, in the twenty-first century, their lives are profoundly influenced by our actions. On an increasingly human planet, other species find themselves as unrecognized citizens of our nations. Some animals work for us; some live alongside us; many live with us; and we utilize countless more. Yet there's no formal democratic recognition of their presence as subjects, workers, or residents of a shared world. Today, decisions we make directly impact most species in all the ecosystems of the world. The deep reach of an animal like us – with a wide range of behavioural choices – places many species and individual animals in vulnerable positions. That combination of vulnerability and the absence of any formal status invites us to consider whether something like animal dignity might assist in offering other species some security, particularly where other ethical avenues from welfare to personhood-based rights are limited or ineffective. But is dignity the right concept to do this work for us (and them)?

Let's return to Rich's joke. Unless an amphibian is placed on an endangered species list, the frogs in our world have no foundational status like dignity – neither their needs nor their sensations, neither their experiences nor their wellbeing matter to us enough to alter what we do to them or how we see them. Yet the success and provocation of Rich's joke relies on our awareness that it *is* possible to see frogs in ways that relate to our own intuitions about dignity.

Consider that the project of human dignity is often directed at the special *kind* we are. Human dignity recognizes *human* specialness. As suggested by Debes, by way of Stephan Darwall, human dignity is a form of 'recognition-respect' that includes the formal claim to respect our distinctive qualities. Yet the nervous laughs that follow a sequence of jokes about frog dissection stem from the possibility that dignity might relate to *other* special kinds. Rich knows this. He relies on it for the success of his humour. He has the child's report state that 'frogs are a wonder of biology.' The use of 'wonder' is a provocation. When frogs become a pointless exercise in a child's education, it feels like a kind of violation of their – for want of a better word – *frogness*. The frogs have been stripped of their wonder-inducing reality and distinctiveness. Can we consider that frogs are special 'kinds' whose dignity is violated when they are denigrated in certain ways by us and we cease to see them as *wonder*ful?

Figure 2 Wild frog, credit Jo-Anne McArthur / NEAVS / We Animals Media.

However, to understand why some people might be threatened by non-human animal dignity (even if it turns out that it is conceptually consistent), we need to acknowledge the history of human dignity in the twentieth century. When dignity gained its modern, moral conception, our societies were reckoning with world events that had taken us to the Holocaust, to torture during war and imprisonment, and to staggering forms of denigration that no regional law had succeeded in preventing. The atrocities of the Second World War had revealed the need for an inviolable moral status that should be recognized for all individuals, regardless of their relative status or power. Dignity was summoned to fill that gap.

Dignity was plucked from a floating stock of concepts, perhaps, for two significant reasons: first, it borrowed from our deferential instincts as a hierarchical creature. The old *Dignitas*, the perceptions of rank captured by the term, when applied generally, called on us to imagine everyone as a figure worthy of respect, even awe. Second, it retained the old, religious notions of *imago Dei*, of deportment and respect for our bodies and the bodies of others as the earthen vessels of our souls, and, by this, leaned into our impulses to sense shame and humiliation, and to know vulnerability – each a facet of core human needs and experiences.

Yet the brilliance of dignity as a conceptual resource was that it packed in all that complexity under one simple demand: to always first look on another being as having a worth beyond measure. What is more, for those generations that struggled to make sense of the horrors of war, no other language could sufficiently capture – at least not succinctly – the wrongs at the core of a Fascist mentality that justified shaving the head of a young woman, rendering her naked, ushering her into a cubicle, gassing her and throwing her body into a tangle of other anonymous bodies in a pit of earth as if she was little more than a *thing*.

These kinds of extraordinary violences are concentrations of multiple wrongs and abuses that are achieved both physically *and* mentally. Dignity was invoked to tackle *both* the physical and the mental wrongs. It is extremely important to modern understandings of dignity and its role in our lives that we understand that twin purpose. Dignity invocations disrupt the potential for a mental and a physical violation by framing our relations to another (or to ourselves) as one of fundamental worth.

But the assertion that our dignity status originates entirely in being a member of the human species or even, in more acute versions, in *not* being an animal, only truly makes sense when we recognize that this claim was viewed as necessary in the wake of colossal acts of dehumanization that recruited animal and biological metaphors to denigrate humans. This is a key feature of the history of dignity, and one that I will return to in the conclusion.

Today, partly because of this history, where we have been counselled for so long to resist seeing humans in animal terms, *animal* dignity is a profoundly difficult mental leap to make. Yet, if we can overcome this, we can see a related necessity for the concept of dignity in the treatment of the frogs. Notions such as disregard or the subjection of pain can't sufficiently capture what is wrong with the pathetic treatment of the frogs. There is something *undignified* about a spread-eagled, anaesthetized animal whose life and death have been rendered meaningless. The frog, in all its wonder, is but a fleeting resource in the school day, to be disposed of without gratitude.

And so, some of the most important work that the term and concept 'dignity' does in our world is to capture forms of denigration that not only grossly disrupt the distinct needs of particular 'kinds' (e.g., humans) but also debase an individual or group of individuals by acting towards them in ways that suggest they have no worth in and of themselves. In simpler terms, dignity seeks to uphold the qualities of a state of being that is of unique and irreducible value, and to prevent harms that follow from status denigration.

Frameworks from ecofeminism have also made important contributions on denigration and systemic injustices. In making associations between the invisibility of women and non-human animals in industrial, capitalist economies as part of a wider pattern of female oppression and the exploitation of nature, ecofeminists alert us to the role of visibility and dignity in limiting violations. (See, for example Carol J. Adams and Lori Gruen, *Ecofeminism: Feminist intersections with other animals and the Earth*, 2022).

It is enormously challenging, even revolutionary, for some to truly consider looking at another species of animal as if they have unique and irreducible value (it is easy to immediately hear the derisive tone of someone asking, 'What next: the dignity of *slugs*?'). It is challenging in part because nearly ninety per cent of the human population eats or wears other animals, often under circumstances that we each know are distressing and life-limiting for that creature. In most parts of the world, other animals are *almost only a means of some sort*.

There are gradations here – some very significant. There's a considerable difference between Indigenous worldviews that sacralize other species and offer respect and gratitude for the species they kill, and the cultures of factory farming or industrial fisheries of large, urbanized societies. That said, almost no human societies are unquestionable paragons of human–non-human animal relations. It is important for our societies to reckon with the track record of our species. *Homo sapiens*, indeed, likely hominids prior to our speciation to *Homo sapiens*, are implicated in the endangerment and extinction of numerous large mammals. Humans are predatory and competitive animals, and we have tended to disrupt and destroy ecosystems as we've migrated around the world. Often, as the traditional knowledge of Indigenous Peoples can show us, only the persistence of generations of experience can engender cultures of respect that soften or mitigate these patterns.

Of course, dignity violations *presuppose* the presence of moral alternatives. Moral agency was, of course, the aspect of human behaviour that Kant placed at the centre of human worth – the ability to will a universal moral action. Yet while moral agency *generates* duties, it is not a condition for dignity. It is true that we stick out like a single strange fruit on our evolutionary branch. We have cognitive and emotional capacities and cultural behaviours that have peeled us away from the fabric of the living world and placed us in stark relief against the order of life. The consequences are both destructive and dizzyingly exciting. Still, as Danielle Celermajer once said to me in an email exchange, 'what is exceptional about humans is not that only our dignity ought to be recognized but that we ought to recognize the dignity of others.'

It has always tested our intellects to come up with sound logics about morality given our natural, amoral origins. Animal dignity may help amid this confusion. Moral systems based on respecting and formally recognizing uniqueness within the biotic community allow us to acknowledge what is wonderful in all animals, including humans. An emphasis on distinctiveness rather than superiority also unites us with other species that exist within their own adaptive worlds of being, their own *umwelts*. This is a non-hierarchical conception of the world that admits diversity.

And from this we can venture to ask whether 'dignity' has always been 'animal dignity' but has, to date, only been recognized and applied to humans. Yet if dignity is grounded in uniqueness and having a unique biological world, then dignity has always been a consequence of animality. That is an idea that will recur throughout this collection and at the close.

As said, the strongest challenge to the idea of animal dignity is that dignity refers to qualities that only humans possess; even that dignity is *synonymous* with human uniqueness. But there has always been a fundamental problem at the heart of human dignity in reducing the irreducible to a set of human-only criteria. Taken together, the contributions in this collection refute the exceptionalist claim first by questioning the historical validity of the argument and second by considering its logic. In so doing, we hope that animal dignity clarifies rather than undermines the wider concept of dignity and brings it into harmony with the reality that humans are both moral agents *and* animals. Further, the importance of distinctiveness and diversity to animal dignity theories can help resolve any concerns that the exceptional qualities of humans might be collapsed into a category 'animal' along with crows and cattle. The fundament of animal dignity is that it is based on heterogeneity.

Our volume is radical, not only for being the first of its kind to give due attention to animal dignity but for the way we have chosen to present the materials. Dignity is an intuitive and domesticated term, and one that spills into many different arenas of life, from the private to the public sphere, from university halls to farms to zoos to medical facilities to public spaces to courts of law. Rather than deny or ignore the promiscuous nature of dignity, this book and its style are modelled around the way that dignity manifests in our lives. Academic discourse and personal essay, humour and scholarship are deliberately brought together to mirror the way dignity shows up. This practical approach to reflecting on dignity seeks not only to further our understanding of what the concept means but also to point to where the concept is useful.

When I asked my eight-year-old son whether he knew the word 'dignity' and what it meant, he paused and then replied: 'It's a hard thing to explain but easy to understand.' He's right, of course, and it's not a trivial distinction. Dignity thrives as a psychological event and as a *lived* experience. As my son's intuition suggests, we might not be able to exactly describe dignity at first, and yet we all somehow know what we mean when presented with some specifics. And so, this volume considers not just *what* animal dignity is but *where* it is. Under what circumstances is dignity relevant in our relations with other species?

The first section of the book begins with two succinct overviews of the concept of dignity, and some historical roots through to animal dignity. The second section reflects on what might ground the dignity status of animals. What is it about animals that means we should attribute dignity to them? Is it all animals or only some? The final section considers the normative functions of animal dignity. What difference could the concept of dignity make to other animals and how does it differ from current rights or welfare approaches? In simple terms, how might animal dignity matter?

The reflections in this volume work together to present both what is common to dignity in all its manifestations and what, if anything, is *specific* to animal dignity. Are these commonalities reducible to another, better concept or are they fundamental to dignity? Is dignity 'squishy' for a good reason? Indeed, is its imprecision in some ways its strength?

Is there something about dignity that can only be fully recognized through the relations and moments in which we summon the term? Some of our contributions challenge aspects of human exceptionalism to show that other animals share many of the traits that we believe ground the worth and status of humans. Others propose that any singling out of capacities of any kind is a fundamental error in the formal concept of dignity.

The contributions to this volume suggest some areas of consensus that can be extracted to offer a tentative set of claims about the core concept of animal dignity, as well as some promising practical approaches to what follows from this. At the close of this volume, I suggest some ways forward.

A word on who this book is for. While there is sufficient detail and scholarship to invite further scholarly engagement, this book aims to reach wider audiences than an academic discourse alone. There is a long practical branch of philosophy that exploits dialogue or fiction to surface philosophical truths or make them lucid to non-specialists, from the dialogues of Plato and Hume to the creative modes of Nietzsche, Rousseau, and Thoreau. As such, each section begins with a short lyrical treatment of ideas by creative writers – a prelude – that offers us a glimpse of dignity, most often where dignity has been invoked in life. These are not written in the language of philosophy but in personal narrative.

We hope that the book will be of interest to scientists who work with non-human animals, environmentalists, policymakers, decision-makers in the public sphere, conservationists, veterinarians, and farmers, for instance, as well as students who are interested both in dignity as a concept and in historical and philosophical approaches to other animals. We also hope that the book is digestible enough for general publics. It is our commitment both to being honest about the spaces in which dignity becomes significant and to embracing wide-ranging debate that is expressed in the design of this book.

Dignity has proven useful to thousands of people who have lived experience of a moment or a relation in which the concept mattered. It has yet to do much work for non-human animals. Yet the concept of dignity is still blossoming and undergoing change. We may find that dignity is not done with us (or other members of this planet's biotic community) just yet.

References

C. J. Adams and L. Gruen. (eds.) (2022), *Ecofeminism: Feminist Intersections with Other Animals and the Earth*, 2nd edn, London: Bloomsbury Academic.
Bayertz, K. (ed.) (1996), *Sanctity of Life and Human Dignity*, Dordrecht: Springer Netherlands.
Bird, C. (2013), 'Dignity as a moral concept', *Social Philosophy and Policy*, 30(1–2): 150–176.
Cataldi, S. (2002), 'Animals and the concept of dignity: Critical reflections on a circus performance', *Ethics and the Environment*, 7(2): 104–126.
Debes, R. (ed.) (2017), *Dignity: A History*, New York: Oxford University Press.
Düwell, M., J. Braarvig, R. Brownsword, D. Mieth, N. van Steenbergen, and D. Düring. (2014), *The Cambridge Handbook of Human Dignity: Interdisciplinary Perspectives*, Cambridge: Cambridge University Press.
Foster, C. (2012), 'Putting dignity to work', *Lancet*, June 2(379): 2044–2045.
Fuh, D. (2020), 'Human dignity', in *Humanitarianism*, Leiden: Brill.
Gruen, L. (2011), *The Ethics of Captivity*, New York: Oxford University Press.
Holloway, K. and F. Grandi. (2018). 'Dignity in displacement: A review of the literature' (HPG Integrated Programme 2017–19). Available from https://www.odi.org/publications/11148-dignity-displacement-review-literature
Kateb, G. (2011), *Human Dignity*, Cambridge, MA: The Belknap Press of Harvard University Press.
Kirchhoffer, D. (2020), 'Dignity, autonomy, and allocation of scarce medical resources during COVID-19', *Journal of Bioethical Inquiry* 17(4): 691–696.
Macklin, R. (2003), 'Dignity is a useless concept', *British Medical Journal*, December 20(327): 1419–1420.
Morreall, J. (1981), 'Humor and aesthetic education', *Journal of Aesthetic Education* 15(1), 55–70.
Nussbaum, M. (2006), *Frontiers of Justice: Disability, Nationality, Species Membership*. Cambridge, MA: Belknap Press of Harvard University Press
Pinker, S. (2008), 'The stupidity of dignity', *The New Republic*, 28 May, 2008, pp. 28–31. Available from https://newrepublic.com/article/64674/the-stupidity-dignity (accessed 24 March 2023).
Rachels, J. (1986), *The Elements of Moral Philosophy*, New York: Random House.
Wein, T. (2020). 'A review of the literature on dignity in international development', *The Dignity Project*, 17. Available online: https://dignityproject.net/ (accessed 25 January 2023).
White, E. B. and K. S. White. (1941), 'The preaching humorist,' *The Saturday Review of Literature*, New York, 18 October 1941, p. 16.
Zuolo, F. (2016). 'Dignity and animals: Does it make sense to apply the concept of dignity to all sentient beings?', *Ethical Theory and Moral Practice* 19(5): 1117–1130.

PART ONE

Defining the Concept: *What is Dignity?*

Summary

Early on in his introduction, philosopher Remy Debes reminds us of the steps that must be taken to offer a good account of animal dignity. They are not *particular* to animal dignity, but rather to dignity whomever it concerns.

The first step is to make sense of what dignity is. Debes confronts the primary objections to animal dignity from the modern moralized idea of *human* dignity. He then suggests some ways that animal dignitarians might rebut those objections and strengthen their claims.

Debes argues that we must first settle disagreements over dignity claims to see whether the concept applies to other species. He singles out three common claims: that dignity refers to a fundamental value status that should not be exchangeable for any other measure of worth; that dignity affords a normatively special status; and that dignity originates in the unique value inherent in humans. It is this third claim that presents the greatest challenge to animal dignitarians because a reasonable account of animal dignity must refute the claim that dignity is a unique property of humans.

Debes's correction of the commonest distortions in the history of the concept lays some of the ground. In particular, he offers a close reading of four historical misconceptions, including those surrounding the preeminence of Immanuel Kant. Not only are Kant's assertions about the moral exceptionalism of humans not precisely synonymous with his notion of dignity, but Kant's influence as an originator of the Western concept of dignity has been subtly but importantly overstated. Tidying up the history of ideas can assist in legitimizing our admission of non-human animals within the purview of dignity claims, not necessarily by revising or disturbing what we take dignity to mean but by recognizing that the work dignity does in the world isn't necessarily or logically exclusive to humans. What's more, as Debes counsels us to remember, we have all been 'beneficiaries of a very slow expansion of the concept of dignity.'

Suzy Killmister offers an overview of the main philosophical approaches to animal dignity. She notes that the focus on the human capacity for moral agency in neo-Kantian versions shows little promise as the basis of animal dignity. Instead, Killmister points to the conferralist position, as exemplified by Jeremy Waldron, or the Capabilities Approach, associated with Martha Nussbaum, as offering the best philosophical approaches for a robust account of animal dignity.

For Killmister, examining the properties of dignity violations is key. Dignity violations, she emphasizes, commonly involve an element of denigration. She challenges animal dignitarians to formalize an argument that being 'lowered in the eyes of the human community is bad for animals'. For example, could denigration lead to further abuses? Does it matter in whose eyes the animal is denigrated, whether ours or those of their own (if a social species) community?

The piece of nonfiction that opens this section, from novelist and essayist Jonathan Safran Foer, offers testimony for the potential consequences of an entrenched state of denigration among a population of animals; in this case, factory-farmed chickens. It's worth holding in mind whether the potential harms to the animals are fully captured by welfare considerations, or whether being strung upside down and smeared in faeces constitute special kinds of denigration for which only the notion of dignity will suffice and that only the invocation of dignity might prevent.

PRELUDE II
33,000 Birds
Jonathan Safran Foer

It's hard to get one's head around the magnitude of 33,000 birds in one room. You don't have to see it for yourself, or even do the math, to understand that things are packed pretty tight. In its Animal Welfare Guidelines, the National Chicken Council indicates an appropriate stocking density to be eight-tenths of a square foot per bird. That's what's considered animal welfare by a 'mainstream' organization representing chicken producers, which shows you how thoroughly co-opted ideas about welfare have become – and why you can't trust labels that come from anywhere but a reliable third-party source. It's worth pausing on this for a moment. Although many animals live with far less, let's assume the full eight-tenths of a square foot. Try to picture it. (It's unlikely you'll ever get to see the inside of a poultry factory farm in person, but there are plenty of images on the Internet if your imagination needs help.) Find a piece of printer paper and imagine a full-grown bird shaped something like a football with legs standing on it. Imagine 33,000 of these rectangles in a grid. (Broilers are never in cages, and never on multiple levels.) Now enclose the grid with windowless walls and put a ceiling on top. Run in automated (drug-laced) feed, water, heating, and ventilation systems. This is a farm.

Now to the farming. First, find a chicken that will grow big fast on as little feed as possible. The muscles and fat tissues of the newly

---

* '33,000 birds' is an excerpt from *Eating Animals* (2009) by Jonathan Safran Foer, reprinted by permission of Little, Brown, an imprint of Hachette Book Group, Inc.

Figure 3 Chicken unable to stand, credit Stefano Belacchi / Equalia / We Animals Media.

engineered broiler birds grow significantly faster than their bones, leading to deformities and disease. Somewhere between one and four percent of the birds will die writhing in convulsions from sudden death syndrome, a condition virtually unknown outside of factory farms. Another factory farm-induced condition in which excess fluids fill the body cavity, ascites, kills even more (five percent of birds globally). Three out of four will have some degree of walking impairment, and common sense suggests they are in chronic pain. One out of four will have such significant trouble walking that there is no question they are in pain.

For your broilers, leave the lights on about twenty-four hours a day for the first week or so of the chicks' lives. This encourages them to eat more. Then turn the lights off a bit, giving them maybe four hours of darkness a day – just enough sleep for them to survive. Of course, chickens will go crazy if forced to live in such grossly unnatural conditions for long – the lighting and crowding, the burdens of their grotesque bodies. At least broiler birds are typically slaughtered on the forty-second day of their lives (or increasingly the thirty-ninth), so they haven't yet established social hierarchies to fight over. Needless to say, jamming deformed, drugged, overstressed birds together in a filthy, waste-coated room is not very healthy. Beyond deformities, eye damage, blindness, bacterial infections of bones, slipped vertebrae, paralysis, internal bleeding, anaemia, slipped tendons, twisted lower legs and necks, respiratory diseases and weakened immune systems are frequent and longstanding problems on factory farms.

Scientific studies and government records suggest that virtually all (upwards of ninety-five percent of) chickens become infected with E. coli (an indicator of faecal contamination) and between thirty-nine and seventy-five percent of chickens in retail stores are still infected. Around eight percent of birds become infected with salmonella (down from several years ago, when at least one in four birds was infected, which still occurs on some farms). Seventy to ninety percent are infected with another potentially deadly pathogen, campylobacter. Chlorine baths are commonly used to remove slime, odour, and bacteria.

Of course, consumers might notice that their chickens don't taste quite right – how good could a drug-stuffed, disease-ridden, shit-contaminated animal possibly taste? – but the birds will be injected (or otherwise pumped up) with 'broths' and salty solutions to give them what we have come to think of as the chicken look, smell, and taste. (A recent study by Consumer Reports found that chicken and turkey products, many labelled as natural, 'ballooned with ten to thirty percent of their weight as broth, flavouring, or water.')

The farming done, it's now time for 'processing.' First, you'll need to find workers to gather the birds into crates and 'hold the line' that will turn the living, whole birds into plastic-wrapped parts. You will have to continuously find the workers, since annual turnover rates typically exceed one hundred percent. (The interviews I did suggest turnover rates of around one hundred and fifty percent.) Illegal aliens are often preferred, but poor recent immigrants who do not speak English are also desirable employees. By the standards of the international human rights community, the typical working conditions in America's slaughterhouses constitute human rights violations; for you, they constitute a crucial way to produce cheap meat and feed the world. Pay your workers minimum wage, or near to it, to scoop up the birds – grabbing five in each hand, upside down by the legs – and jam them into transport crates. If your operation is running at the proper speed – one hundred and five chickens crated by a single worker in three and a half minutes is the expected rate according to several catchers I interviewed – the birds will be handled roughly and, as I was also told, the workers will regularly feel the birds' bones snapping in their hands. (Approximately thirty percent of all live birds arriving at the slaughterhouse have freshly broken bones as a result of their Frankenstein genetics and rough treatment.) No laws protect the birds, but of course there are laws about how you can treat the workers, and this sort of labour tends to leave people in pain for days afterward, so, again, be sure you hire those who won't be in a position to complain – people like 'Maria,' an employee of one of the largest chicken processors in California, with whom I spent an afternoon. After more than forty years of work, and five surgeries due to work-related injuries, Maria no longer has enough use of her hands to do the dishes. She is in such constant pain that she spends her evenings soaking her arms in ice water, and often can't fall asleep without pills. She is paid eight dollars an hour, and asked that I not use her real name, for fear of retribution.

Load the crates into trucks. Ignore weather extremes and don't feed or water the birds, even if the plant is hundreds of miles away. Upon arrival at the plant, have more workers sling the birds, to hang upside down by their ankles in metal shackles, onto a moving conveyer system. More bones will be broken. Often the screaming of the birds and the flapping of their wings will be so loud that workers won't be able to hear the person next to them on the line. Often the birds will defecate in pain and terror. The conveyer system drags the birds through an electrified water bath. This most likely paralyzes them but doesn't render them insensible.

Other countries, including many European countries, require (legally, at least) that chickens be rendered unconscious or killed prior to bleeding and scalding. In America, where the USDA's interpretation of the Humane Methods of Slaughter Act exempts chicken slaughter, the voltage is kept low – about one-tenth the level necessary to render the animals unconscious. After it has travelled through the bath, a paralyzed bird's eyes might still move. Sometimes the birds will have enough control of their bodies to slowly open their beaks, as though attempting to scream. The next stop on the line for the immobile-but-conscious bird will be an automated throat slitter. Blood will slowly drain out of the bird, unless the relevant arteries are missed, which happens, according to another worker I spoke with, 'all the time.' So you'll need a few more workers to function as backup slaughterers – 'kill men' – who will slit the throats of the birds that the machine misses. Unless they, too, miss the birds, which I was also told happens 'all the time.'

According to the National Chicken Council – representatives of the industry – about one hundred and eighty million chickens are improperly slaughtered each year. When asked if these numbers troubled him, Richard L. Lobb, the council's spokesman, sighed, 'The process is over in a matter of minutes.' I spoke to numerous catchers, live hangers, and kill men who described birds going alive and conscious into the scalding tank. (Government estimates obtained through the Freedom of Information Act suggest that this happens to about four million birds each year.) Since faeces on skin and feathers end up in the tanks, the birds leave filled with pathogens that they have inhaled or absorbed through their skin (the tanks' heated water helps open the birds' pores). After the birds' heads are pulled off and their feet removed, machines open them with a vertical incision and remove their guts. Contamination often occurs here, as the high-speed machines commonly rip open intestines, releasing faeces into the birds' body cavities.

Once upon a time, USDA inspectors had to condemn any bird with such faecal contamination. In the 1970s, the poultry industry convinced the USDA to reclassify faeces so that it could continue to use these automatic eviscerators. Once a dangerous contaminant, faeces are now classified as a 'cosmetic blemish.' As a result, inspectors condemn half the number of birds. Perhaps Lobb and the National Chicken Council would simply sigh and say, 'People are done consuming the faeces in a matter of minutes.'

Next the birds are inspected by a USDA official, whose ostensible function is to keep the consumer safe. The inspector has approximately two seconds to examine each bird inside and out, both the carcass and the organs, for more than a dozen different diseases and suspect abnormalities. He or she looks at about twenty-five thousand birds a day. Journalist Scott Bronstein wrote a remarkable series for the Atlanta Journal-Constitution about poultry inspection, which should be required reading for anyone considering eating chicken. He conducted interviews with nearly a hundred USDA poultry inspectors from thirty-seven plants. 'Every week,' he reports, 'millions of chickens leaking yellow pus, stained by green faeces, contaminated by harmful bacteria, or marred by lung and heart infections, cancerous tumours, or skin conditions are shipped for sale to consumers.' Next the chickens go to a massive refrigerated tank of water, where thousands of birds are communally cooled. Tom Devine, from the Government Accountability Project, has said that the 'water in these tanks has been aptly named "faecal soup" for all the filth and bacteria floating around. By immersing clean, healthy birds in the same tank with dirty ones, you're practically assuring cross-contamination.' While a significant number of European and Canadian poultry processors employ air-chilling systems, ninety-nine percent of US poultry producers have stayed with water-immersion systems and fought lawsuits from both consumers and the beef industry to continue the outmoded use of water-chilling. It's not hard to figure out why. Air-chilling reduces the weight of a bird's carcass, but water-chilling causes a dead bird to soak up water (the same water known as 'faecal soup').

One study has shown that simply placing the chicken carcasses in sealed plastic bags during the chilling stage would eliminate cross-contamination. But that would also eliminate an opportunity for the industry to turn wastewater into tens of millions of dollars' worth of additional weight in poultry products. Not too long ago there was an eight percent limit set by the USDA on just how much absorbed liquid one could sell consumers at chicken meat prices before the government took action. When this became public knowledge in the 1990s, there was an understandable outcry. Consumers sued over the practice, which sounded to them not only repulsive, but like adulteration. The courts threw out the eight percent rule as 'arbitrary and capricious.' Ironically, though, the USDA's interpretation of the court ruling allowed the chicken industry to do its own research to evaluate what percentage of chicken meat should be composed of fouled, chlorinated water. (This is an all-too-familiar outcome when challenging the agribusiness industry.) After industry consultation, the new law of the land allows slightly more than eleven percent liquid absorption (the exact percentage is indicated in small print on packaging – have a look next time). As soon as the public's attention moved elsewhere, the poultry industry turned regulations meant to protect consumers to its own advantage. US poultry consumers now gift massive poultry producers millions of additional dollars every year as a result of this added liquid. The USDA knows this and defends the practice – after all, the poultry processors are, as so many factory farmers like to say, simply doing their best to 'feed the world.' (Or in this case ensure its hydration.)

What I've described is not exceptional. It isn't the result of masochistic workers, defective machinery, or 'bad apples.' It is the rule. More than ninety percent of all chickens sold for meat in America live and die like this. In some ways factory systems may differ considerably, for example in the percentage of birds that are accidentally scalded alive each week during processing or in the amount of faecal soup their bodies absorb. These are differences that matter. In other ways, though, chicken factory farms – well run or poorly run, 'cage-free' or not – are basically the same: all birds come from similar genetic stock; all are confined; none enjoy the breeze or the warmth of sunlight; none are able to fulfil (or usually any) of their species-specific behaviours like nesting, perching, exploring their environment, and forming stable social units; illness is always rampant; suffering is always the rule; the animals are always only a unit, a weight; death is invariably cruel. These similarities matter more than the differences.

Chapter 1
A Place for Animals? Rethinking the History of Human Dignity

Remy Debes

The concept of human dignity typically refers to the basic worth or status that purportedly belongs to all persons equally. In this sense of the term, which might be called its moralized connotation, dignity is often taken as the normative grounds of universal human rights; but if not rights, at least the basis of certain interpersonal duties, including respect, care, and toleration. This justificatory relation between dignity and rights, or dignity and duty, has led many to wonder whether dignity extends to non-human animals. If so, is it anything like human dignity? And if it is like human dignity, could there be an overlapping basis of human and animal rights? Do we have duties to respect or care for animals as we do humans? Can their dignity be humiliated or degraded, like ours? Or do animals have their own distinctive basis of dignity, perhaps something like the 'wild dignity' postulated by the influential animal ethicist, Lori Gruen (2011: 151–5)? If so, what does *their* dignity entail?

---

* The content in the section headed 'Four origin stories of dignity' draws from Remy Debes (2023), 'Dignity', in E. N. Zalta and U. Nodelman (eds.), *The Stanford Encyclopedia of Philosophy* (Spring 2023 Edition). The author thanks the editors of the SEP for permission to reproduce this content here.

Answering these questions will not be easy. This is because, on the one hand, the concept of dignity is multifaceted. Alongside its contemporary moralized meaning, the term has been used to signify the idea of rank, station, honour, uniqueness, beauty, poise, gravitas, integrity, self-respect, self-esteem, a sense of self-worth, a sacred place in the order of things, supreme worth, and even the apex of astrological significance. On the other hand, dignity is contentious. Even when talking about humans, theorists differ on how the various meanings of dignity connect. Specifically, there is no consensus on how or even whether the moralized connotation of 'basic worth or status' has any principled connection to dignity's other possible meanings.

Moreover, even if we delimit our attention to the moralized connotation of dignity, we confront at least two further challenges as we try to extrapolate and apply the concept. First, we must adjudicate competing claims about the *defining criteria* of dignity. That is, we need to determine the distinguishing properties or characteristics of the basic worth or status, that a satisfactory account of dignity must explain. Or, to put this one other way, regardless of why we think humans *have* dignity, we need to settle competing claims about what the relevant worth or status *is*. For example, it is often claimed (1) that dignity is 'incommensurable' with other values; (2) that dignity picks out a normatively 'special' status (i.e., one that justifies unique inter-personal responsibilities); or (3) that dignity is 'innate' or 'inherent' in humans. Which of these definitional criteria about dignity are correct? How do they fit together? What exactly do they entail? And what other defining properties or characteristics might there be?

Second, we must say what *grounds* the basic worth or status, which the defining criteria of dignity purports to pick out. In other words, what is it about *being* human that makes it true that we have the relevant kind of worth or status that the criteria specify. For example, some argue that we have dignity in virtue of possessing a soul, or in virtue of the fact of our divine creation. Some take an Aristotelean turn and claim that we have dignity in virtue of our distinctive human 'function' or capacities. Others take a Kantian turn and argue that dignity is grounded on our capacity for agency, or a particular aspect of this capacity, such as autonomy, or the ability to make choices. Still others have looked beyond rationalist paradigms of human nature to claim that dignity is grounded on our capacities for empathy, caring relationships, or individual personality. Do all these offer an equally good answer to the defining criteria? Might human dignity have more than one grounds?

Locating and defending the place of non-human animals in this complex, shifting, and disputed landscape is bound to be difficult. To some, it might also seem objectionably anthropocentric to even try. On their view, to formulate animal dignity by reference to human dignity is to genuflect to assumptions of human exceptionalism.

This hesitation is understandable. The concept of human dignity has indeed been influenced at points in its history by assumptions of human exceptionalism, even human supremacy. However, and ironically, much of the history that tends to raise these worries turns out to be more unquestioned platitude than substantial fact. Hence, the premise of this chapter: Regardless of whether one ultimately accepts or rejects a comparative approach to *animal* dignity, it helps to understand the history of *human* dignity. Or better, because closer to what follows, it helps to not *mis*understand that history. So, let us first set the record straight on the history of human dignity. Then we can reconsider the worry about human exceptionalism.

Two final caveats are in order before we begin. First, what follows is an examination of the Western tradition. This is not because the concept of human dignity or its associated ideals cannot be found elsewhere. On the contrary, it is because both the idea and the ideals of human dignity have been claimed to exist in a wide range of non-western traditions (albeit, usually under different terminology.) And this breadth of possible sources risks turning any attempt at a genuinely global history of dignity into something superficial, if not simply mistaken. Second, the history of dignity includes sceptics as well as proponents. Moreover, these sceptics are not univocal. They have issued differing challenges, metaphysical, theological, political, practical, legal, and psychological. However, a proper treatment of the sceptical side of dignity's history is beyond the scope of this chapter.

From the present to the past

In one sense, the moralized idea of human dignity is relatively recent. Until the late nineteenth century, neither the English term 'dignity,' nor its

Latin root *dignitas*, nor the French counterpart *dignité*, had any stable currency as meaning 'the unearned status or worth of all persons', let alone any association as the basis of universal rights and equal respect. Instead, 'dignity' picked out a value that distinguished *between* persons, usually in hierarchical ways. In everything from Hobbes's *Leviathan* (1651) to Samuel Johnson's *Dictionary* (1755) to Webster's *Compendious Dictionary* (1806), dignity typically connoted special merit or high social station – something like the 'rank of elevation' that Johnson officially gave it. This is not to suggest that prior to the late nineteenth century the term 'dignity' was never connected to the moralized idea of basic human worth or status. But such cases were rare and not very influential, at least not in their own day. Correspondingly, the moralized meaning of dignity remained uncommon until the twentieth century, when it quickened considerably after appearing in the preamble to the *Universal Declaration of Human Rights*, ratified by the United Nations in 1948. That famous declaration asserted the 'inherent dignity' of humans as the 'foundation of freedom, justice and peace in the world'. Thereafter, the concept of dignity began to populate all manner of political, legal, constitutional, jurisprudential, and humanitarian claims.[1]

Initially, the force of these claims drew on the felt urgency to formulate official responses to the atrocities of the Second World War, and the attending hope to codify legal and social guardrails that might prevent similar 'barbarous acts', as the UN *Declaration* puts it. Later social causes, however, added new impulses to the growing dignitarian culture in the West. For example, one thinks immediately of the American Civil Rights Movement, second wave feminism, or the struggle for same-sex marriage rights. But also important were highly publicized episodes of global inequities and racial violence, such as the 1983–85 Ethiopian famine, the 1989 Tiananmen Square massacre, the 1990s exposure of *Nike* child labour factories, the genocidal wars in Rwanda and Darfur, and the twenty-first century Black Lives Matter movement.[2] As Western society struggled to express its anger and grief over moral crises like these, we have increasingly turned to the idea of human dignity.

The question is: how did this conceptual sea change come about? How did 'dignity' transform from an idea largely indicative of a *difference* in human value or status, to one that marks fundamental human *equality*? And what might this history tell us about the full scope of dignity? For example, how might this history bear on the ethics of non-human animals?

These remain unsettled questions. Although there is a vast literature on the general subject of dignity, and although one finds all manner of interesting historical leads in that literature, these are usually only tidbits of history used by authors and theorists as stepping-stones to some further, non-historical point. The result is a great many half-told stories about dignity's past. This said, the last decade has witnessed growing interest in the history of human dignity. And as the historical contours of dignity have started to resolve, some of the old stories about its origins have been challenged – not so much because they are entirely false, but because they are half-truths. Four such half-true platitudes are especially notable.

Four origin stories of dignity

The revolutionary platitude

The Western creed of human dignity stems from the proleptic wisdom of eighteenth-century political radicals such as Thomas Jefferson, Alexander Hamilton, or Gilbert du Motier, the Marquis de Lafayette. At the founding of new liberal states like America, or the reformation of existing ones like England and France, political sages like these put forward the inviolable and inherent value of individual human beings.

In fact, one looks in vain for dignity in the founding documents of the new Western republics. The term is not used in any existing copy of the Magna Carta (1215). And while it does show up much later in the English Bill of Rights (1689), its use there lacks any of our contemporary moralized meaning. For example, no one was yelling '*Liberté, égalité. . . dignité*' during the French Revolution. And, for all its fiery rhetoric about the equal and 'inalienable' rights of man, the US *Declaration of Independence* does not speak of human dignity. Nor does the US Constitution. Indeed, it was not until the Mexican Constitution of 1917 and the Weimer Constitution of 1919, that the term appeared in any state constitution with its moralized meaning, and even in these cases it is debatable.[3]

Moreover, we must keep in mind that the revolutionary platitude is challenged by the testimony and arguments of an entirely different set of nineteenth-century political radicals from Sojouner Truth, David Walker, Anna Wheeler, and William Thompson, to Lucy Stanton, Susan B Anthony, Frederick Douglass, James Rapier, and Ida B. Wells. Through their speeches, pamphlets, autobiographies, and books, voices like these vividly remind us that the revolutionary platitude was contradicted by the lived reality within the new Western republics – a reality defined by systematic, often bloody oppression.

In short, it is far more historically accurate to think of ourselves as the beneficiaries of a very slow expansion of the concept of dignity. This process that took a few baby steps in the eighteenth century, began to quicken gradually during the nineteenth century, but in certain respects was still unfolding in the twentieth century, perhaps even the late twentieth century. For example, according to Tina Beattie (2013: 259–74) and David Hollenbach (2013: 123–39), the Western 'universalization' of human dignity was still taking important steps in the 1960s, when the Catholic Church partly reconciled itself to secular ideas of human rights and human dignity as part of the Second Vatican Council, especially its 1965 decree, *Dignitatis humanae*.[4]

More generally, various scholars have shown that the conceptual spread of human dignity was at least as much a by-product of slow cultural changes, as it was the result of some philosophical 'breakthrough' or 'revolutionary' proclamation. For example, during the evolution of the bourgeoisie social class in the late eighteenth century, the 'working man' began to rethink himself and his social place in a way consistent with the moralized sense of dignity (Henderson, 2017: 269–90). This rethinking wasn't cashed out in the terminology of dignity, but it was an important shift in the collective mindset that we can think of as preparing the way. Similarly, but even more generally, the nineteenth century witnessed efforts to make various contingent and non-inherent attributes of persons the grounds for why one should take for granted the kind of equal status that dignity implies. For example, as old aristocratic and patriarchal value systems began to falter, we find efforts to convert less-respectable attributes of persons into respectable ones – attributes such as being a labourer, or a woman being intellectual rather than merely chaste (LaVaque-Manty, 2017: 301–22). Movements like these, while slow, and even contraindicated by the revolutionary platitude, facilitated the conceptual shift towards our present-day idea of human dignity.

The Kantian platitude

The early modern concept of dignity originates with Immanuel Kant, who in his 1785 *Groundwork for the Metaphysics of Morals*, argued that all persons have an inherent value, or dignity, in virtue of their rational autonomy. This value commands a distinct kind of moral respect, which we express by abiding certain strict limits in our treatment of others. Most notably, Kant defended the categorical duty to treat persons always as 'ends in themselves' and never as 'mere means' (Kant, 1996 [1785]: 4:429).

This is the greatest dogma about dignity in philosophy. But there are good reasons to rethink it, in favour of a more complicated history of ideas. First, although it is well known that Kant is indebted to Rousseau in a few ways, recent scholarship suggests that this debt runs much deeper than is generally understood on the points of 'humanity' and 'dignity'.[5] Some have even argued that, strictly speaking, it is a longstanding interpretive mistake to think that Kant *grounds* the obligation to respect 'persons' on any absolute inner value that humans possess; and that 'dignity' is not the name Kant gave to such a value anyway (Sensen, 2011: 71–9; Meyer, 1987: 319–32). Second, even if we set these disputes aside, contemporary philosophers have greatly overestimated Kant's historical influence on the development of the Western, and especially the Anglophone, notion of moral respect for persons. Not only did Kant have sparing influence on British thought before 1830, but what influence he did have both before and after this point was variously circumscribed. In England, for example, all early discussion of Kant took place outside the university in the pages of popular literary journals. Kant did enjoy a brief flash of popularity in these journals at the very end of the eighteenth century, but what was conveyed in these journals was greatly simplified, even trivialized. Moreover, there was little discussion of his ethics, with most attention given to his theoretical, theological, and political views – the last mostly based on his essay on *Perpetual Peace*. And in this last respect, English readers were by and large leaning *away* from Kant, partly because they had become rather nationalistic, with a growing suspicion of German

Enlightenment thought and culture (Micheli, 2005: 302–14; Copleston, 1966: 148–54).

And so it was that, already by 1798, the influential *Critical Review* complained that, 'The philosophy of Kant is little known in this country' (Unknown, 1798: 445–48). Indeed, after 1806 Kant's name virtually disappeared from English periodicals for decades (Micheli, 2005: 202–314).[6] Translations of Kant's work, which had already been rare, were not in demand. And his practical philosophy was especially slow to find its way into English. Most notably, the *Groundwork* was not professionally translated into English until 1836, when J. W. Semple, a Scotsman, offered the first serious edition.[7] However, even this translation was not easily accessible until a revised edition appeared in 1869, 'at a third of the original price' (Unknown, 1869: 452).

On top of these corrections in the history of ideas, we can add a philosophical one, drawing on the work of Stephan Darwall. Only certain conceptions of dignity, Darwall contends, will support the kind of inferences about respect that could justify using dignity to ground human rights. Namely, those conceptions that render dignity as a kind of authoritative standing to make 'second-personal' claims – that is, claims by one person *to* another. However, the original insight for *this* crucial point, Darwall argues, does not originate with Kant. It comes from the natural lawyer Samuel Pufendorf.[8]

Writing a century before Kant, Pufendorf argued that human beings have perfect natural rights (rights owed to one another) in virtue of a certain moral 'standing' that we assign to one another as an essential part of being sociable beings. More exactly, whenever we address another person directly – for example, with a claim like 'You must allow me to speak' – we *already* treat them as an accountable, responsible being. Otherwise, why address them at all? The same is true when they address us. And this includes cases where we address others in a way that *offends* their equal standing. Indeed, this is precisely when 'dignity' becomes morally urgent. Thus, Pufendorf writes: 'There seems to him to be somewhat of *Dignity* [*dignatio*] in the appellation of **Man**: so that the last and most efficacious Argument to curb the Arrogance of insulting Men, is usually, *I am not a Dog but a Man as well as yourself*' (Pufendorf, 1934, I.VII.I: 100).[9] This remark by Pufendorf may be the first use of the actual term 'dignity' in the Western tradition (here in its

Latin cognate), where it carries the significance of our contemporary moralized notion.

The *imago Dei* platitude

The moralized concept of dignity does not originate in the early modern era. It was explicitly celebrated as early as the Renaissance, in Giovanni Pico della Mirandola's 1486, *Oration on the Dignity of Man*. Moreover, Pico's oration is drawn from the older, Judeo-Christian doctrine of *imago Dei* (based on Genesis 1:26 and Wisdom 2:23), which tells us that we are made 'in the image of God', and that this likeness grounds our distinctive moral worth or status.

This story about dignity is to Christian theology what the Kantian dogma is to philosophy. And like the Kantian dogma, it is usually misleading if not false. For example, the Renaissance scholar Brian Copenhaver has shown that history flatly contradicts the claim that Pico was talking about human dignity in a sense akin to our contemporary moral-political notion. In the first place, Copenhaver notes, the speech was a failure when Pico first delivered it, in large part because it was entangled with Kabbalah mysteries for how humans can escape the body to *increase* their status by becoming angels. Second, not only did Pico never publish it, but also, the actual title that catches our attention today – the one with the word 'dignity' in it – postdates Pico. Adding to this reversal of fortunes, the medievalist Bonnie Kent marshals extensive evidence from the scholastic tradition against the *imago Dei* platitude (Kent, 2017: 73–97). Specifically, although she confirms that both 'dignity' and the doctrine of *imago Dei* were widely discussed by medieval Christian scholars in the Latin West, she demonstrates that these discussions did not intersect in a way that supports an inference to our contemporary moral-political notion of dignity.

To be clear, as Kent also argues, not all interpretations of the Christian tradition, including the doctrine of *imago Dei*, are beholden to this historical platitude (Kent, 2017).[10] Still, the platitude is repeated often enough to guard against it, in favour of seeking out more nuanced, balanced, and careful explorations of the place of 'dignity' in the Judeo-Christian theological tradition.[11]

The Ciceronian platitude

'Dignity' derives from the Latin *dignitas*. And although many if not most Romans used *dignitas* only in its merit sense, a few, and Cicero in particular, had a proleptic understanding of *dignitas* that anticipated today's moral-political sense. This historical claim has attracted more attention lately, as evidenced by its endorsement by widely cited scholars of human dignity such as Christopher McCrudden (2008) and Michael Rosen (2012). However, as the celebrated classicist, Miriam Griffin carefully demonstrates, the textual support for this view is very thin. Straightforward lexical analysis of Roman sources, she argues, offers sparing evidence for connecting *dignitas* to our present day, moralized sense of dignity. Moreover, even if we branch out to other ancient Roman concepts to see if dignity might be hiding under different terminology, we run into a fundamental challenge. 'Stoics and Roman moralists,' Griffin explains, 'think in terms of *officia*, obligations or duties or functions that our nature, properly understood, imposes on *us*.' Correspondingly, '[t]he entitlements and rights of those at the *receiving end* of our actions is not a prominent aspect of their thinking' (Griffin, 2017: 49). Admittedly, in some cases this Roman view entailed a kind of treatment of others that *accords* with our modern notion of dignity. But this treatment towards others was not grounded in any right that *they* have in virtue of 'the worth of a human being per se' (ibid.: 64). In short, Griffin warns that in looking for a Roman precursor to our modern notion of dignity, 'we are swimming against the current' (ibid.: 49).[12]

Human dignity as human distinctiveness: Finding a place for all animals

The idea that humans occupy a morally special or distinctive place has found expression in the religion, philosophy, literature, and art of virtually all societies, modern and ancient. Connected to that idea and those expressions is an enduring struggle to understand what this peculiar 'place' is and entails. And sometimes, as we noted at the outset, the answers that result are marked by human exceptionalism. The chorus in Sophocles' *Antigone*, for example, lauds man as the most 'wondrous' of all things in the world, a prodigy who cuts through the natural world the way a sailor cuts through the 'perilous' surging seas that threaten to engulf him.[13] Similarly, the Judeo-Christian doctrine of *imago Dei* is often conjoined to a loud claim for human dominion over the earth. Excluding God and angels, the doctrine implies that humankind is pre-eminently valuable. Or there is Kant's famous claim that humans do not have a price, only a 'dignity' – a kind of worth or status that puts them above all fungible or exchangeable values.

Many similar historical claims could be found. However, it is crucial to keep in mind that none necessarily connects to human dignity. More exactly, a claim about human exceptionalism does not in itself amount to, or even imply a bona fide *concept* of human dignity, let alone a *theory* of human dignity. As the previous section illustrates, both the moralized idea of human dignity (as basic worth or status), and dedicated theories of human dignity are by and in large relatively recent innovations. There are exceptions, to be sure, with Kant being the most obvious. But even the exceptions, as we saw with Kant himself, were not immediately influential. All in all, then, the fact that human history is littered with claims to human supremacy and human exceptionalism, does not require us to carry forward an attitude of exceptionalism in our contemporary, twentieth-century concept of human dignity.

More important, we must not assume that every historical aspiration to explain human *distinctiveness* reduces to a claim or assumption about human *exceptionalism*, especially as the former connects to the concept of human dignity. The essential point of the concept of dignity is not to mark the exceptional virtue, value, or status of humans. The point is to explain the virtue, value, or status of humans in a way that articulates the distinctive normative function that this worth, status, or virtue is supposed to have. That is, the fundamental point of the concept of dignity is to mark a peculiar kind of treatment, or way of being regarded, which humans are owed and can demand in virtue of their dignity.

This must be underlined. Explaining dignity's distinctive normative function, or its 'distinct set of concerns', is constitutive of most theories of human dignity, including both those that lean towards exceptionalism and those that do not.[14] From Cicero's ancient claim about the superior capacities of the 'human race'; to Oscar Schachter's 1983 claim that dignity's import outside legal contexts underlines the need 'to treat it as a distinct subject' (1983: 854); to Teresa Iglesias's 2001 attempt to defend the distinctiveness of each individual human as a 'bedrock truth' of interpersonal experience; to George Kateb's 2011 claim that human dignity turns on the unique role humans have as 'stewards' of the earth, which stewardship justifies thinking that 'humanity is the greatest type of being' (2011: 3–4) – these are all ways of chasing up the 'distinctiveness' point. Each of these authors leverages their argument into some kind of claim about the *special* treatment or regard humans owe to others and themselves as beings with dignity, albeit, not always by invoking the terminology of 'dignity'. For example, consider Simone Weil, writing in the shadow of WWII, and who inspired Iglesias: 'There is something sacred in every man, but it is not his person. Nor yet is it the human personality. *It is this man;* no more nor less. . . *The whole of him.* The arms, the eyes, the thoughts, everything. Not without infinite scruple I would touch anything of his' (Weil, [1950] 1986: 70–1). This is the distinctiveness point *par excellence.*

To reiterate, it is true that sometimes human distinctiveness runs into human exceptionalism. But not always. And this brings us back to my cautionary note: A proper account of human dignity must pick out a distinctive worth or status belonging to humans. However, this is not equivalent to demanding a worth or status that belongs distinctively to humans. Indeed, a theory of human dignity should not make the latter demand – not, at least, at the outset.

To be sure, dignity must *at least* belong to humans. For those interested in human dignity, the theory must fit humans. Second, it is our human experiences, intuitions, and history that provide the basic source material for conjecture about what dignity is and demands. Still, we can use humans and the human experience as our touchstones for working out the distinctive normative function of dignity *without* demanding, definitionally, that no other being can be attributed with dignity except humans. The one simply does not entail the other. Once we work out the normative function of dignity, well, if the account we settle on extends to animals, plants, or rocks, that is fortuitous for them.

And there is also this: To demand that dignity belongs distinctively to humans risks ruling out the best options for explaining the *grounds* of human dignity. For example, suppose rationality should turn out to be the most defensible explanation for why humans have dignity. That is, suppose it does the best job of both explaining and justifying why we have the kind of dignity that the definitional accounts articulate, including especially the distinctive normative function of dignity. Would we want to yield these grounds simply because we discovered that crows or chimps or whales were rational, or that Martians really have been trying to communicate with us for millennia? Surely not.

Further, there is no pre-theoretical reason to deny that there could be multiple ways of satisfying any given criteria of dignity. Humans, or any being for that matter, might have more than one purchase on the relevant conceptual space. Depending on the defining criteria we commit ourselves to, one might coherently argue that we have dignity in virtue of both autonomy *and* sentience; or autonomy *and* divine creation; or divine creation *and* a capacity for empathy; or even all these together, or something else entirely. Again, it depends on the criteria we settle on. The overarching point is that, in principle, this is a way of thinking about dignity, which has a place for all animals.

Notes

1. I am not suggesting that the UN Declaration was the sole catalyst to the conceptual expansion of human dignity. It was not. Relatedly, Lori Gruen has suggested that the UN declaration turns on a 'political' notion of human dignity. It identifies, she argues, a 'social value,' like justice or peace, which 'societies should strive to promote in order for members of those societies to achieve well-being' (Gruen, 2011: 152). I think this is half-right. The UN Declaration does position dignity politically in the way that Gruen suggests. But it takes itself to be appealing to a moral truth. In other words, a moral notion of human dignity *grounds* the political one. For more discussion of the role of dignity in the UN Declaration, see my article 'Dignity's Gauntlet' (Debes, 2009); see also Schachter (1983).
2. Black Lives Matter was founded by three black women in 2017, after the murder of seventeen-year-old Trayvon Martin. However, the movement was electrified in the spring of 2020 when the world collectively watched a police officer slowly suffocate George Floyd under his knee, exposing the sometimes lethal consequences of racial inequities.
3. See e.g., McCrudden (2008) and Debes (2009 and 2017), for further discussion.
4. Beattie argues, however, that this reconciliation came at some cost to the full potential of human dignity.

5 For a general overview of Kant's relationship to Rousseau, see esp. Beiser (1992). For examples of arguments deepening the debt on the points of humanity and dignity, see e.g., Hanley (2017) and Sensen (2017).

6 A few exceptions exist, such as Coleridge's musings on Kant, or the entry on 'Philosophy' in John Wilkes's 1825 *Encyclopaedia Londinensis*, which was essentially a summary and partial defence of Kant's system of philosophy.

7 In a translator's note to the text, Semple (1836) mentions an earlier anonymous translation, which appeared under the title *Kant's Essays* in 1799. But according to Semple, these essays, 'rendered by a foreigner' (probably John Richardson), were very hard to obtain. For further discussion, see Debes (2021).

8 See Darwall (2012 and 2017).

9 Note further that for Pufendorf, we also have a moral duty to *be* sociable, which duty derives directly from God's command and authority. Darwall (2017), however, argues that this can be severed from Pufendorf's core insight.

10 Importantly, Kent notes that some exceptions to this trend in Christian theology can be found, for example, in John Scotus Eriugena and Robert Grosseteste. Or consider Soskice (2013).

11 For a good lead on human dignity in the Jewish Tradition, I recommend Lorberbaum (2015).

12 See also Meyer (1987); and Lebech (2008), esp. p. 46 n. 22. Further challenges to the Roman trope and contrasting discussion can be found between Darwall (2017), McCrudden (2008), Killmister (2020) and Etinson (2020).

13 Verses 332 ff., cited in Debes (2009), at p. 52.

14 The phrasing of 'distinct set of concerns' is from Adam Etinson (2020)

References

Beattie, T. (2013), 'The vanishing absolute and the deconsecrated God: A theological reflection on revelation, law, and human dignity', in C. McCrudden (ed.), *Understanding Human Dignity*, Oxford: Oxford University Press, 259–274.

Beiser, F. (1992), 'Kant's intellectual development, 1746–1781', P. Guyer (ed.), in *The Cambridge Companion to Kant*, Cambridge: Cambridge University Press, 26–61.

Copleston, F. (1966), *A History of Philosophy*, Vol. VIII, Mahwah, NJ: Paulist Press, 148–154.

Darwall, S. (2012), 'Pufendorf on morality, sociability, and moral powers', *Journal of the History of Philosophy*, 50: 213–238.
Darwall, S. (2017), 'Equal dignity and rights', in R. Debes (ed.), *Human Dignity: A History*, New York: Oxford University Press, 181–201.
Debes, R. (2009), 'Dignity's gauntlet,' *Philosophical Perspectives* 2(1): 45–78.
Debes, R. (2017), 'Introduction', in R. Debes (ed.), *Human Dignity: A History*, New York: Oxford University Press.
Debes, R. (2021), 'Respect: A history', in R. Dean and O. Sensen (eds.), *Respect: Philosophical Essays*, New York: Oxford University Press, 1–28.
Etinson, A. (2020), 'What's so special about human dignity?', *Philosophy & Public Affairs,* 48(4): 353–381.
Griffin, M. (2017), 'Dignity in Roman and Stoic thought', in R. Debes (ed.), *Human Dignity: A History*, New York: Oxford University Press.
Gruen, L. (2011), *Ethics and Animals: An Introduction*, New York: Cambridge University Press, 151–155.
Hanley, R. (2017), 'Rethinking Kant's debts to Rousseau', *Archiv für Geschichte der Philosophie* 99(4): 380–404.
Henderson, C. (2017), 'On bourgeois dignity: Making the self-made man', in R. Debes (ed.), *Human Dignity: A History*, New York: Oxford University Press, 269–290.
Hollenbach, D. (2013), 'Human dignity: Experience and history, practical reason, and faith', in C. McCrudden (ed.), *Understanding Human Dignity*, Oxford: Oxford University Press, 123–139.
Iglesias, T. (2001). 'Bedrock truth and the dignity of the individual', *Logos* 4(1): 114–134.
Kant, I. (1996 [1785]), *Groundwork for the Metaphysics of Morals*, in M. Gregor (trans. and ed.), *Practical Philosophy: The Cambridge Edition of the Works of Immanuel Kant*, New York: Cambridge University Press.
Kant, I. (1836), *The Groundwork for the Metaphysics of Morals*, trans. J. W. Semple, Edinburgh: T. & T. Clark.
Kateb, G. (2011), *Human Dignity*, Cambridge, MA: Belknap Press of Harvard University Press.
Kent, B. (2017), 'In the image of God: Human dignity after the Fall', in R. Debes (ed.), *Human Dignity: A History*, New York: Oxford University Press, 73–97.
Killmister, S. (2020), *Contours of Dignity*, Oxford: Oxford University Press.
LaVaque-Manty, M. (2017), 'Universalizing dignity in the nineteenth century', in R. Debes (ed.), *Human Dignity: A History*, New York: Oxford University Press, 301–322.
Lebech, M. (2008), *On the Problem of Human Dignity: A Hermeneutical and Phenomenological Investigation*, Würzburg: Königshausen & Neumann.
Lorberbaum, Y. (2015), 'Human dignity in the Jewish tradition', in M. Düwell, J. Baarvig, R. Brownsword, and D. Mieth (eds.), *The Cambridge Handbook of Human Dignity: Interdisciplinary Perspectives*, Cambridge: Cambridge University Press, 135–144.

Malpas, J. (2007), 'Human dignity and human being,' in J. Malpas and N. Lickiss (eds.), *Perspectives on Human Dignity: A Conversation*, Dordrecht: Springer, 29–26.

McCrudden, C. (2008), 'Human dignity and judicial interpretation of human rights', *European Journal of International Law* 19(4): 655–724.

Meyer, M. (1987), 'Kant's concept of dignity and modern political thought', *History of European Ideas* 8(3): 319–332.

Micheli, G. (2005), 'The early reception of Kant's thought in England 1785-1805,' in G. Ross and T. McWalter (eds), *Kant and His Influence*, London: Continuum International, 202–314.

Pufendorf, S. (1934), *On the Law of Nature and Nations*, trans. C. Oldfather, C. and W. A. Oldfather, Oxford: Clarendon Press.

Rosen, M. (2012), *Dignity: Its History and Meaning*, Cambridge, MA: Harvard University Press.

Schachter, O. (1983), 'Human dignity as a normative concept', *The American Journal of International Law* 77: 848–854.

Sensen, O. (2011), 'Human dignity in historical perspective: The contemporary and traditional paradigms', *European Journal of Political Theory* 10(1): 71–79.

Sensen, O. (2017), 'Dignity: Kant's revolutionary conception' in R. Debes (ed.), *Human Dignity: A History*, New York: Oxford University Press, 237–262.

Soskice, J. (2013), 'Human dignity and the image of God', in C. McCrudden (ed.), *Understanding Human Dignity*, Oxford: Oxford University Press.

UN Declaration of Human Rights: https://www.un.org/en/about-us/universal-declaration-of-human-rights

Unknown (1798), *The Critical Review, Or Annals of Literature*, vol. 23 (August, 1798, 445–448).

Unknown (1869), *The Contemporary Review*, London: Strahan & Co.: 452.

Weil, S. ([1950] 1986), 'Human personality', in S. Miles (ed.), *Simone Weil: An Anthology*, New York: Weidenfeld & Nicolson.

Chapter 2
Philosophical Approaches to Dignity, and their Applicability to Non-Human Animals

Suzy Killmister

Academic philosophy has seen a resurgence of interest in the concept of dignity in recent decades. For the most part, however, these philosophical discussions have centred on the dignity of human beings, along with its moral and political import. As such, comparatively little attention has been paid to the possibility and significance of dignity for non-human animals.[1]

Approaching the topic from the other direction, some philosophers advocating for animal welfare have expressed scepticism towards the utility of dignity as a concept. For instance, Will Kymlicka notes that:

> The one concept in the moral toolbox that many people find more awkward or unnatural to apply to animals is 'dignity'. If someone terrorizes a cow with a cattle prod, there is no question that this harms her basic interests and her well-being, assaults her subjectivity, exploits her vulnerability, renders her precarious, instrumentalizes her, and undermines her capabilities and flourishing. [. . .] But does

the routinized violence of factory farming violate cows' 'dignity'? This is less clear.

(Kymlicka, 2018: 770)

Kymlicka's scepticism is rooted in his observation that 'dignity talk is saturated with the idea that dignity involves not being treated as an animal' (Kymlicka, 2018: 771), and so the concept is ill-suited to being applied to non-human animals. Even more strongly, Federico Zuolo (2016) holds that 'it seems impossible to outline a coherent account of animal dignity.'

Such reservations notwithstanding, dignity is an immensely evocative and powerful moral concept. As such, it is worth considering whether the admittedly human-centric philosophical conceptions of dignity that have been developed in recent decades could potentially be extended to non-human animals.

The Kantian approach

Those who work with the concept of dignity within academic philosophy are often quick to note that it is highly contested – while it is possible to identify core themes in how it is theorized, there is no indication of any kind of consensus emerging. That said, it would be hard to deny the influence of Immanuel Kant on philosophical discussions of dignity, whether as an inspiration or a foil. His is thus an appropriate account to commence with.

For Kant, dignity refers to a worth above all price, meaning that it can never be sacrificed or traded for another good. From this position, Kant develops the principle that those with dignity must never be used merely as means, but always also as ends in themselves. As he is typically interpreted, Kant grounds this worth in a particular rational capacity: the capacity to determine the moral law for ourselves. Kant himself took it as given that non-human animals lack this capacity (though he was open to the possibility of other rational agents, such as angels or aliens, possessing it). This meant that for Kant, non-human animals *can* be used as mere means; insofar as we have reason to treat animals well, according to Kant, it's because of what mistreatment does to *us*, as moral agents, not because of what we owe to animals themselves.

Few contemporary philosophers follow Kant in critiquing the mistreatment of animals in such anthropocentric terms.[2] His continuing influence on theories of dignity, however, is profound. In areas such as human rights and medical ethics, for instance, it is common to hear philosophers appeal to the dignity of persons as the basis of their rights, and to explain this dignity in terms of the agent's capacity for autonomy.

If dignity is thought of in this neo-Kantian way, its applicability to non-human animals is highly circumscribed. While some philosophers countenance the possibility that some animals, such as great apes, possess the relevant capacities, and thus have dignity and all that follows from it, it is commonly assumed that most non-human animals are not autonomous in the distinctly Kantian sense.

As such, while it is arguably useful in many other contexts, this conception of dignity is not an immediately promising one for those whose primary interest lies in animal welfare. A key reason for this is the view's anthropocentrism. Kantians take a particularly human capacity as the grounds of moral worth, and as the standard against which all other creatures are to be measured. Unsurprisingly, since the human form of life defines the terms of this standard, other creatures come up short. This approach thus takes humans' capacity for a particular kind of autonomy to set us apart, morally speaking, from the rest of the natural world. Dignity then becomes a label to justify elevating human interests above those of other animals (Kymlicka, 2018).

Yet, as our understanding of the complexity of the animal world improves, there may be the possibility of extending something like the Kantian approach to non-human animals. If dignity is grounded in the possession of certain rational capacities, and if other animals do indeed possess those rational capacities, then they too would have dignity. One downside of this strategy, however, is that it still presupposes a morally critical dichotomy between rational and non-rational creatures, reserving moral duties only for the former. An amended Kantian approach could work to expand the realm of moral considerability beyond the human, but it would be difficult to avoid reinforcing a moral hierarchy between species.

Capabilities approaches

There is an alternative philosophical approach that retains the idea of dignity as an inherent moral status but broadens its foundation. Such theories typically share with neo-Kantians the connection between having dignity and having particular capacities; but instead of reducing dignity to autonomy, they look to the wider range of properties that define our humanity. For example, John Tasioulas claims that humans have dignity because we:

> belong to a species which is in turn characterized by a variety of capacities and features: a characteristic form of embodiment; a finite life-span of a certain rough duration; capacities for physical growth and reproduction; psychological capacities, such as perception, self-consciousness, and memory; and, specifically rational capacities such as the capacities for language-use, for registering a diverse range of normative considerations (including evaluative considerations, prudential, moral, aesthetic, and others besides), and for aligning one's judgments, emotions, and actions with those considerations.
> (Tasioulas, 2015: 54)

However, while many non-human animals share at least some of these capacities, Tasioulas not only denies they have dignity but also takes this to mean humans are morally superior to non-human animals. For Tasioulas, then, dignity is 'a status that is shared equally by all human beings, elevating them above non-human animals.'

Such statements are not uncommon within contemporary philosophical accounts of dignity. George Kateb, for instance, takes there to be 'two basic propositions that make up the concept of human dignity', which are that 'All individuals are equal: no other species is equal to humanity.' (Kateb, 2011: 6). Responding to the re-emergence of such assertions within theories of human rights, Will Kymlicka has accused what he terms the 'new dignitarians' of shaping the human rights project such that it is 'characterized by ideologies and practices of species hierarchy, and in that respect is complicit in the ongoing moral catastrophe of our relations with non-human animals' (Kymlicka, 2018: 764).

To the extent that a theory builds into its definition that dignity is exclusively held by humans, it is obviously a very poor candidate for extending to non-human animals. The general strategy of taking dignity to be an inherent moral status held in virtue of species-specific capacities does, however, have potential. Martha Nussbaum is a central case in point. In her development of the capabilities approach, Nussbaum is careful to distance herself from the Kantian tradition, with its exclusive focus on what separates us from animals, and instead holds that 'our dignity just is the dignity of a certain sort of animal' (Nussbaum, 2006: 132). More precisely, she explains that for each species, we can identify core capabilities that make them the kind of creature they are. These capabilities both underpin the creature's dignity as a member of that species and determine what is required for them to live a dignified life. As such, 'the capabilities approach sees the world as containing many different types of animal dignity, all of which deserve respect and even awe' (Nussbaum, 2006: 159).

Similarly, Pablo Gilabert appeals to human dignity as the foundation of human rights. That is, he holds that humans have human rights because we have status dignity, and we have status dignity because we have normatively significant capabilities such as 'sentience, knowledge, prudential and moral reasoning and choice, aesthetic appreciation, self-awareness, creative production, social cooperation, and sympathy' (Gilabert, 2019: 127). Moreover, echoing Nussbaum, Gilabert holds that what we have human rights *to* is a feature of our dignity: we have rights to those things that are necessary for the development and exercise of the very capabilities that ground our status dignity. Importantly, Gilabert rejects the idea that a dignitarian foundation for human rights must single out capabilities that are particular to human beings: 'We should avoid the (unfortunately common) assumption that the basis of human dignity must be constituted by what distinguishes human beings from other entities. What is crucial for human dignity is the valuable features that human beings have. Some of those features (such as sentience) are also present in other animals.' (Gilabert, 2019: 204). A key implication of such an approach, shared with Nussbaum, is that other animals will have their own form of status dignity, grounded in the normatively significant capabilities relevant to their species; and this status dignity will ground rights to the development and exercise of those capabilities.

Capabilities approaches to dignity extend straightforwardly to non-human animals and have the additional benefit of providing a clear connection between the moral status a creature has, and how she ought to be treated. This makes dignity more than just an evocative slogan, providing a principled basis for opposing specific forms of mistreatment. Moreover, such approaches reject the idea that there is necessarily a moral hierarchy between human dignity and the dignity of other animals, further strengthening its critical potential in the domain of animal welfare.

Dignity as conferred

The previous two approaches share a commitment to seeing dignity as an inherent moral status; where they come apart is simply in what properties they take to ground that status. The final approach to be considered departs from that commitment. Instead of taking dignity to be inherent, these theories take dignity to be something that we confer on one another. For some theorists what is conferred is a status, which then commands a form of respect – much as it does for those who take dignity to be inherent. For other theorists, by contrast, dignity is not a status that we possess, but rather names a certain kind of relationship. In Colin Bird's memorable phrase, dignity is 'abroad' – it lives in the space between people (Bird, 2014).

Jeremy Waldron is the most prominent advocate of the idea that dignity is conferred. In his *Dignity, Rank and Rights*, he argues that we should think of dignity as a quasi-legal status, constituted by a bundle of rights. So, rather than dignity being a prior status that entails its bearer has certain rights, for Waldron the rights are prior, with dignity naming the status that is constructed through a distinct set of rights and privileges, analogously to how citizenship is a status constituted by its own distinct set of rights and privileges. Importantly, Waldron ties the status of dignity to *rank*: to have dignity is to occupy an elevated social position. However, whereas historically the status of dignity was restricted to the aristocracy, nowadays all humans share the same elevated rank:

> [E]very man a duke, every woman a queen, everyone entitled to the sort of deference and consideration, everyone's person and body sacrosanct, in the way that nobles were entitled to deference or in the way that an assault upon the body or the person of a king were regarded as a sacrilege.
>
> (Waldron, 2012: 34)

Importantly, though, the levelling up of status that Waldron lauds carries with it a dark underbelly: as Diego Rossello has pointed out, on such a view, dignity 'operates as a device of equalization *precisely by lifting the human up away from the animal*' (Rossello, 2017: 3, emphasis added).

While Waldron himself is thus not a promising ally in theorizing about animal welfare, key elements of his theory could nonetheless potentially be repurposed to that end. Waldron's dignity is simply a status we have chosen to confer on one another.[3] As such, it has the benefit of not presupposing some inherent moral hierarchy between human and non-human animals, in contrast to the Kantian approach discussed above. This leaves open the possibility that we could go on to confer dignity on other animals – whether as part of the very same status we humans have constructed for ourselves; as a new elevated status for all non-human animals; or as separate ranks for each species, in line with the capabilities approach. Whatever the case, animal dignity, like human dignity, would be constituted by a specific bundle of rights (or, more broadly, norms of treatment).

We can perhaps see something like this process already in play with the category of pet. What differentiates a pet from any other animal is not some inherent difference in capacities, but rather a social rank that we have chosen to confer on some animals but not others, which carries with it a complex array of special rights and privileges.[4] While our obligations towards pets are not typically described in the language of dignity, the nature of this relationship nonetheless bears a striking resemblance, structurally speaking, to the way Waldron understands the development of human dignity.

Such an approach does raise the challenge, though, of explaining *why* we should confer such a status – whether on ourselves or on other species. The worry is that if we justify it based on the inherent properties of those on whom we do the conferral, the account simply collapses back into a neo-Kantian or capabilities approach. If, instead, we take the conferral to be independent of inherent properties, the account risks arbitrariness. Federico Zuolo puts the point thus:

> [If] dignity-conferring relations are totally independent of non-relational properties possessed by the dignified individual, any kind of being in any circumstance may be dignified provided that there is a human individual capable of dignifying it who is willing to do so. In this sense, not only animals and plants, but also inanimate objects

may be dignified. However, on this account, the attribution of dignity may end up being an arbitrary act lacking proper good motivations, thus risking losing its moral properties which make dignity so important.

(Zuolo, 2016)

While such a challenge is formidable, it is not necessarily insurmountable. It does indicate, though, where the weak point of such an account would lie, and hence where justificatory work would need to focus.

This leaves the final way of conceiving of dignity: i.e., as a certain kind of relationship. On this view, dignity is tightly connected to social standing, and it emerges when we treat one another with markers of respect. As Linda Barclay puts it, 'dignity is secured when our exchanges with each other conform to whatever our social norms are for treating one another as social equals' (Barclay, 2018: 64). Adam Etinson holds a similar view: 'dignity's concern is with social status and its markings – or what we sometimes call "honor". What it requires is that we avoid subjecting people to the specific (socially oriented) harm of humiliation or degradation and, more positively, that we help protect them from such harm, too' (Etinson, 2020: 335). I draw a similar connection between dignity and humiliation: 'To have one's social dignity violated [. . .] is to be made to do or be something that is taken to be debasing or degrading by one's community. More precisely, it's to be made to do or be something that *lowers one in the eyes of one's peers*' (Killmister, 2020: 50).

One of the distinctive aspects of this approach to dignity, in contrast to the others canvassed here, is the specificity of the wrong of dignity violations. For neo-Kantians, dignity violations are co-extensive with moral wrongs, while for those adopting a capabilities approach, dignity violations are composed of any impediment to the species-relevant capacities of the individual. On the relational approach, by contrast, not all setbacks to welfare, or violations of rights, will constitute dignity violations – there needs to be an element of denigration at play.

While none of the authors noted above explicitly rule out the applicability of this relational conception of dignity to non-human animals, they do develop it in ways that are highly focused on the social practices of human beings. This is unsurprising, since what it is to be

Figure 4 Bear in zoo, credit Jo-Anne McArthur / Born Free Foundation / We Animals Media.

treated as an equal, or humiliated, depends crucially on the details of the social practices that shape our lives. But this nonetheless leaves open the possibility both that (some) animals participate in our social world, and hence are vulnerable to being denigrated within it; and that (some) animals have their own complex social worlds that our actions can negatively affect.

With respect to the former possibility, inviting others to see particular animals as objects of ridicule, for instance in a circus act, would constitute a violation of their dignity, because it would lower those animals in the eyes of the audience (Cataldi, 2002). More ambitiously, such an account could also potentially be used to argue that there is an element of denigration involved in placing *any* wild animal in captivity, or in a position of dependency, since such actions presuppose the subordination of those animals to human desires. The key challenge in developing such a position, though, would be to show why such treatment constitutes a *wrong* to the animal, especially if it doesn't directly undermine their wellbeing in the kinds of ways captured by a capabilities approach. This is especially challenging because the kinds of psychological harms that humans suffer in the face of public denigration require a self-conception that is arguably absent for most non-human animals (Sangiovanni, 2017).

What's needed is an argument that being lowered in the eyes of the human community is bad for animals, and that this is independent of their ability to recognize that social fact. One possible argument would look to the likely long-term consequences of denigration. As Barclay (2018: 66) points out, with respect to humans, 'when people are regularly treated as social inferiors, they can be particularly vulnerable to maltreatment and abuse.' This, she argues, is because treatment shapes how we see particular kinds of people, and hence how we feel we ought to interact with them going forward. As such, 'The failure to treat people with cognitive impairments as social equals, and the subsequent reinforcement of stigmatized cultural schemas around their inferiority, can perpetuate [. . .] violence, neglect, and maltreatment.' (Barclay, 2018: 66). Analogously, when animals are regularly treated as expendable, or as mere entertainment, this shapes the way they are seen, and corrodes inhibitions against maltreatment and abuse.

The above line of argument focuses on the position animals hold within the human social world. The relational approach account could, however, also be used to argue against certain forms of treatment on the grounds of what they do to animals within their *own* social worlds. If what we do to, or with, other animals lowers them within the social hierarchies of their own kind, perhaps by rendering them incapable of navigating those social relationships, this could constitute an indirect dignity violation.

Notes

1 For some notable exceptions, see Meyer (2001); Nussbaum (2006); Cataldi (2002).

2 Some do, however. See for, instance, Formosa (2017), who agrees with Kant that we only have indirect moral duties to animals, with the direct duties owed either to those persons who care for the animal, or to ourselves (since mistreatment of animals could corrode our moral virtues).

3 In later work Waldron (2015, 2017) does attempt to offer a justification for the elevated status of humans, on the grounds of our capacities.

4 Interestingly, this conferral sometimes applies to all members of a particular species, for instance dogs and cats (at least in contemporary Western societies); while in other cases, such as with rabbits or rats, it depends upon the individual animal's relationship to humans.

References

Barclay, L. (2018), 'Dignitarian medical ethics', *Journal of Medical Ethics* 44(1): 62–67.
Bird, C. (2014), 'Dignity as a moral concept', *Social Philosophy and Policy* 30(1–2): 150–176.
Cataldi, S. (2002), 'Animals and the concept of dignity: Critical reflections on a circus performance,' *Ethics and the Environment* 7(2): 104–126.
Etinson, A. (2020), 'What's so special about human dignity?', *Philosophy & Public Affairs* 48(4): 353–381.
Formosa, P. (2017), *Kantian Ethics, Dignity, and Perfection*, New York: Cambridge University Press.
Gilabert, P. (2019), *Human Dignity and Human Rights*, New York: Oxford University Press.
Kateb, G. (2011), *Human Dignity*, Cambridge, MA: The Belknap Press of Harvard University Press.
Killmister, S. (2020), *Contours of Dignity*, Oxford: Oxford University Press.
Kymlicka, W. (2018), 'Human rights without human supremacism', *Canadian Journal of Philosophy* 48(6): 763–792.
Meyer, M. (2001), 'The simple dignity of sentient life: Speciesism and human dignity', *Journal of Social Philosophy* 32(2): 115–126.
Nussbaum, M. (2006), *Frontiers of Justice: Disability, Nationality, Species Membership*, Cambridge, MA: Belknap Press.
Rossello, D. (2017), 'All in the (human) family? Species aristocratism in the return of human dignity', *Political Theory* 45(6): 749–771.
Sangiovanni, A. (2017), *Humanity without Dignity: Moral Equality, Respect, and Human Rights*, Cambridge, MA: Harvard University Press.
Tasioulas, J. (2015), 'On the foundations of human rights', in S. Cruft, M. Liao, and M. Renzo (eds.), *Philosophical Foundations of Human Rights*, Oxford: Oxford University Press.
Waldron, J. (2012), *Dignity, Rank, and Rights*, New York: Oxford University Press.
Waldron, J. (2015), 'Is dignity the foundation of human rights?', in S. Cruft, M. Liao, and M. Renzo (eds.), *Philosophical Foundations of Human Rights*, Oxford: Oxford University Press.
Waldron, J. (2017), *One Another's Equals: The Basis of Human Equality*, Cambridge, MA: Harvard University Press.
Zuolo, F. (2016), 'Dignity and animals: Does it make sense to apply the concept of dignity to all sentient beings?' *Ethical Theory and Moral Practice* 19(5): 1117–1130.

PART TWO

Approaches to Dignity: *What are the Grounds for Animal Dignity?*

Summary

The essays gathered in this section speak to the next step that must be taken in offering a robust account of animal dignity. After considering what properties constitute the concept of dignity, we must consider on what grounds other animals fit the concept. A question to which we will return is whether it is reasonable to approach dignity as if it is a measure of any kind. Are calculable or hierarchical, qualifiable criteria antithetical to the concept of dignity? If dignity today is a moral concept that exists most particularly as respect-recognition (see Darwall, 1977, in Düwell *et al.*, 2014) for a being in and of itself, where and how might meaningful boundaries emerge to avoid ceding dignity to such things as pathogens? What are the limits of dignity?

We open with a piece of creative nonfiction from science journalist, Sy Montgomery. She offers a personal account of her meetings with cephalopods, touching on general intelligence and the ability to engage in social relations – two criteria commonly considered as qualifiers for dignity – but ultimately reaching beyond smarts to species distinctiveness.

Historian Harriet Ritvo reveals some of the historical thinking about intelligence in nature, most particularly in the Victorian era. Not only are we prone to biases in how we interpret signals of intelligence in non-human animals, but such measures have rarely encouraged the recognition of much, if any, dignity. Her work is a reminder that hierarchies of biological attributes as part of the core criteria of dignity is associated with the earlier, Ciceronian notions of dignity as standing (which were also prone to distorted views about intelligence and skills across human societies) rather than the modern, moralized conception that most of us accept today.

Lori Gruen, a philosopher who has contributed significant early work to the literature on animal dignity, claims that dignity is a product of just, attentive social relations. She terms animal dignity as 'wild dignity', a relational and non-anthropocentric property, with 'wild' coming to stand for the realities of non-human existence beyond the human gaze. 'Wild dignity,' she writes, 'is like political dignity but more expansive, it includes other animals within their own social networks as evaluated through ours.'

Many of the later contributions to this section complement one another. Each presents dignity as becoming visible through a special, moralized kind of attention. Cognitive scientist, Alexandra Horowitz discusses the serious illness and dying days of her dog to assert that dignity attributes should flow from the animal rather than from us – we (or any kind of moral agent) are, if you like, the receivers of dignity 'signals', but the information flows from the communicator, in this case, a dog. As such, due attention to the distinctive qualities of both animal types and individual variation among types is essential for the emergence of a just set of relations. Dignity recognition derives its logic not only from attending to and respecting differences across the forms of beings but also among individuals themselves.

For Deborah Slicer – who narrates experiences with a trio of different animal kinds from bears and horses to wasps – the special attention by which humans recognize animal dignity (or human dignity) is 'unsentimental, detached, unselfish, objective attention,' to paraphrase Iris Murdoch. To catch sight of dignity, to invoke dignity from the human perspective, is to attend with open heart and mind to the worlds of others. Or, in the words of Danielle Celermajer, whose contribution completes this section, dignity (for any being) is foreclosed to humans unless 'we pay close attention to others in their own right.' From this, Celermajer tells us, emerges 'a dignity of their world.'

The respectful attention or perspective in each case is grounded in the distinctiveness not only of the species kind but of the individual organism (or superorganism) in sight. For a moral agent, recognizing dignity is an act of imagination that gives meaning to and resets action. Note, this is not *all* the work dignity does but rather one of the primary instruments by which we bring dignity into play in establishing a positive set of relations.

But does this mean that what we name as dignity requires a dignifier to exist? Against the claims of philosophers who argue strongly that dignity *only* exists in relations, most animal (and human) dignitarians appear to believe that the concept captures a real property of our world. Species and organismal distinctiveness – biological distinctiveness – coupled with the agential characteristics of animals (amplified by but not limited to sentience and aspects of intelligence) are most often given as the grounds for the respect that emerges when we pay due, moral attention to another being in pursuit of their own flourishing and persistence. The contributions that follow discuss the kind of moral attention that is so particular to how we, as moral agents, come to see dignity.

Reference

Düwell, M., J. Braarvig, R. Brownsword, and D. Mieth (eds.). (2014). *The Cambridge Handbook of Human Dignity: Interdisciplinary Perspectives*, Cambridge: Cambridge University Press.

PRELUDE III
Ways of Seeing an Octopus
Sy Montgomery

The definition of dignity that comes up first in the dictionary is 'the state of being worthy of honour and respect'. If you believe in a Creator, everything (animate or not) that He or She created is worthy of our honour or respect – our reverence, even. If we understand evolution, we should be in awe of every kind of life that has emerged. All of animate creation – every animal, plant, fungus, protist, even bacterium – is worthy of awe and respect.

It's easy to see the dignity of a majestic tiger laying up with its kill or an elephant matriarch leading her herd. But what of slimy invertebrates, like slugs – or octopuses?

Not long ago, I met a banana slug named Duke (to refer to whom one uses the pronoun they/them, since slugs are hermaphrodites) whose dignity was clear to me. Duke was sleeping when we first met, but once they slid onto my hand, their eye stalks arose, their lower tentacles emerged, and they began cruising along my skin. Duke encircled my wrist, exploring the landscape of me with curiosity and courage. As I watched this small, boneless, common, and often overlooked animal investigate their world, they showed me their own

---

* 'Ways of Seeing an Octopus' by Sy Montgomery is an adaptation of her prior essay, 'Deep Intellect', which appeared in the Nov/Dec 2011 issue of *Orion Magazine*.

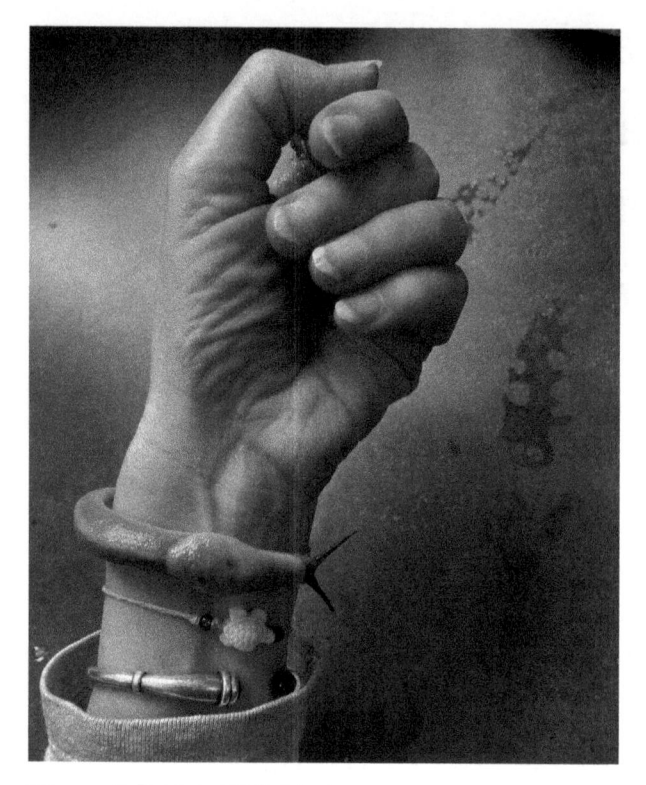

Figure 5 Duke, credit Sy Montgomery.

inherent dignity. Surely, I thought, even this tiny, humble animal is worthy of our respect?

Perhaps, for many, the dignity of slugs seems remote. But the case of our growing recognition of and respect for cephalopods offers hope. When it comes to recognizing the dignity of the octopus, what matters is to pay attention. The more we have paid attention to cephalopods on their own terms, the more we have found to respect.

§

On an unseasonably warm day in the middle of March, I travelled from New Hampshire to the moist, dim sanctuary of the New England Aquarium, hoping to touch an alternate reality. I came to meet Athena, the aquarium's forty-pound, five-foot-long, two-and-a-half-year-old giant

Pacific octopus. For me, it was a momentous occasion. I have always loved octopuses. No sci-fi alien is so startlingly strange. Here is someone who, even if she grows to one hundred pounds and stretches more than eight feet long, could still squeeze her boneless body through an opening the size of an orange; an animal whose eight arms are covered with thousands of suckers that taste as well as feel; a mollusc with a beak like a parrot and venom like a snake and a tongue covered with teeth; a creature who can shape-shift, change colour, and squirt ink.

But most intriguing of all, recent research indicates that octopuses are remarkably intelligent. Many times, I have stood mesmerized by an aquarium tank, wondering, as I stared into the horizontal pupils of an octopus's large, prominent eyes, if she was staring back at me – and if so, what was she thinking? Not long ago, a question like this would have seemed foolish, if not crazy. How can an octopus know anything, much less form an opinion? Octopuses are, after all, 'only' invertebrates – they don't even belong with the insects, some of whom, like dragonflies and dung beetles, at least seem to show some smarts. Octopuses are classified within the invertebrates in the mollusc family, and many molluscs, like clams, have no brain. Only recently have scientists accorded chimpanzees, so closely related to humans we can share blood transfusions, the dignity of having a mind. But now, increasingly, researchers who study octopuses are convinced that these boneless, alien animals – creatures whose ancestors diverged from the lineage that would lead to ours roughly five to seven hundred million years ago – have developed intelligence, emotions, and individual personalities. Their findings are challenging our understanding of consciousness itself.

I had always longed to meet an octopus. Now was my chance: senior aquarist Scott Dowd arranged an introduction. In a back room, he would open the top of Athena's tank. If she consented, I could touch her. The heavy lid covering her tank separated our two worlds. One world was mine and yours, the reality of air and land, where we lumber through life governed by a backbone and constrained by jointed limbs and gravity. The other world was hers, the reality of a nearly gelatinous being breathing water and moving weightlessly through it. We think of our world as the 'real' one, but Athena's is 'realer' still: after all, most of the world is ocean, and most animals live there. Regardless of whether they live on land or water, more than ninety-five per cent of all animals are invertebrates, like Athena.

The moment the lid was off, we reached for each other. She had already oozed from the far corner of her lair, where she had been hiding, to the top of the tank to investigate her visitor. Her eight arms boiled up, twisting, slippery, to meet mine. I plunged both my arms elbow deep into the fifty-seven-degree water. Athena's melon-sized head bobbed to the surface. Her left eye (octopuses have one dominant eye like humans have a dominant hand) swivelled in its socket to meet mine. 'She's looking at you', Dowd said. As we gazed into each other's eyes, Athena encircled my arms with hers, latching on with first a dozen, then hundreds of her sensitive, dexterous suckers. Each arm has more than two hundred of them.

The famous naturalist and explorer William Beebe found the touch of the octopus repulsive. 'I have always a struggle before I can make my hands do their duty and seize a tentacle', he confessed. But to me, Athena's suckers felt like an alien's kiss – at once a probe and a caress. Although an octopus can taste with all of its skin, in the suckers both taste and touch are exquisitely developed. Athena was tasting me and feeling me at once, knowing my skin, and possibly the blood and bone beneath, in a way I could never fathom. When I stroked her soft head with my fingertips, she changed colour beneath my touch, her ruby-flecked skin going white and smooth. This, I learned, is a sign of a relaxed octopus. An agitated giant Pacific octopus turns red, its skin gets pimply, and it erects two papillae over the eyes, which some divers say look like horns. One name for the species is 'devil fish'. With sharp, parrotlike beaks, octopuses can bite, and most have neurotoxic, flesh-dissolving venom. The pressure from an octopus's suckers can tear flesh (one scientist calculated that to break the hold of the suckers of the much smaller common octopus would require a quarter ton of force). One volunteer who interacted with an octopus left the aquarium with arms covered in red hickeys. Occasionally an octopus takes a dislike to someone. One of Athena's predecessors at the aquarium, Truman, felt this way about a female volunteer. Using his funnel, the siphon near the side of the head used to jet through the sea, Truman would shoot a soaking stream of salt water at this young woman whenever he got a chance. Later, she quit her volunteer position for college. But when she returned to visit several months later, Truman, who hadn't squirted anyone in the meanwhile, took one look at her and instantly soaked her again.

Athena was remarkably gentle with me – even as she began to transfer her grip from her smaller, outer suckers to the larger ones. She seemed to be slowly but steadily pulling me into her tank. Had it been big enough to accommodate my body, I would have gone in willingly. But at this point, I asked Dowd if perhaps I should try to detach from some of the suckers. With his help, Athena and I pulled gently apart. I was honoured that she appeared comfortable with me. But what did she know about me that informed her opinion? When Athena looked into my eyes, what was she thinking?

§

Measuring the minds of other creatures is a perplexing problem. As scientist Alexa Warburton put it, 'How do you prove the intelligence of someone so different?' One yardstick scientists use is brain size, since humans have big brains. But size doesn't always match smarts. As is well known in electronics, anything can be miniaturized. Small brain size was the evidence once used to argue that birds were stupid – before some birds were proven intelligent enough to compose music, invent dance steps, ask questions, and do maths.

Octopuses have the largest brains of any invertebrate. Athena's is the size of a walnut – as big as the brain of the famous African grey parrot, Alex, who learned to use more than one hundred spoken words meaningfully. That's proportionally bigger than the brains of most of the largest dinosaurs. Another measure of intelligence: you can count neurons. The common octopus has about one hundred and thirty million of them in its brain. A human has one hundred billion. But this is where things get weird. Three-fifths of an octopus's neurons are not in the brain; they're in its arms. 'It is as if each arm has a mind of its own', says Peter Godfrey-Smith, a diver, professor of philosophy at the University of Sydney, and an admirer of octopuses. For example, researchers who cut off an octopus's arm (which the octopus can regrow) discovered that not only does the arm crawl away on its own, but if the arm meets a food item, it seizes it – and tries to pass it to where the mouth would be if the arm were still connected to its body.

'Meeting an octopus', writes Godfrey-Smith, 'is like meeting an intelligent alien.' Their intelligence sometimes even involves changing colours and shapes. One video online shows a mimic octopus alternately

Figure 6 Octopus, credit Istock.

morphing into a flatfish, several sea snakes, and a lionfish by changing colour, altering the texture of its skin, and shifting the position of its body. Another video shows an octopus materializing from a clump of algae. Its skin exactly matches the algae from which it seems to bloom – until it swims away. For its colour palette, the octopus uses three layers of three different types of cells near the skin's surface. The deepest layer passively reflects background light. The topmost may contain the colours yellow, red, brown, and black. The middle layer shows an array of glittering blues, greens, and golds. But how does an octopus decide what animal to mimic, what colours to turn? Scientists have no idea, especially given that octopuses are likely colourblind. But new evidence suggests a breathtaking possibility.

Woods Hole Marine Biological Laboratory and University of Washington researchers found that the skin of the cuttlefish *Sepia officinalis*, a colour-changing cousin of octopuses, contains gene sequences usually expressed only in the light-sensing retina of the eye. In other words, cephalopods — octopuses, cuttlefish, and squid — may be able to see with their skin. The American philosopher Thomas Nagel once wrote a famous paper titled 'What Is It Like to Be a Bat?' Bats can see with sound. Like dolphins, they can locate their prey using echoes. Nagel concluded it was impossible to know what it's like to be a bat. And a bat is a fellow mammal like us – not someone who tastes with its suckers, sees with its skin, and whose severed arms can wander about, each with a mind of its own. Nevertheless, there are researchers still working diligently to understand what it's like to be an octopus.

§

Jennifer Mather is the lead author of *Octopus: The Ocean's Intelligent Invertebrate*, which includes observations of octopuses who dismantle Lego sets and open screw-top jars. Co-author Roland Anderson reports that octopuses even learned to open the childproof caps on Extra Strength Tylenol pill bottles – a feat that eludes many humans with university degrees. In one experiment, Anderson gave octopuses plastic pill bottles painted different shades and with different textures to see which evoked more interest. Usually, each octopus would grasp a bottle to see if it were edible and then cast it off. But to his astonishment, Anderson saw one of the octopuses doing something striking: she was blowing carefully modulated jets of water from her funnel to send the bottle to the other end of her aquarium, where the water flow sent it back to her. She repeated the action twenty times. By the eighteenth time, Anderson was already on the phone with Mather with the news: 'She's bouncing the ball!'

This octopus wasn't the only one to use the bottle as a toy. Another octopus in the study also shot water at the bottle, sending it back and forth across the water's surface, rather than circling the tank. Anderson's observations were reported in the *Journal of Comparative Psychology*. 'This fit all the criteria for play behaviour', said Anderson. 'Only intelligent animals play – animals like crows and chimps, dogs and humans.' Aquarists who care for octopuses feel that not only can these animals play with toys, but they may need to play with toys.

An Octopus Enrichment Handbook has been developed by Cincinnati's Newport Aquarium, with ideas of how to keep these creatures entertained. One suggestion is to hide food inside Mr. Potato Head and let your octopus dismantle it. At the Seattle Aquarium, giant Pacific octopuses play with a baseball-sized plastic ball that can be screwed together by twisting the two halves. Sometimes the molluscs screw the halves back together after eating the prey inside. At the New England Aquarium, it took an engineer who worked on the design of cubic zirconium to devise a puzzle worthy of a brain like Athena's. Wilson Menashi, who began volunteering at the aquarium weekly after retiring from the Arthur D. Little Corporation sixteen years ago, devised a series of three Plexiglas cubes, each with a different latch. The smallest cube has a sliding latch that twists to lock down, like the bolt on a horse stall. Aquarist Bill Murphy puts a crab inside the clear cube and leaves the lid open. Later he lets the octopus lift open the lid. Finally, he locks the lid, and invariably the octopus figures out how to open it. Next, he locks the first cube within a second one. The new latch slides counterclockwise to catch on a bracket. The third box is the largest, with two different locks: a bolt that slides into position to lock down, and a second one like a lever arm, sealing the lid much like the top of an old-fashioned glass canning jar. All the octopuses Murphy has known learned fast. They typically master a box within two or three once-a-week tries. 'Once they "get it",' he says, 'they can open it very fast' – within three or four minutes. But each may use a different strategy. George, a calm octopus, opened the boxes methodically. The impetuous Gwenevere squeezed the second-largest box so hard she broke it, leaving a hole two inches wide. Truman, Murphy said, was 'an opportunist'. One day, inside the smaller of the two boxes, Murphy put two crabs, who started to fight. Truman was too excited to bother with locks. He poured his seven-foot-long body through the two-inch crack Gwenevere had made, and visitors looked into his exhibit to find the giant octopus squeezed, suckers flattened, into the tiny space between the walls of the fourteen-cubic-inch box outside and the six-cubic-inch one inside it. Truman stayed inside half an hour. He never opened the inner box – probably he was too cramped.

 Three weeks after I had first met Athena, I returned to the aquarium to meet the man who had designed the cubes. Menashi, a quiet grandfather with a dark moustache, volunteers every Tuesday. 'He has a real way with octopuses', Dowd and Murphy told me. I was eager to see how Athena behaved with him. Murphy opened the lid of her tank, and Athena rose to the surface eagerly. A bucket with a handful of fish sat nearby. Did she rise so eagerly sensing the food? Or was it the sight of her friend that attracted her? 'She knows me', Menashi answered softly. Anderson's experiments with giant Pacific octopuses in Seattle prove Menashi is right. The study exposed eight octopuses to two unfamiliar humans, dressed identically in blue aquarium shirts. One person consistently fed a particular octopus, and another always touched it with a bristly stick. Within a week, at first sight of the people, most octopuses moved toward the feeders and away from the irritators, at whom they occasionally aimed their water-shooting funnels. Upon seeing Menashi, Athena reached up gently and grasped his hands and arms. She flipped upside down, and he placed a capelin in some of the suckers near her mouth, at the centre of her arms. The fish vanished. After she had eaten, Athena floated in the tank upside down, like a puppy asking for a belly rub. Her arms twisted lazily. I took one in my hand to feel the suckers – did that arm know it had hold of a different person than the other arms did? Her grip felt calm, relaxed. With me, earlier, she seemed playful, exploratory, excited. The way she held Menashi with her suckers seemed to me like the way a long-married couple holds hands at the movies. I leaned over the tank to look again into her eyes, and she bobbed up to return my gaze. 'She has eyelids like a person does', Menashi said. He gently slid his hand near one of her eyes, causing her to slowly wink.

§

Biologists have long noted the similarities between the eyes of an octopus and the eyes of a human. Canadian zoologist N. J. Berrill called it 'the single most startling feature of the whole animal kingdom' that these organs are nearly identical: both animals' eyes have transparent corneas, regulate light with iris diaphragms, and focus lenses with a ring of muscle. Scientists are currently debating whether we and octopuses evolved eyes separately, or whether a common ancestor had the makings of the eye. But intelligence is another matter. 'The same thing that got them their smarts isn't the same thing that got us our smarts', says Mather, 'because our two ancestors didn't have any smarts.'

Half a billion years ago, the brainiest thing on the planet had only a few neurons. Octopus and human intelligence evolved independently. 'Octopuses', writes philosopher Godfrey-Smith, 'are a separate experiment in the evolution of the mind'. And that, he feels, is what makes the study of the octopus mind so philosophically interesting. The octopus mind and the human mind probably evolved for different reasons. Humans – like other vertebrates whose intelligence we recognise (parrots, elephants, and whales) – are long-lived, social beings. Most scientists agree that an important event that drove the flowering of our intelligence was when our ancestors began to live in social groups. Decoding and developing the many subtle relationships among our fellows and keeping track of these changing relationships over the course of the many decades of a typical human lifespan, was surely a major force shaping our minds.

But octopuses are neither long-lived nor social. Athena, to my sorrow, may live only a few more months – the natural lifespan of a giant Pacific octopus is only three years. If the aquarium added another octopus to her tank, one might eat the other. Except to mate, most octopuses have little to do with others of their kind. So why is the octopus so intelligent? What is its mind for? Mather thinks she has the answer. She believes the event driving the octopus toward intelligence was the loss of the ancestral shell. Losing the shell freed the octopus for mobility. Now they didn't need to wait for food to find them; they could hunt like tigers. And while most octopuses love crab best, they hunt and eat dozens of other species – each of which demands a different hunting strategy. Each animal you hunt may demand a different skill set: Will you camouflage yourself for a stalk-and-ambush attack? Shoot through the sea for a fast chase? Or crawl out of the water to capture escaping prey?

Losing the protective shell was a trade-off. Just about anything big enough to eat an octopus will do so. Each species of predator also demands a different evasion strategy – from flashing warning colouration if your attacker is vulnerable to venom, to changing colour and shape to camouflage, to fortifying the door to your home with rocks. Such intelligence is not always evident in the laboratory. 'In the lab, you give the animals this situation, and they react', points out Mather. But in the wild, 'the octopus is actively discovering his environment, not waiting for it to hit him. The animal makes the decision to go out and get information, figures out how to get the information, gathers it, uses it, stores it. This has a great deal to do with consciousness.'

So, what does it feel like to be an octopus? Philosopher Godfrey-Smith has given this much thought, especially when he meets octopuses and their relatives, giant cuttlefish, on dives in his native Australia. 'They come forward and look at you. They reach out to touch you with their arms', he said. 'It's remarkable how little is known about them . . . but I could see it turning out that we have to change the way we think of the nature of the mind itself to take into account minds with less of a centralized self'. 'I think consciousness comes in different flavours', agrees Mather. 'Some may have consciousness in a way we may not be able to imagine.'

§

In May, I visited Athena for a third time. I wanted to see if she recognised me. But how could I tell? Scott Dowd opened the top of her tank for me. Athena had been in a back corner but floated immediately to the top, arms outstretched, upside down. This time I offered her only one arm. I had injured a knee and, feeling wobbly, used my right hand to steady me while I stood on the stool to lean over the tank. Athena in turn gripped me with only one of her arms, and very few of her suckers. Her hold on me was remarkably gentle. I was struck by this, since Murphy and others had first described Athena's personality to me as 'feisty'. 'They earn their names', Murphy had told me. Athena is named for the Greek goddess of wisdom, war, and strategy. She is not usually a laid-back octopus, like George had been. 'Athena could pull you into the tank', Murphy had warned. 'She's curious about what you are.' Was she less curious now? Did she remember me?

I was disappointed that she did not bob her head up to look at me. But perhaps she didn't need to. She may have known from the taste of my skin who I was. But why was this feisty octopus hanging in front of me in the water, upside down? Then I thought I might know what she wanted from me. She was begging. Dowd asked around and learned that Athena hadn't eaten in a couple of days, then allowed me the thrilling privilege of handing her a capelin. Perhaps I had understood something basic about what it felt like to be Athena at that moment: she was hungry. I handed a fish to one of her larger suckers, and she began to move it toward her mouth. But soon she brought more arms to the task and covered the fish with many suckers – as if she were licking her fingers, savouring the meal.

A week after I visited Athena, I was shocked to receive this e-mail from Scott Dowd: 'Sorry to write with some sad news. Athena appears to be in her final days, or even hours. She will live on, though, through your conveyance.' Later that same day, Dowd wrote to tell me that she had died. To my surprise, I found myself in tears. Why such sorrow? I had understood from the start that octopuses don't live very long. I also knew that while Athena did seem to recognise me, I was not by any means her special friend. But she was very significant to me, both as an individual and as a representative from her octopodan world. She had given me a great gift: a deeper understanding of what it means to think, to feel, and to know. I was eager to meet more of her kind. And so, it was with some excitement that I read this e-mail from Dowd a few weeks later: 'There is a young pup octopus headed to

Boston from the Pacific Northwest. Come shake hands (x8) when you can.'

§

How could I resist such an invitation? In fact, almost from the moment the new octopus arrived – her name was Octavia – I was enchanted. I visited her almost every week until nearly the day she died.

Octavia and I became very good friends indeed. How do I know this? When I would open the lid to her tank, after our first few, shy meetings, she invariably chose to come over to visit and play with me. She did not always do this with others, and in truth, there were some people she simply did not like.

Once, I was gone on an expedition overseas and missed several of our weekly visits. When I returned, we literally flew into each other's arms. She flushed red with excitement as she jetted to my side, and she stayed with me, hugging me with her suckers and looking into my face, for an exceptionally long time.

That Octavia cared about me, and not just vice versa, was even more obvious during her last days of life. Even when she was old and sick and dying, even when she had no desire to eat the fish I offered her, when I came to visit, she rose, with great effort, from the bottom of her tank to greet me, to hold me in her arms, tasting and feeling my skin, and looking into my eyes.

Despite an evolutionary divide of half a billion years, Octavia and I clearly understood and cared for each other. What does friendship feel like to an octopus? This I can't answer. But I can tell you what her friendship meant to me: ours was one of the most treasured relationships in my life – for she opened to me a new universe of compassion, reverence and love for all living creatures, no matter now unalike we might seem.

References

Mather, J., R. C. Anderson, and J. B. Wood. (2010), *Octopus: The Ocean's Intelligent Invertebrate*, Illustrated edn, Portland, OR: Timber Press.
Nagel, T. (1974), 'What is it like to be a bat?', *The Philosophical Review* 83(4) 435–450.

Chapter 3
On Standing
Harriet Ritvo

The ways in which people have treated other animals, and especially the subset of those ways that seem more or less positive, reflect the variety of our relationships with them. Consideration has often been based on affection, as with pets, or on economic considerations, as with fellow labourers, or on fear, as with a range of large or ferocious creatures. Of course, those relationships do not necessarily confer the kind of respect implicit in the term 'dignity', which, according to the *Oxford English Dictionary*, refers to 'the quality of being worthy or honourable'. That kind of standing has tended to be reserved for animals who seem to possess mental qualities that resemble those that we attribute to our own species. The definition of those qualities, never the subject of detailed consensus, has also tended to shift over time, as we have gained a fuller appreciation of the intellectual capacities of other species, so that, for example, tool use and even symbolic communication no longer serve as firm boundaries separating them from us.

Even with regard to humans, the umbrella term 'intelligence' has long accommodated a range of interpretations, so it is not surprising that it has been still less specific when applied to others. This was apparent, for example, in the scale of animal intelligence that George Romanes, a younger colleague of Charles Darwin, included in *Mental Evolution in Man* (1888). He ranked animals according to what he perceived as their percentage of human intellectual capacities. At the top, with equal standing and equal numbers (but nevertheless only twenty-eight per cent), were anthropoid apes and dogs, who shared what Romanes termed 'indefinite morality'. One step below (twenty-seven per cent), due to their 'use of tools', were monkeys, cats, and elephants, and a step below them (twenty-six per cent), due to their 'understanding of mechanisms', were rodents, ruminants, and other (non-canine or feline) carnivores. Thus, even though Romanes grouped these diverse (albeit exclusively mammalian) creatures at the top of his scale, he valued them for very different mental strengths. (It is worth mentioning that he did not think that any of them approached human intelligence very closely.)

In his earlier *Animal Intelligence* (1882) Romanes had examined the varied capacities of non-humans in greater detail, beginning with molluscs and arthropods before working up to elephants, carnivores, and primates. He felt that elephant intelligence had generally been overestimated (perhaps as much a comment on human observers as on the elephants themselves), but he nevertheless ranked them below only apes and dogs in their 'higher mental faculties' (singling out sympathy and vindictiveness, as well as the coordinated activities of elephant herds). He argued that cats, on the other hand, though 'highly intelligent', were routinely underestimated (this continues to be the case), because they lacked the sociability and docility of dogs – qualities that had allowed dogs, whose emotional life was more highly developed than that of any other animal, to benefit from the elevating influence of humans. (Despite their aloofness, however, he felt that cats had derived at least some intellectual benefit from domestication.)

Romanes lamented that, because of their unsuitability for domestication and their general uselessness, the intelligence of non-human primates had not been as frequently observed as that of the other highly ranked animals, and, for the same reason, it had not been enhanced by association with people. He nevertheless argued that their similarity to humans, demonstrated by their sympathy for each other and by their lively curiosity, as well as their general intelligence, justified his high estimation of them.

Romanes was writing as a scientist, but his opinions resonated with those of contemporaries whose expertise reflected different relationships to non-humans. The animal protection movement assumed a recognizably modern form in the course of the nineteenth century in

Britain and elsewhere. In 1822 Parliament enacted protections for livestock, and the SPCA (later RSPCA) was established soon afterwards to enforce the law. Legal protection was extended to pet species and species involved in animal combats in subsequent decades. This trajectory did not suggest that cattle were more deserving of protection than, for example, dogs; it rather reflected official reluctance to penetrate private domains of home and family. (This reluctance extended to human victims: children received legal protection later than animals – the NSPCC was an offshoot of the RSPCA).

Legal protection never extended far down Romanes' scale. And when animal dignity, or even claim to consideration, conflicted with that of humans, there was not much question about which took precedence (which is not to say that there was no question at all). In particular, Victorian legislators, along with many humane activists, were reluctant to interfere with elite practices. Thus, in the sporting realm, while animal baiting and combat, which attracted miscellaneous audiences, were targeted, fox hunting was mostly not, although current critiques were available then. Similarly, although the initial attempt to regulate scientific experimentation on animals was passed by Parliament in 1876 (the first such law anywhere, and the model for many similar laws in other countries), it was viewed by antivivisectionists as enabling rather than controlling the practice.

Such regulations have been repeatedly revised and strengthened in the intervening century and a half, but they continue to reflect the rankings embodied in Romanes' chart. Like earlier legislation, current regulation of experimentation gives greatest consideration to animals perceived as closest to us, whether intellectually or emotionally or socially, at least in the US and the UK. There is more elaborate (or sympathetic) acknowledgment of their pain and suffering, and, in some cases, animals must be provided with stimulation to allay the boredom and stress of laboratory life. Small rodents and fish have become the preferred experimental subjects, at least in part because their use is less heavily constrained than that of dogs, cats, and primates.

Of course, it is hard to characterize preferential treatment in such circumstances as constituting dignity, even though it clearly evidences relative consideration or standing. Indeed, dignity seems elusive for most animals who live among humans, no matter how privileged. Primates in some (certainly not all) zoo settings – like dogs and cats in loving homes – enjoy far better living conditions, but whether even those circumstances allow them much dignity is at least open to question.

References

Romanes, G. (1882), *Animal Intelligence*, London: Kegan Paul, Trench.
Romanes, G. (1888), *Mental Evolution in Man*, London: Kegan Paul, Trench.

Chapter 4
Wild Dignity
Lori Gruen

Dignity is often thought to be a quality that inheres in humans, like a kernel of light that lifts humans above all others. But there are at least two problems with this idea. First, how is it that some people, like many of the incarcerated people I have taught, feel their dignity is systematically violated, if every human being has it inherently? Humans who are incarcerated are often dehumanized, subjected to numerous indignities daily. They are under constant surveillance, told what to do and when, and have their bodies intruded upon without consent. And incarcerated people aren't alone in feeling that their dignity is violated or overlooked – many people of colour, immigrants, gender non-conforming people, and disabled people experience exclusion from those thought to have dignity. If dignity inheres in all humans, how can there be so many circumstances when it is lost or fails to be acknowledged?

The second problem has to do with the possibility that it isn't all and only humans who can be said to have dignity. Some humans are systematically denied dignity when they are 'treated like animals' and, as I'll suggest, many animals can be denied dignity when they are exposed to 'de-animalizing' conditions.[1]

There are a group of scholars who argue that to solve the first problem and establish that all humans, no matter the conditions they live under, have dignity they must double down on the second problem and strongly assert that no non-human animals can have dignity. These scholars believe that having dignity is what makes humans distinct. Will Kymlicka has identified this group as the 'new dignitarians' – theorists who advocate for human dignity as a central argument in securing global human rights. These new dignitarians tend to argue that dignity is a concept that must be exclusively applied to humans in order to distinguish human beings from other 'things', which do not have dignity but only relative worth. Some of the new dignitarians go so far as to say that thinking of animals as having dignity tarnishes the very concept of dignity that all and only humans share.[2]

Yet there are certainly instances in which it makes good sense to apply the concept of dignity to non-human beings. In my book *Ethics and Animals* (2021) I recount Suzanne Cataldi's discussion of her visit to the Moscow Circus observing bears in bright-coloured clown collars holding balloons and prancing around on tiptoes pushing baby strollers like clumsy 'overweight ballerinas' (Cataldi, 2002: 106). Surely there is something wrong with making bears appear as ballerinas or other animals appear as clowns beyond the suffering that inevitably occurs in their training? I argued that by getting animals to do these things, the animal's dignity is being undermined.

When animals are forced to be something other than who they are, when they are made to be ridiculous, presented as laughable spectacles, as they often are in the entertainment industry, this is disrespectful of their animal dignity. When an individual is denied the opportunity to behave in ways that are fitting for beings like her, for example, when a highly social elephant is held alone in a zoo or when an orca whale or dolphin is kept in a small tank, her dignity is being undermined. Similarly, when individuals are forced to perform acts involuntarily that aren't part of their behavioural repertoires, like dancing with tutus on, or making clown lips, or walking on two legs and pushing a baby carriage, their dignity is being violated. This violation is in addition to and distinct from any suffering that an animal may endure, it is a relational harm that also happens when who they are as sentient beings that can make choices is intentionally obscured from view, leaving a distorted image of their lives and experiences in our minds.

But, you might think, the animals themselves don't necessarily care that they are being laughed at, ridiculed, and misunderstood. Most other animals either don't have the capacity or the desire to think about what humans think of them. People who spray-paint their dogs and

Figure 7 Elephant, close up, credit Adam Oswell / We Animals Media.

enter them into extreme grooming contests to see which dog looks the most like a ninja turtle, battleship, dinosaur, or panda, claim the dogs like it. And many animals appear to enjoy performing 'stupid pet tricks'. Some animals do seem embarrassed or guilty under certain circumstances, although as Alexandra Horowitz has shown, this is most likely a product of their 'owner's' expectations (Horowitz, 2009). Seeing other animals as embarrassed, ashamed, or indignant, or alternatively suggesting they enjoy being made to look absurd, always runs the danger of being a human projection. Attributing dignity or noticing events that violate the dignity of other animals, critics may suggest, is simply another expression of our human inability to perceive anything outside of our anthropocentric perspective.

Even if we oppose strong anthropocentrism – the view that maintains that human perspectives are superior perspectives – we cannot avoid the inevitability of our perspective always being a human one. Nonetheless, focusing on an animal's dignity can move us closer to a position that both reveals and decentres human arrogance.

§

One of the traditional philosophical views that lies at the heart of discussions of human dignity, that of Immanuel Kant, is inescapably anthropocentric. Kantian dignity posits that there is a property that inheres in humanity, usually tied to the human capacity of reason, in virtue of which we recognize and respect each other's dignity. Variations of the Kantian view can also be found in a variety of discussions of dignity, including dignity that is grounded not only in the capacity of rationality but in other properties that tend to be associated with human personhood – properties such as self-consciousness and self-reflection, the ability to imagine oneself into a future, and the capacity to value one's projects and goals.

Within standard formulations of animal ethics, even those that aren't so bold as to posit that animals have dignity, there has been tremendous effort to identify these dignity-conferring capacities beyond the human. There are robust efforts to try to show, for example, that elephants are self-conscious and aware of their futures, that chimpanzees value their own goals, and that whales engage in self-reflection by modifying their songs when they encounter new melodies.

But looking for specific and static properties that inhere in animals, properties to which dignity can be attached, ignores the social and relational significance of dignity. Dignity-evoking capacities exist when they are recognized and appreciated by others within specific social contexts. Dignity, particularly animal dignity, may be most sensibly understood as a relational property.

Consider political dignity in the human context, which is akin to a social or civic demand for recognition and respect. Political dignity doesn't rely on the idea that there is a property or set of properties that all humanity has in virtue of which we respect each other and recognize dignity. Rather, this account constructs dignity to promote human social flourishing. The Preamble to the Universal Declaration of Human Rights recognizes the dignity 'of all members of the human family', and that recognition 'is the foundation of freedom, justice and peace in the world'. Political dignity, whether it rests on some inherent property or not, ultimately can be understood as identifying a social value, like justice and peace, that societies should strive to promote for members of those societies to achieve well-being. We can think of political dignity as conducive to social harmony and human fulfilment. What is important about this conception, and what makes it different from Kantian dignity, is that political dignity is embedded in social relations.

I suggest we think of animal dignity as 'wild dignity' that focuses on the context of expression as well as a dynamic, as opposed to essentialist or static, understanding of dignity. Wild dignity is like political dignity but more expansive, it includes other animals within their own social networks as evaluated through ours. Wild dignity is a relational notion, not unlike the sort of political dignity that suggests that 'human dignity is not a metaphysical property of individual human beings, but rather a property of relations between human beings – between, so to speak, the dignifier and the dignified' (Luban, 2009: 214).

It may be helpful to think of the question of dignity as arising when there is a compromised relation – between the dignity violator and the dignity deserver. Philosopher Elizabeth Anderson also suggests that we understand dignity as a relational concept, and she applies it to other animals, but she frames it in problematic anthropocentric terms. She writes, 'The dignity of an animal, whether human or non-human, is what is required to make it [sic] decent for human society, for the particular, species-specific ways in which humans relate to them' (Anderson, 2004: 283). I think Anderson's instinct is right that dignity only comes into play when non-humans are part of a social world in which questions of dignity arise. When animals are living in the wild, free from our interference, or at least mostly free from our interference, we might see their behaviour as majestic or awesome and perhaps we might think of them as dignified, although the term seems odd in that context. When other animals become part of a human context, as they do when we hold them captive, their wild dignity becomes a meaningful concept, because it is in these contexts where it is most likely violated. Making other animals 'decent for human society' is precisely what it means to deny them their dignity. When we project our needs and tastes onto them, try to alter or change what they do, and when we prevent them from controlling their own lives, we deny them their wild dignity. In contrast, we dignify the wildness of other animals when we respect their behaviours as meaningful to them and recognize that their lives are theirs to live. We may not like it that some animals are aggressive, that some smell badly or throw or eat excrement, destroy plants, masturbate, or hump each other or us. Often, in captivity, animals are forced to stop doing the things that make them indecent to 'human society' and made to do things that they don't ordinarily do (like pushing a baby carriage in a circus) because humans want them to. This is an exercise of domination, and it violates their wild dignity, even if it doesn't cause any obvious suffering.

While recognizing and promoting the dignity of other animals most likely leads to an enhancement of their wellbeing, the valuer who appreciates the dignity or recognizes and protests an indignity, has something significant at stake in aptly responding in the right contexts as well.[3] When accurately perceiving the dignity evoked (or indignities experienced), the valuer is exercising her own moral perception and agency since being perceptive about dignity-enhancing or dignity-diminishing activities is a central part of our ethical capacity to treat others as they should be treated.

Dignity, understood relationally, can be compromised or undermined even when the individual whose dignity is at stake does not object or complain. And dignity can be promoted or respected even if the individuals whose dignity is being preserved are unaware that efforts are being made to do so. Of course, in the case of dignity promotion, the individuals are likely to suffer less, and that is something that directly impacts their well-being. I would hope that by focusing not just on minimizing suffering but also on preventing indignities, the likelihood of inadvertently causing pain or distress will be minimized and wellbeing may be promoted. That other animals are not necessarily concerned about such things as dignity does not tell against their having it and recognizing their dignity can benefit them.

By viewing dignity as relational, we get a sense of how it is that denying dignity marks others as 'rightly' excluded and it also illuminates the ways our own perceptions and valuations become distorted in that process. We see that denying dignity is part of what keeps others as 'others'. The status hierarchies that dignity has historically been used to uphold are also relational, of course, although often those who promote them fail to register it. The specific human-centred hierarchies that are adopted maintain that the dignity of humans (and some humans at that) depends on the denial of dignity to others.

But a relational conception of dignity also explains why concerns about dignity are often expressed in the contexts in which it has been or might be denied. It is rarely the case that we comment on or admire the dignity of people being respectful of one another in the ordinary course of things. But, in a country like America, when a police officer singles out a black youth to stop and frisk or when a bus driver doesn't stop for a Hispanic woman carrying her groceries or when macho guys harangue lesbians walking out of a theatre, we are concerned not just with the indignities experienced by the youth and women, but we are struck by the lack of respect on the part of the offenders. They have failed to properly value the individuals with whom they are interacting and in that lose some of their own worth as moral beings. In respecting someone's dignity, a valuer recognizes the worth of that individual, a worth they share, and values it accordingly.

Importantly, recognizing that dignity is a relational concept is not the same as reducing it to the mere whims of the perceiver or that dignity is a social projection about the worth of another. Clearly animals are not getting the respect they deserve – they are being used and killed on a massive scale as a matter of routine – so relying on common attitudes or a human-centred conception of dignity will not lead to the promotion of animal dignity. But the relational notion of dignity does capture both the contextual nature of the notion – the larger non-ideal historical, social, political, racialized, and gendered landscape it emerges within – as well as the broader normative implications of the recognition of dignity or the failure to recognize dignity on the valuer, the community of valuers, and the individual whose dignity should be respected.

Wild dignity is a relational, non-anthropocentric account of dignity that can help us see the ways in which so many animals are being harmed, not just by violent institutions and practices that cause them to suffer, but also by the ways in which their dignity is being denied. The 'wild' part of wild dignity evokes a sense of other species beyond their human entanglements, even if we are thinking of domesticated animals who necessarily live with humans. Recognizing wild animal dignity also helps us develop and envision more expansive and more inclusive ways of respecting others, humans and non-humans alike.

Notes

1. For an important discussion of the de-animalization of both humans and animals in captivity, see Guenther (2013).
2. For a full discussion, see Kymlicka (2018).
3. For a related discussion of animal dignity, see Crary and Gruen (2022).

References

Anderson, E. (2004), 'Animal rights and the values of non-human life', in C. Sunstein and M. Nussbaum (eds.), *Animal Rights: Current Debates and New Directions*, New York: Oxford University Press.

Cataldi, S. (2002), 'Animals and the concept of dignity: Critical reflections on a circus performance', *Ethics and the Environment* 7(2):104–126.

Crary, A. and L. Gruen. (2022), *Animal Crisis: A New Critical Theory*, Oxford: Polity Press.

Gruen, L. (2014), 'Dignity, captivity, and an ethics of sight', in L. Gruen (ed.), *The Ethics of Captivity*, New York: Oxford University Press.

Gruen, L. (2021), *Ethics and Animals: An Introduction*, 2nd edn, Cambridge: Cambridge University Press.

Guenther, L. (2013), *Solitary Confinement: Social Death and Its Afterlives*, Minneapolis: University of Minnesota Press.

Horowitz, A. (2009). 'Disambiguating the "guilty look": Salient prompts to a familiar dog behavior', *Behavioural Processes* 81(3): 447–452.

Kymlicka, W. (2018), 'Human rights without human supremacism', *Canadian Journal of Philosophy* 48(6): 763–792.

Luban, D. (2009), 'Human dignity, humiliation and torture', *Kennedy Institute of Ethics Journal* 19(3): 211–230.

Chapter 5
Dignity in Dogs
Alexandra Horowitz

In what would turn out to be the last year of his life, Finnegan at first gradually, then quickly, lost use of his hind legs almost completely, until he could not run or even walk unassisted. The rest of his spirit was intact, and he looked at me balefully, ears back, eyes seeming to ask the question, *Why can I not?* I tried to answer by modifying his world to meet him in his changed state. When the stairs became slippery, we carpeted the stairs. When even carpeted, they were too formidable to ascend, I hoisted his rear legs as he powered himself up. When descent became precarious, I swooped all sixty pounds of him in my arms and slowly backed down the stairs, setting him on the bottom step to launch himself. As he became unable to support any of the weight of his rear quarters, we needed to support his weight with a strap under his belly and walk with him, pausing when he wanted to sniff a patch of grass, or hurrying up when he was keen on greeting a dog down the street. The paralysis included control of the bladder; we dressed him in a kind of dog diaper and changed it throughout the day. His bowels moved involuntarily, so we lay pads under him wherever he rested and began to read his behaviour for when he needed to defecate. Presented with a wheelchair, he initially baulked, although in his final days he acceded to its use – getting treats when he'd follow us down the sidewalk – and soon would race ahead of us on the sidewalk or path from smell to smell, from dog to dog.

    I could read his distress at his inability to partake in the ordinary moments of his life: jumping up on the couch; chasing a squeaking ball;

sitting in the prime spot by the kitchen; greeting me first at the door. So I lifted him to the couch; supported him while rolling the ball; brought the tastiest morsels to him; went to meet him where he lay on returning home.

We tried to meet him where he was in every respect. Because he was *our Finnegan* – this charming, earnest, and enthusiastic character who had been an essential member of our family for fourteen years. And also because he was a sentient, feeling, aware creature who needed help from us.

Finnegan died at fourteen and a half years old. Sitting with our grief, we are nonetheless gratified for every day that we got to know him, to tickle his ears, to listen to his breathing, to be caught by his gaze, to watch him run madly, to feel the weight of his head resting on our legs. In quiet moments, though, I wonder whether it was dignified, our strapping him in a wheelchair for a walk or our letting him defecate inside when he could no longer hold himself up outside. Was his dignity *as a dog* intact?

§

It is commonly stated that it is merciful to euthanize a pet, such as a dog, who is suffering from a disease, or even for reasons of advanced age or what the owner interprets as intransigent behavioural problems. It is certainly legal – unlike euthanasia of humans in most of the world. Not only is it considered merciful, but it is also at times claimed to be 'just', the righteous response of a pet owner who has an obligation to a pet deemed to be suffering, as the pet cannot reflect on their suffering, only experience it (Cavanaugh, 2016).

If we put aside the question of pet animals' self-reflection for a moment – an empirical claim, without support – the notion of the obligation, or the responsibility, of the owner resounds. The responsibility of the owner, in other words, might be to euthanize a pet at the appropriate time to maintain that pet's dignity: 'a death with dignity', as it is often described (Ashe, 2018).

Indeed, when researching the expected progression of the disease, degenerative myelopathy, that was affecting Finn, I noted that he had already advanced past the stages of evolution of the disease that veterinary science describes. It appeared that this was not because the disease caused other animals' deaths. Instead, I suspect this can be

Figure 8 Dog, credit Jo-Anne McArthur / We Animals Media.

explained by the probability that other owners euthanized their dogs before the disease progressed to the degree it had with Finn.

There is no definitive statistic as to the number of pet euthanasias performed each year but is estimated to be around five or six million in the United States alone. Writing about the phenomenon, Jessica Pierce and Ross Taylor note that while the statistic is under-discussed, there is a growing literature on the subsequent feelings of guilt of some owners who request this procedure for their animals (Pierce and Taylor, 2019: 163). While a veterinarian who performs the procedure is likely to reassure the client about its appropriateness, few people feel prepared to determine when to end the life of an animal who has been a part of the family. Even if 'merciful', the act of euthanasia is, by its finality, destructive of a relationship between person and dog.

At play in these different approaches to dignity in a dog's late life may be two ways to think about their dignity in an owned-animal (pet) environment. They may not be contradictory. In both cases, what is at issue is the dog's ability to exist *as the sort of thing they are*. My family and I tried to enable this for Finn by extending his couch-jumping, puddle-running, dog-sniffing capacities when they were diminished. Or one may do this by ending the dog's life altogether when they are so diminished. In common is the recognition of the partial or complete loss of important, dog-specific capacities, and the acknowledgement that some of these capacities are critical for their flourishing. In both cases, it seems to be additionally important that, done right, the dog is being treated with dignity by the person: the dog bears dignity because they are part of a dignity-affirming relationship.

Not all ways of treating dogs are so affirming, of course. I think immediately of two kinds of cases where the dog's dignity is undone by their way of being treated. One is to do with our occasional lack of imagination (as humans) for what the experiences of a non-human might be like. To dress a dog in a tutu (as a costume, or for 'fun'), or to shame them for perceived misdeeds (as boredom-derived inappropriate chewing): these are distortions of the dog that are not benign.

The second kind of case is complementary: included within dog-specific capacities and desires are often behaviours that humans would find undignified to do themselves. Finnegan, for instance, loved to sniff other dogs in a way inconsistent with the personal space humans of all cultures recognize. He was definitely interested in smelling the crotch of a visiting human. He liked rolling in foul-smelly things. He ate deer poop with alacrity. He humped the occasional leg. He responded to our return with people-toppling exuberance.

People often work to restrict dogs' abilities to do these things. These are cases in which human treatment of dogs reflects a mistranslation of dignity *for dogs* – for certainly it is dignified to greet social others in a species-typical fashion (in the case of sniffing closely); to move too closely to smell the smelliest part of our bodies; to pursue scents that are pleasurable. And these are cases in which our desire to treat them *like us* – the tutu, the shaming – compromises their ability to be *like themselves.* To treat them with dignity we must use *their* sense of dignity. I cannot be sure what this is, but I suggest that it is those behaviours that they do voluntarily without fear of reprisal: the living into who they are.

And sometimes we must help them get to their own dignity. To give them a chance to be themselves, to release them from their leash when able, to respect their reluctance to go on that noisy street, to accede to their desire to sniff something long and deeply. As dogs are still property, their lives circumscribed by where and what we allow, we are partial arbiters of how their life will go.

By analogy with the rights conferred on humans by our claim of intrinsic dignity,[1] to grant Finn, or any dog, dignity would be to give him the right to be unrestricted in his ability to 'be a dog', to live their life to the full extent of their capacity: making choices and expressing species-appropriate desires and behaviours. To 'flourish' as a dog (Gruen, 2011: 38; Nussbaum, 2011: 237–8). One could make the claim that the very fact of the captivity of the species *Canis familiaris*, having been partially designed – *shaped* – by us out of wolves to look like and act like what we prefer – extracts some dignity from us both. And yet it can be reinserted by carefully attending to that which the dog needs to flourish in their dogness, even with that constraint to their lives.

While Finn, as the dog of a dog-cognition researcher, was subjected to much scrutiny during his life – I generated many hypotheses for studies from simply watching him – in his last year I gazed at Finn every day with extra attention. I minded his moods and marked what he needed, wanted, and could not do. For his part, he developed new ways of communicating with us – using his snout to move our hands to a part of his body that needed support, or to point at a place he would like to be carried – and found new pleasures. He flourished. And he flourishes still, in the synapses of my brain, the sinews of my heart – and here, on this page with us.

Note

[1] 'Dignity' is presented as a human trait, constitutive of human rights: opening both the EU Charter of Fundamental Rights and the UN's Universal Declaration on Human Rights.

References

Ashe, C. (2018), 'Why Do We Give Our Pets Death with Dignity but Not Ourselves?' Slate.com, 16 August.

Cavanaugh, T. A. (2016), 'Dignity, pet-euthanasia and person euthanasia', in J. Mizzoni (ed.), *G.E.M. Anscombe and Human Dignity*, Aston, PA: Neumann University Press, 117–142.
Gruen, L. (2011), *Ethics and Animals: An Introduction*, Cambridge: Cambridge University Press.
Nussbaum, M. (2011), 'The capabilities approach and animal entitlements', in T. L. Beauchamp and R. G. Frey (eds.), *The Oxford Handbook of Animal Ethics*, Oxford: Oxford University Press, 228–253.
Pierce, J. and R. Taylor. (2019), 'Last moments: Witnessing and representing the death of pets', in T. K. Shackelford and V. Zeigler-Hill (eds.), *Evolutionary Perspectives on Death*, Switzerland: Springer, 161–176.

Chapter 6
The Heart of the Scorpion
Kathleen Dean Moore

Day One. The sky shone black in the Death Valley desert that night, and the stars seemed closer and denser than they should have been. I recognized the constellation Scorpius crawling up the dusty edge of the southern sky, but the light from uncountable stars drowned out the other constellations. In that wild, wind-swept night, it was not hard to imagine an extra-terrestrial's view of the tiny Earth, spinning through its celestial night. The effect was intensified by a circle of blue light that wandered over the desert sand, spotlighting one saltbush after another, as if a star ship were hovering in the night, beaming its blue light on one Earthly astonishment after another. But these were not aliens; rather, our two grandsons with an ultraviolet flashlight, searching for scorpions.

We found one, they shouted, as gleefully surprised as an alien might be, and the whole family rushed across the sandflat to see.

In the UV light, the scorpion glowed chartreuse. It was tiny, small enough to perch comfortably on a dime. I had to kneel on the sand to get close enough to bring into focus its two lobster-like pincers and the stinger curved over its back. But soon the boys left us in the dark and found another scorpion in another saltbush. It would seem that dozens of scorpions had left their burrows to move through the night, hunting small flies or other, even smaller, scorpions. If the small scorpions are out wandering, it occurred to me, so probably are larger ones, and I stood up awkwardly, keeping my hands far away from star-shadows in the sand. I knew that a small scorpion's sting would hurt no more than a sweat bee's. I knew also that although there are twenty species of scorpion worldwide whose sting can kill a grown writer on her knees in the dark, none of them live in Death Valley. I shouldn't have worried, but I did.

The boys were, of course, full of excited questions. How do they hunt? Why do they glow green like that? If they are cannibals, how do they mate? – an astute question for a kid. The boys had never imagined that they would ACTUALLY FIND A SCORPION, and here they had found dozens, or that they would be SO COOL, and here the scorpions were, undeniably cool.

I didn't have answers to their questions then, but I knew a man who did. Many years ago, we camped in this desert with our friend Phil Brownell, an Oregon State University zoologist, who was studying the sensory biology of scorpions. At the end of each day, as the air began to lose its creosote-spiced heat and fill instead with the smell of frying onions, Phil would saunter into camp with three scorpions hanging from both hands, each one pinned by its stinger between the knuckles of two fingers. I had called him as soon as we got home.

§

As long as I've known him, Phil has been devoted to scorpions. Never has there been an animal, he said, so brilliantly, so perfectly able to thrive in so challenging a habitat. They evolved from arthropod ancestors in the Silurian and Devonian Oceans, 400 million years ago. *Imagine swimming with a scorpion as long as your leg*, Phil said. But freshly evolved vertebrates, fishes with teethed jaws, ate the aquatic scorpions almost to extinction. The ones who survived were those who gradually backed into the most inhospitable places on earth – the sand deserts. Scorpions became among the first successful terrestrial animals. Phil would nominate them for the most intriguing too. Sure, they have a bad press. But that's hardly fair for such an ancient and extraordinary animal. The night that Phil and Sir David Attenborough talked scorpions into the wee hours, the great nature filmmaker averred that scorpions are the poster child of this truth: that the more people know about an animal, the more they come to respect them. *If you can get people to change their fear of scorpions into awe and reverence. . .* he told Phil, *they would have to accept all others, everywhere.*

§

Day Two. Late the next night, we leaned back in camp chairs and squinted into the great awning of stars. *There's the Big Dipper*, the boy pointed out to his little brother. *So that would be the Little Dipper, and there is the North Star.* We worked to find Leo, the great lion, usually hanging out on the far side of the Big Dipper, but that night he was just more stars in a sea of stars. I pointed to the south instead. *That bright star is Antares. That is the heart of Scorpius.* The boys followed my pointing finger and found it low on the southern horizon, pulsing in the desert air. *And if you've got Antares, you can get Scorpius. See it there? Those three stars are its head and pincers, but you might not see the long curl of its tail. There's an exoplanet somewhere up there in Scorpius,* I told the boys. Astrobiologists are excited about it, because it's relatively near to Earth and has a zone of temperatures that can hold life.

 The boys looked for Orion but did not find him in the late spring sky. In winter, Orion stands astride the Western sky with his legs akimbo and a dagger on his belt. Orion, the Great Hunter, boasted he would kill all the animals on Earth. But Artemis, the true and wise goddess of the hunt, sent a scorpion to kill Orion instead, which the scorpion managed to do after a nasty battle. Zeus put the scorpion in the sky, at the farthest distance from Orion, and put the double-star Antares at the scorpion's heart. Antares, from *ant-* (against) + *ares* (the god of war). At its heart, the scorpion is a war protestor who saved the animals from the hunter's hubris.

§

Although scorpions need to hunt to live, they don't eat much, Phil told me. Good-sized scorpions might do just fine on one cricket a year, an economy that works well in the dry and hungry desert sands. They achieve this by sitting still, shutting their systems down to the metabolic rate of a tick, rousing themselves only when a likely meal comes by – which may not happen for months on end.

To find their prey, scorpions use vibrational information from the sand. This is the part that Phil has studied for most of his professional life. Special waves, called Rayleigh waves, are surface waves that ripple across the ground, Phil told me, the way the shifting of an earthquake sends surface waves through a city, knocking down buildings. The smallest scuff on the sand is conveyed outward mostly along its surface, with compressional 'sound' waves also penetrating its depths. So, the desert that seems dead to us is actually alive with information, and the denizens of the desert are fine-tuned to the news, both to find prey and to avoid becoming prey.

With her head poked down into the ancient sands of the Namib desert, for example, a golden mole can hear the vibration of insects chewing roots on nearby shrubs and dig straight to them. On the other hand, a sand-swimming snake, sensing a disturbance, will stop breathing and shut down the beating of its heart – five, even ten minutes – to avoid sending out a vibration that will catch the attention of a predator or approaching prey. The scorpion's sensitivity to sand waves is just as exquisite. Imagine, Phil suggested, that each of your eight legs has grown a sense organ just above a sandshoe of long hairs delicately supporting it on the surface. These sense even the smallest surface vibrations of the sand in waves maybe as small as a hydrogen atom. So here, in the darkest night, a scorpion can map every beetle, every snake, every drop of rain or shifting dune, every boy dancing around it, every kneeling writer, and know if they are coming or going, north or south, up or down.

But don't think for a minute that scorpions can't also see, Phil warns. They can gather light at the limit of sensitivity known for any animal, even a single photon of light in the colour blue-green. So, there's every reason to think they can see dim light even better than humans. Can they make out the North Star, the Great Dipper, the wash of the Milky Way, even their own image shimmering in the dark sky and the dazzling star of their own hearts? Phil didn't know. But he has gathered evidence that scorpions can navigate by orienting relative to bands of light in the night sky, like the Milky Way, and to polarized light on the horizons at night. Imagine this, a tiny little animal ploughing alone through the waves of sand, buffeted by gales, holding its course by the light of the stars.

§

Day Three. In the dusty, sizzling heat of the next afternoon, we heard a woman's voice crying out again and again. We struggled to make out what she said. Then a pickup rolled onto the sandflat where we were camped. Standing in the open bed, a women called to us: Have you seen a yellow Labrador retriever? We had not, but we would watch for her. The dog's name is 'Tracie,' we learned, and she is a service dog, trained to help a hearing-impaired woman. Earlier, the group had climbed far up into the dunes, leaving the dog with a friend back at camp. At some point, the friend had let the dog off-leash. Tracie had charged into the dunes. And had not returned.

A Labrador retriever missing in the infinite sun of desert sand and scrub with no water for fifty miles in any direction? She must have become lost, or she would have returned. Or she could be following some inner map of fealty toward wherever home was – Los Angeles? Reno? We spent the next day trying to track her and had no luck, but the boys' father reported an ancient metate, a concave stone for grinding corn, and the boys stopped to examine the centre portion of a spear point chipped from yellow chert. When the day finally cooled and the stars began to poke out, there was still no sign of Tracie.

§

I can vaguely understand why the yellow stars of Scorpius shine so brightly in the night sky. But why do the tiny scorpions in the saltbush shine with that citrus chartreuse? Brighter than frogs, brighter than spring grass, the only things I've seen this colour are cartoons of space invaders, the little green men. Not so, Phil told me. There are plants in the desert that shine that otherworldly fluorescence; in wet years, the flowers of a perennial evening primrose bloom brightly fluorescent and attract pollinating moths. *Of course, of course*, the boys exulted when I'd called them to pass this news along. *The scorpion is disguising itself as a flower. And when a moth flutters down to feed, the scorpion grabs it with its pincers. Awesome!*

The wonder of this strategy thrilled the boys, but even more wonderful than the scorpion's green shine, in my opinion, is its blue blood. The scorpion's heart is strung out in multiple chambers along the top of its back. The blood doesn't flow through vessels or capillaries, but floods throughout the scorpion's body. The blood is light blue because the carrier for its oxygen is copper, not the iron that accounts for the red colour of mammalian blood. Imagine, I told the boys, a tiny animal who bleeds as blue as the desert sky at dawn.

§

Day Four. The desert where we camped is bordered by several US Naval Air bases, home to some of the most sophisticated fighter jets in existence, perhaps including the 'adaptable and lethal' F-89 Scorpion. Pilots have to test-fly the fighters somewhere, I suppose, so they fly them over Death Valley – at what seems like one hundred feet. That morning just past dawn, we felt them coming, a buzz in our sternums, and then saw a pair of them, far in advance of their sound. They screamed flat overhead, banked so they were flying on the point of one wing, made a tight turn around the sand dune, disappeared, and then suddenly reappeared, screeching over our heads while we slammed our hands over our ears and ducked.

The pilots roared out of the valley. They must have been exquisitely trained to manoeuvre in a tight space at extraordinary speed, up to Mach 3.0, which is good in case they are engaged in a dogfight to save a small democracy or. . . well, to defend supplies of petrofuel, which the jets burn at 385 gallons a minute. But what this did to the scorpions, so acutely attuned to vibrations, one can only imagine.

§

So now we have our characters assembled, and we can begin the thought experiment. Consider: 1. The scorpion. 2. The Labrador retriever. 3. The fighter pilot. Of these three, which animal is best? That is, which is most worthy of dignity and respect? It may be a trick question, but in fact, it's a question that has preoccupied humans for at least three thousand years. It seems clear that, in the European tradition at least, the Man, the fighter pilot, has long been the clear winner.

Aristotle carefully charted the Great Chain of Being, a rigid hierarchy from God to Man to cattle, all the way 'down' to clams. The Middle Ages added a couple of ranks of angels and archangels between God and Man, but never quarrelled with the pecking order, except to debate where Black men fit. For itself, Christianity started equitably enough: *And God said, Let the waters bring forth abundantly the moving creatures that hath life, and fowl that may fly above the earth in the open firmament of heaven.* That was day five. For one damn day, all the animals enjoyed God's equal regard and respect. *And it was good, it was very good.*

But the very next day, number six, God enthroned Man at the top of the Chain: *Subdue [the Earth]: and have dominion over the fish of the sea, and over the fowl of the air, and over every living thing.* In subsequent centuries, extractive capitalists danced drunkenly on the back of the 'substandard', subjugated natural world. Even visionary Aldo Leopold, who advocated expanding *the sphere of our moral concern* to include the land, never questioned that Man squats squarely at the centre of that sphere of worth.

But now we have been to the desert, and we have been shown what we had not seen before. So let us ask again, which of our three animals truly is the apogee of evolution? Which is most beautiful? Which is most clever? Which is the most perfectly suited to its purposes? Which is most worthy – not relative to human ends, but in itself? And which, in a moral world, should be treated with reverence and respect? A good case could be made for the fighter pilot, who is surely useful, maybe essential, in a civilization built on war. Perhaps an equal case could be made for the loyal yellow lab, who managed, it must be said, to stagger back to camp to resume her service after two sizzling hot days. And the ancient, infinitely patient, cleverly complicated, extravagantly florid, stargazing scorpion, tuned and trembling to the frequency of the Earth?

Every one of these is astonishing. Each one is wonderful and to be wondered at. But that is not the main point. It's not beauty or cleverness of design or efficacy that makes a man or a dog or a scorpion worthy of care and respect – although those are miraculous enough. In my judgement, the most important point is that every one of these shares the urge to live. Or, as Albert Schweitzer put it, *the most immediate fact of man's consciousness is the assertion 'I am life that wills to live in the midst of life that wills to live.'*

Figure 9 Scorpion, credit Philip Brownell.

Every living thing is the *urge to live* packaged by evolution into wildly creative, unpredictable, divergent, and often extravagantly beautiful forms. *Life* is the astonishing fact of the universe – life, and its insistence on life's continuing. In my judgement, the urgency toward life is as close as we will come to the sacred, and no wonder we fall to our knees in the dark. Reverence, awe, respect, dignity – call it what you will – every living being deserves this in equal measure, because every living being has in equal measure the hunger for life – enclosed, as it may be, in flight jacket, yellow pelt, or hairy fluorescent-green cuticle.

§

Day Five. Before you zip into your tent, I asked the boys on our final night in the desert, will you turn off your flashlights and walk with me into the warm wind one last time? We will listen for the sound of a sand dune as it slides down its slip face; the tinkling song may stop our breath and still our hearts. Maybe we will reach out to hold each other's hands, the night will be that beautiful. We will see the soft hips and flanks of the shining sand itself, which once was a mountain, which once was a sea where scorpions swam. When we lift our eyes, we will look through the sparkling spirals of the galaxy to which we belong, as the sand belongs, as the animals belong. Look up to the south, and for all we know, we may be looking into the curious eyes of life-loving creatures on Gliese, only twenty-two light years away. It is the evening of the fifth day, when all of creation is one. The night will tell us: *We are not the kings of this universe, but oh how blessed we are to be among its creations*.

Chapter 7
'An Old Joy': Ways of Attending to Dignity

Deborah Slicer

Horses: Lu and Noah

Horses don't all particularly like us. They don't have to like us. Some don't want much to do with us, in fact. As the revered horseman Tom Hunt once said, 'You have to give something you never gave to get something you never had.' With these horses, the giving is all on you. And after a few decades of this kind of giving, they might develop some little curiosity about you. If you persist from a non-predatory distance, they might eventually even treat you like another horse, now and then. A toothy rummaging around the hair shafts should you wander, hatless, inside a grooming session. A gentle lean-into during a bout of loneliness one starry winter night.

You can climb up top of these horses' backs and have a very pleasant ride through fields, across creeks, up mountainsides, when they feel like it. And sometimes they do feel like it. Though what they like is very different for each individual of course. Lu liked the woman-strong rub-rubs all over her Rubenesque self. At home, Lu was the boss mare with big responsibilities. And before that, she led strings of pack mules and other riders into the way-back country for days at a time, into lion and griz scent, through fast-running rivers that chilled her belly, through September snow squalls, a solid eight days of lousy food, rude mules snuzzling her rear end. But on Saturday trail rides she preferred the middle or last (closest to the trailhead) position. Let somebody else find out if a rock is really a rock or a black bear.

This is, of course, *when* she feels like it. When she doesn't: give it up. Insouciance is only the beginning of a really bad day. Experts say: nip it in the bud.

'See to it that the colt be kind, used to the hand, and fond of men when he is put out to the horse-breaker. He is generally made so at home and by the groom, if man knows how to manage so that solitude means to the colt hunger and thirst and teasing horse flies, while food, drink, and relief from pain come from man. For if this be done, colts must not only love men, but even long for them' (Xenophon, 2006: 21).

'[T]he ultimate objective of training must be to guide the horse with invisible aids. Two creatures, the one who thinks and the other who executes the thought must be fused together' (Podhajsky,1965: 55).

On a more contemporary view: 'Respect is hard to get and easy to lose; therefore you should strive to maintain it. [F]irst. . . you get a horse's respect by proving you're the alpha animal (primary or superior animal, the leader) while on the ground. This is where the relationship starts. . . This relationship should be one with you as the leader and the horse, the follower,' says Pat Parelli, one of the several mostly male authors of the recent and popular Natural Horsemanship school, which aims to 'understand the horse's mind in order to control his feet' (Parelli, 1993: 24). At least, in our eyes, horses have minds now, sort of.

'Leading' that is coerced, isn't leadership; it's bullying. But horses don't want human leaders anyway. As in any relationship, they want clear, consistent communication and respect. What could we possibly offer horses as leaders? We're pathetic runners, a huge handicap from the perspective of an animal whose constant worst fear is being eaten. With eyes in the front of our heads, we cannot scan for predators three hundred and forty degrees on the horizon, and our mononuclear brains can't process two different images at once. So, for most practical purposes, we're more than half-blind. The scent of lion piss or water ten miles distant hardly register, if we notice at all. Thunder that human ears hear at noon, the horse hears at eleven. Sadly, we will never feel the reassuring tremor of the earth as a six-ton pack string concusses the ground beneath us. But a horse feels all this in her very bones.

No wonder they prefer their own kind, instead of us. And some horses prefer other horses *and* don't particularly like us. For the horses who do not especially like us, one of the primary turn-offs has to do with a certain failure of moral perceptiveness.

Egregious, everyday failures might include clambering up on a horse's back when she isn't in the mood to wear a human being on her back or putting a rope halter around her head, then 'leading' her away from dinner on some human being's whim to ride or bathe her or to tie her head to a post to comb out her mane. Subtler transgressions include standing too close, giving her the 'predator eye', using 'aids' ineptly or in other ways communicating poorly.

Lu is extremely intolerant of sloppy communication – pinning her ears or snapping or making her entire body completely deaf to my existence. The horses who don't like us are less forgiving of our arrogant behaviour than other horses, abruptly walking away from the offender, nudging them out of their space or even biting. And if the horse is hot-headed – and here I introduce the second horse, Noah – watch out. A bite means business. Instead of a nose nudge, prepare for a well-aimed kick. Even after a minor, forgivable insult, you won't get near Noah for days, despite wheedling with carrots and cookies.

Iris Murdoch gave us the notion of 'attention' or 'love' – sight that is independent of the 'greedy organism of the self.' The goal of such vision is 'unsentimental, detached, unselfish, objective attention.' The work of attention goes on continually. And as we attend and practice loving in Murdoch's sense, we imperceptibly build 'up structures of value round about us,' so that at 'crucial moments of choice most of the business of choosing is already over. . . The moral life, on this view, is something that goes on continually, not something that is switched off in between the occurrence of explicit moral choices. What happens in between such choice is indeed what is crucial' (Murdoch, 1997, 329). Such attention is a lifetime's project.

In Denise Levertov's well-known poem 'Come into Animal Presence', 'presence' is something 'holy', 'sacred', a near-relation of what an animal-friendly contemporary Kantian like Christine Korsgaard (2018) may well call 'dignity'. 'Only the sight that saw it faltered and turned away from it,' says Levertov. But 'those who are sacred have remained so / holiness does not dissolve.' 'An old joy returns in holy presence' (Levertov, [1960] 1991).

When Noah is quite done with his ride, he will say so, in Horse – an irritable ear, a slight hesitation moving forward, after which you are summarily launched skyward, landing in an undignified heap in some hawthorn clutch, and often left there while he trots merrily homeward.

'What is this joy? That no animal/faulters, but knows what [he] must do?'

Bears

Bears are huge presences, and not just because of their physical size and strength.

In English, we have the unfortunate notion that a 'bear-like' person is clumsy, ill-mannered, and lacking social graces and education. This is nothing at all like the physically graceful, incredibly restrained, socially intelligent Ursus herself. I've lived in proximity to black and Grizzly bears in rural Montana for decades. I have had many sightings and a handful of brief encounters, but never any conflict. Unhappy human–bear encounters, inevitably human-caused, certainly happen in this part of the country, but it's astonishingly rare considering how we force bears to live in 'war zone conditions,' to cite scientist G. A. Bradshaw.

'While humans might enjoy a weekend in the wilderness, the bears are on the job. The constant stress of hunting, habitat appropriation, noise and intrusive hiking, biking and ATVs in North America has intensified the natural press for food' (Bradshaw, 2020: 31).

What follows is a recent encounter during which the black bear's perceptiveness, judgments, and behaviour were extraordinarily gracious, even *beautiful* (to borrow again from Iris Murdoch, who tells us that goodness and beauty are 'largely part of the same structure' (Murdoch, 1997: 332). By contrast, my own thinking and behaviour were coarse and ill-mannered. I thank Bradshaw for helping me better understand what happened from the bear's perspective. It is an example of the role of scientific knowledge in enabling us to *attend* to another animal properly and thereby also respect that animal's dignity.

If you're a bear, late summer and fall are all about consuming calories and making fat. Opportunists' diets range from berries to succulent plants, nuts, occasional carrion, and protein-rich insect life. In August, on the west side of Montana's Mission Mountain range, the Salish and

An Old Joy: Ways of Attending to Dignity

Figure 10 Guard bear, credit Nancy Erickson.

Kootenai nations, exemplary neighbours to bears, close trails to McDonald Peak so that Grizzly bears can gorge in peace on beetles and cutworms in the talus on top. Hawthorn berries are favourites among bears in the valley floor, and that's where I encountered the black bear, standing on her hind legs, lipping, dexterously, a berry-full hawthorn bush. Three-year-old, nearly exhausted wild apple trees were fruiting nearby, their bowed branches spilling hundreds of small, sticky, bee-loved apples on the ground. Days of Edenic gorging.

This is also when the hunter shoulders his rifle and scope (the scope hardly necessary), and in a matter of seconds has a 'really lucky day'. This is when the hound hunter bookmarks the site in his mind and strategizes the topographical possibilities for his dogs, along with the odds, which are good, of this bear coming back here at dusk. The hiker, meanwhile, fumbles his belt for mace and might even spray a chemical wall between himself and the bear, might shake bear bells on his walking stick and shout – 'BE OFF! BEAR, OFF!'

'Bears are haunted,' Bradshaw says. 'Eating is sacred.'[1] A hyperphagic black bear going into winter can eat twenty thousand calories in a hard-working twenty-four hours, or five thousand hawthorn berries in a dedicated day. A malnourished bear cannot reproduce. A malnourished bear might wake from hibernation early when the forest pantry is empty. A malnourished bear might never wake up.

And knowing all that – which I did – you'd expect I'd turn quietly and walk the opposite way when I met that bear.

But I didn't.

Readers familiar with D. H. Lawrence's poem 'The Snake' might remember how the speaker struggles with the 'voice of [his] education' that insists the yellow-brown snake he meets at 'his' water trough must 'be killed,' and how almost simultaneously he also feels 'so honoured' to meet this 'king,' 'like a god,' 'one of the lords of life,' 'my snake' at the trough, a fellow creature who comes for water on a 'hot, hot' 'Sicilian July' day (Lawrence, 1961: 134–7).

But moments later the speaker is overcome by what he later calls 'a pettiness,' his vulgarity, meanness, by his faltering sight, as Levertov might put it, and he throws a 'clumsy log' at this 'lord of life', who 'convulsed in undignified haste / Writhed like lightning and was gone' into that 'horrid black hole.'

My bear did not convulse or writhe or flee in 'undignified haste.' But she came down off her back legs, away from her sacred work, turned, gracefully, as a swan pivots on water.

Waited . . .

You know we can't be here together

'Bears are haunted.'

Then she walked slowly away from her apples and haws, into a tight-braided blind of willow and alder.

Wasps

Sight, or attention, is a prerequisite for recognizing animal 'presence' or what I would call 'dignity'. 'You have to give something you never gave' – 'unsentimental, detached, unselfish, objective attention' – to get 'something you've never had,' an 'old joy' in being present to dignity.

At my home, the bee beach and the bee bath belong to wasps from late June through September. Though bee cousins, wasps do not have the same whiskers on their legs that make bees efficient pollinators. And while a bee is the Mick Jagger of the Hymenoptera world, a wasp's tongue is much shorter and more suited to shallow, disc-shaped flowers, to horsemint or fleabane. Mostly carnivorous, a wasp prefers to stock her larder with cabbage loopers and hornworms, even the occasional bee, rather than with honey.

Of the 13,000 species of North American wasps, the beach and bath attract the striped, tiny tiger kind, the stinging kind, who are famously peevish, irascible, and easily provoked. I find they have a Nijinski-esque physical dignity, peacefully hovering and bobbing around me as I mulch and deadhead. And they're curious, sniffing their antennae along my hand, tasting my salt with their feet. Wasps recognize the faces of perhaps thousands of hive mates, holistically, as we do, and even particular human faces. So perhaps wasps recognize my joyful face by now. I wish I were as discerning. Give me a friend who will fly half a mile on a hot July afternoon, drink a belly-load of water, schlep her water-logged self another half-mile home, where she regurgitates cool drinks into the mouths of pupae and thirsty friends who are stuck in the stuffy hive all day and night taking care of a thousand cooped-up kids. Just imagine.

The bath, a ten-inch violet blue saucer of smooth, flat stones half-submerged in water, is shady and cool where it sits in a bower of pink woods rose, stalks of purple catmint, and scarlet bee balm. Sometimes mint flowers and rose petals drop into the water, which surely wasps smell and taste with their sensual knees and feet.

Wasps wade into the shallow water on their thready legs. They wash their faces and wings with their feet. They stand on the top of stones and. . . *what*? Stand for a long time. Seconds. Then stand some more. Or fly off. Or climb down their stone into the water, twitching their antennae toward another wasp's familiar face.

Unlike the bath, the beach is exposed, sunny, the water deeper and warmer, inside a glacial green-blue birdbath sitting on its pedestal. Three large rough stones, mountainous and cliffy, surround a shady cove, resembling the coast of Cornwall, where wasps float spread-eagled for half a minute, a minute, more. Then fly off. Or else climb up a slippery rock face to the top, to watch other swimmers or doze.

If someone says, 'Do you believe that the Idea of the Good exists?' I reply, not the Idea of *the* Good – universal, fundamentally intellectual, mystical. But this 'magnetic, inexhaustible reality,' this leggy, levitating yellow joy? (Murdoch, 1997: 333). Well, then I say: Yes, oh Yes, to goodness.

In memory of Nancy Erickson (1935–2022), artist, naturalist, and environmentalist, who many years ago gave me a copy of Denise Levertov's poem. For over fifty years her mixed-media art quilts, oil stick paintings, and drawings portrayed the dignity of other animals.

Note

1 G. A. Bradshaw commented that bears are 'haunted' and that 'eating is sacred' in a personal email in 2022.

References

Bradshaw, G. A. (2020), *Talking with Bears: Conversations with Charlie Russell*, Calgary: Rocky Mountain Books.
Korsgaard, C. (2018), *Fellow Creatures: Our Obligations to the Other Animals*, Oxford: Oxford University Press.
Lawrence, D. H. (1961), 'The snake', in *D. H. Lawrence: Selected Poetry*, revised edn, New York: Penguin Books.
Levertov, D. ([1960] 1991), 'Come into animal presence', in C. Merrill (ed.), *The Forgotten Language: Contemporary Poets and Nature*, Salt Lake City, UT: Peregrine Books.
Murdoch, I. (1997) *Existentialists and Mystics: Writings on Philosophy and Literature*, New York: Penguin.
Parelli, P. (1993), *Natural Horse-Manship*, Colorado Springs: Western Horseman, Inc.
Podhajsky, A. (1965), *The Complete Training of Horse and Rider in the Principles of Classical Horsemanship*, Chatsworth, CA: Wilshire Book Company.
Xenophon (2006), *The Art of Horsemanship*, trans M. Morgan, New York: Dover Books.

Chapter 8
Dignity in Their World
Danielle Celermajer

Introduction: Is dignity worth it?

What is it about a being that confers dignity? Across the history of hegemonic or dominant Western philosophy and theology, this question has been answered in ways that place the limits of dignity at the boundary between humans and other beings, especially other animals. One might even say that within these traditions, it is the claim that humans possess qualities that transcend their animality (despite being animals) that determines their possession of dignity (Kant, [1786] 1988). And dignity, in turn, as seen most clearly in the human rights tradition, is held to justify the assertion that humans, uniquely and universally, merit particular types of treatment and must be afforded particularly types of protections (Kateb, 2014). Unfortunately, the human claim to dignity, like the human claim to other qualities such as agency or the capacity to use language, has gone hand in hand with the claim that others don't have dignity, and as such, that it is ethically acceptable (if not required) to treat them in ways prohibited for the dignified (Kymlicka, 2018).

From a certain perspective, the question, 'what is it about a being that confers dignity?', is a problematic one insofar as it already assumes

---

* 'Dignity in Their World' by Danielle Celermajer includes a reworking of a prior version of material that is found in *Summertime: Reflections on a Vanishing Future* (2021) published by Penguin Books Australia.

an exclusivist ethical system and one that privileges humans, or a particular way of being human (Jackson, 2020). This follows for two reasons. As I have noted, the concept has been so historically steeped in worlds of meaning that draw an absolute and hierarchical moral distinction between humans and every*thing* (not every*one*) else, that by using this term, one is setting up an evaluative scheme that, from the outset, demands that others prove they possess 'human' qualities (Kheel, 2007). In other words, the conferral of dignity depends on proximity to (a certain understanding of) humans, rather than looking for the qualities different beings possess and then asking what ethical precepts might follow from them (Plumwood, 2002). This would not be such a problem if being accorded or refused dignity did not matter so much in terms of the ethical status it accords and types of treatments that it forecloses or demands.

There is a larger ontological problem – or a problem with the way that the question imagines the world. As it is framed, the question assumes that the basic unit of being to which dignity might be conferred is the autonomous, distinct individual. Increasingly, however, research across various fields – from biology and physics to philosophy and social theory – has challenged the assumption that the basic building block of biological, physical, social, or ethical being is the individual (Haraway, 2016).

Research is also shedding light on the social and political conditions under which the idea of the primacy of the individual emerged and was consolidated (Pitts, 2010), and the political, biological, and ethical implications of this way of understanding the world (Neimanis, 2019; Gumbs, 2021). It is becoming apparent that 'the individual,' as imagined in hegemonic Western philosophy, does not exist in isolation but is intrinsically entangled in relationships through which identity is continually constituted and sustained, or transformed. This suggests that ethical protection ought to be given not only to individuals but to the relationships within which individuals exist (Winter, 2021). And if we are looking for the qualities that confer dignity, our focus should by necessity extend beyond the individual to ecosystems or relationships.

So, for those concerned with the flourishing of beings other than humans, does it even make sense to try to show that they have dignity? It's tempting to say no. Why put them through a test set up for them to fail? And why use a concept based on distorted understandings of the world? In the abstract, these seem like reasonable arguments. Yet dignity, like rights, plays a critical role in legitimating arguments for why violence, abuse and exploitation are impermissible. In today's world, in which the concept is both familiar and established, the claim to dignity has tremendous practical value for making respectful, just treatment obligatory (Nedelsky, 2020). And in a world where human actions and forms of life are the source of ever intensifying violence against beings other than humans, practical value matters tremendously.

Perhaps one way to navigate this dilemma is by approaching the dignity of other animals in ways that do not start by trying to assimilate them to the existing, anthropomorphic templates of dignity. A better, more respectful approach might be to start by paying close attention to others in their own right, noticing how they are in the world and how their ways of being might constitute them as beings with dignity. Doing so does not mean shattering the coherence of the concept altogether, but rather opening it to a more capacious, less prejudicial reconceptualization.

The passages that follow are borne out of such noticing. I wrote them from my home on the east coast of Australia in the midst of the catastrophe of the black summer fires of 2019–2020. They bear witness to how the animals with whom I live navigate a world that has been rendered both unrecognizable and unliveable by human action.

Grief

As I write this on a Friday afternoon it has been forty-eight hours and he has barely lifted his head. We call him, but it is only when we get right up close that he answers, and only in the softest voice – a voice very different from his usual booming baritone. I just climbed down to where he was lying and finally got him to drink a little water, but he showed no interest in food – not even watermelon, his favourite treat. I had no idea that grief could be so deep for anyone. I have held off telling you that Jimmy is a pig because I appreciate that for many human beings knowing his species would make it impossible to read this as a story about the enormity of loss. But stay with me.

About three years ago a woman who knew that my partner and I offered refuge to a few animals emailed us to ask if we had space for

Figure 11 Dany and Jimmy, credit Danielle Celermajer.

two pigs who had been rescued from the floor of a factory farm when they were three weeks old. They had been discarded as 'wastage'. For the first six months of their lives Jimmy and Katy were so weak and terrified that it seemed doubtful they would live. But they had huddled by each other's side until they had the strength to enter the world. By the time they came to us at the age of four, they were physically huge but unusually timid. It took about two years before Katy would look at me straight on, and whenever the chickens got into their area, Jimmy – all 200-odd kilograms of him – would scurry away in fear.

By 26 December 2019 the fire that had been edging towards our place burned near enough to pose a real threat. Two days later, I telephoned the woman who had raised Jimmy and Katy to see if she could once again offer them sanctuary. She said she had been half-expecting my call. She came the next day to take them home, four hours to the south of us, where we hoped they would be safe until our place was no longer under threat. But the very idea of being 'safe' is yet another casualty of the climate catastrophe. Thirty-six hours later a ferocious fire had enveloped her place, descending upon the inhabitants from three sides, razing the home, turning the fields to ash, and killing Katy.

Given the nature of the fire, everyone presumed that Jimmy was also dead. But then, miraculously, just over a day later, Jimmy appeared, having somehow survived an inferno that had vaporized everything else. The first text I received simply said 'I have found Jimmy'. I assumed she had found his body. Moments later a low-quality video followed showing him at a distance next to a burned-out tree, coming closer and closer until his nose touched the phone camera. The moving image was accompanied by the sound of his snort, a little louder each frame, and my friend's soft words of encouragement: 'I know, I know.'

With roads closed and another catastrophic fire raging through this part of the country only four days after the one that killed Katy, it took us a full week before we could get to Jimmy. A four-hour drive through fire-ravaged country – cindered forests, flattened homes, empty highways – finally took us to him. Any fences that would have kept him from running off had been reduced to ash, but after twenty minutes of our calling his name he appeared, pink on the black. He was clearly coming towards us, but he paused about ten metres away and continued as we did, walking in parallel. It was as if the desire to be close could not quite break through the world in which he had been caught.

Still, his movements were frenetic. He seemed racked by hypervigilance. We could hardly be surprised. His every sense had been assaulted: darkness at dawn; early-morning quiet engulfed in the roar of the flames; the blinding intensity of the fire; the radiant heat that, a week later, still emanated from the ground; the taste of ash. This sensory apocalypse had come upon Jimmy out of nowhere. How could he possibly know when it would return?

After we got Jimmy home, he shuffled over to his mud bath and lowered his huge, hot, shaken body into it. We were overcome with joy as we watched him rediscover the possibility of coolness. He ate watermelon and drank cold water and slept. But he slept alone, not, as he had every night of his life before the fire, next to Katy.

The next morning, he began to look for her. Everywhere. In their house, down in their woods, up under the trees where they had once taken shade from the afternoon sun. He would turn and look and stand very still – listening for her, perhaps smelling the remnants of her presence. And then he stopped. My guess is that now he was home he felt he could cease being hypervigilant. He could let go of some of the terror that had been keeping him in movement. But with that relaxation both the reality of Katy's death and the trauma of his experience came to the fore. He placed his body on the cool of the earth, and there he remained. When he will get up again, and whether he will find a way back to his world, are among the uncertainties we now have to live with.

I sit alone, just down the slope from where Jimmy has been lying. It is way down in the bush over a gully. The light is soft; you can hear the birds and the wind moving through the trees. The air and the earth are cool, and the smell is of leaves and river. I cannot presume to know what he is doing when he lies there, but it seems that he is taking himself back to a more secure ecology, one neither wrought by the terror of the fires nor fuelled by our violence on the earth. He is letting another earth heal him.

When people speak about the fires, they describe being overwhelmed by the enormity of the devastation. We do not have the capacity to grasp this much loss – not only to humans but to other wild and domesticated animals, to the bush, to the ecologies of rivers and moss and the creatures who flourish there, to the possibility of regeneration. I know I don't. But I can hold Jimmy's enormous head in my arms and be present to his broken but miraculous presence.

The dignity of pigs

In paying attention to Jimmy in the immediate aftermath of the apocalyptic fire he survived, I came to recognize in him qualities I had not noticed before. The most immediate was the complexity and depth of his emotions. His emotions altered not only those of the humans in his immediate proximity, but also the emotions and thoughts of the people who read my descriptions of his grief. These responses to Jimmy's grief pointed not only to the fault-lines in human exceptionalism, but also to the communicative power Jimmy and other animals have to encourage humans to experience, feel and think differently. It is all down to our willingness to attend.

I was also struck by his independence – although this is not quite the right word. To those who observed him, it was clear that Jimmy was working out not only how to be in a world without Katy, but whether to be in the world at all. We wanted him to live, and I wanted to push him towards life, but he made it very clear that these choices were not ours to make. We often speak of the capacity of humans to will themselves to live or to will themselves away from life. Other animals can also have this agency.

In the weeks and months that followed Katy's death, we found ourselves trying to come to terms with a world that had been radically destabilized. It soon became evident that the experience of stumbling around the ignorance of how to navigate this type of trauma, and the encounter with our shared and different vulnerabilities, brought us all to new ways of knowing and relating – both human and pig.

The third lesson was how deeply embedded Jimmy was in his world. As I saw him sinking into the earth or lying amidst the trees, it was clear to me that he was profoundly *of* his world. I learned this lesson again when he was dying. While Jimmy survived the assault of the fire at first, only eighteen months later he fell gravely ill. We now believe it was from some disease that had entered him during his time in the fireground. After a few days of his neither eating nor drinking, we became desperate and decided to take him to a veterinary hospital. He did not want to get onto the float, but we were determined to get him to what we had decided was the best form of care.

Before we left, I looked at and finally became present to him, as distinct from being consumed by my own distress at his dying. He had shrunk down into himself and while he had looked ill before, he had still been in the world. Now he seemed to withdraw altogether.

We all stopped and considered what we were doing in his presence. It was obvious to each of us there that we had to open the door of the float and let him walk out. As soon as he did, we knew our mistake had been to think that Jimmy could be abstracted from his world and saved. Jimmy knew that he was of his world. He had lived there, and he would die there.

In Western societies, one of the most frequent applications of the word dignity is in relation to dying, with increasing attention to 'dying with dignity'. I have thought about this a great deal since Jimmy died. For Jimmy, the dignity attached to dying did not end at the boundaries of his body or bounded identity. What flowed from attending first to him, then to the concept of dignity, and then to his dignity was not simply that pigs too have dignity, but that the dignity one learns about attending to a pig is a dignity *beyond* the pig. A dignity of their world.

References

Gumbs, A. P. (2021), 'Undrowned: Black feminist lessons from marine mammals', *Soundings* 78: 20–37.

Haraway, D. J. (2016), *Staying with the Trouble: Making Kin in the Chthulucene*, Durham, NC: Duke University Press.

Jackson, Z. I. (2020), *Becoming Human*, New York: New York University Press.

Kant, I. ([1786] 1988), 'Speculative beginning of human history (1786)', in *Perpetual Peace and Other Essays on Politics, History, and Morals*, trans. and with an introduction by T. Humphrey, Indianapolis, IN: Hackett.

Kateb, G. (2014), *Human Dignity*, Cambridge, MA: Harvard University Press.

Kheel, M. (2007), *Nature Ethics: An Ecofeminist Perspective*, Lanham, MD: Rowman & Littlefield.

Kymlicka, W. (2018), 'Human rights without human supremacism', *Canadian Journal of Philosophy* 48(6): 763–792.

Nedelsky, J. (2020), 'The relational self as the subject of human rights', in D. Celermajer and A. Lefebvre (eds), *The Subject of Human Rights*, Stanford, CA: Stanford University Press: 29–47.

Neimanis, A. (2019), *Bodies of Water: Posthuman Feminist Phenomenology*, London: Bloomsbury.

Pitts, J. (2010), 'Political theory of empire and imperialism', *Annual Review of Political Science* 13: 211–235.

Plumwood, V. (2002), *Environmental Culture: The Ecological Crisis of Reason*, London: Routledge.

Winter, C. J. (2021), *Subjects of Intergenerational Justice: Indigenous Philosophy, the Environment and Relationships*, Oxford: Routledge.

PART THREE

Forms of Dignity: *Are There Separate Cultural Conceptions of Animal Dignity?*

Summary

There is not enough space in this volume for a detailed analysis of different regional or spiritual conceptions of dignity across the world's cultures and communities. Nor is there the opportunity here to untangle such global histories. This is valuable, specialized work that is yet to be done. The ambitions of this section are narrower in scope. Here we offer some scholarship that reconciles the modern, moralized concept of dignity with related traditions extant in other cultures or spiritualities. In some of the countries from which these cultures originate, animal welfare movements are either highly contested or undergoing cultural deliberation. It is reasonable to suggest that in such cases, dignity might act as a more fertile rationale for further ethical or legal considerations of the lives of non-human animals.

We open with testimony from wildlife veterinarian, Nelson Bukamba. Bukamba works to support and save the lives of our closest biological relative, chimpanzees. The current imperilled state of chimpanzees (their populations have more than halved since the 1960s as a direct consequence of our actions) is reason to consider whether an African conception of dignity might strengthen the relative status of chimpanzees.

At present, chimpanzees have been subject to many related dignity violations we recognize among humans. They have been dressed in human outfits for TV adverts, traded as celebrity pets, kept in captivity, placed in zoos, tortured, and killed. Further to this, chimpanzees share many of our characteristics, and are endowed with several skills we lack. Could a recognition of animal dignity assist chimpanzees in their plight?

The presence of chimpanzees in our world is one of the most formidable challenges to the idea that dignity should apply only to humans based on our species. Most philosophers require an abstraction of a biological cognitive process (such as theory of mind) to draw a hard moral border between humans and chimpanzees. Philosophers sometimes collapse disparate biological phenomena, which in science are grounded in empiricism, into a single nebulous concept such as autonomy. A set of adaptations (e.g., mental foraging, shared intentionality, episodic memory, etc.), which are recruited by an animal like us to navigate complex social and environmental challenges, can be reimagined as a unique, morally exceptional capacity. Further empirical work often unsettles such notions, not least because there's little requirement within philosophy to properly understand the underlying biological mechanisms on which many moral axioms are founded.

As a solution, philosophers and theologians rely on broad stroke capacities or characteristics, such as moral agency or the idea of a unique human soul. Yet, these are difficult notions to uphold, when confronted by chimpanzees. Consider that if humans had no moral status prior to the emergence of moral agency or to the moment of ensoulment, could they, by this logic, have been enslaved, exploited, or even killed at any time up to this evolutionary singularity? In other words, could humans have been justifiably extirpated by a superior moral agent before their own inviolable moral status had the opportunity to manifest? Hard borders and biology are poor bedfellows, which is no doubt the reason that many philosophers resist naturalizing morality. *Distinctiveness* rather than *distinctions* is better suited to the realities of the human animal condition.

In any case, despite an older, historical, and lexical relationship with social status, the modern concept of dignity seeks to overcome hierarchies and gift moral status to a life without a qualifier. The creed of the recognition-respect of modern dignity could be summarized as: *to value without measure.*

Bukamba's testimony is followed by an essay on the African concept of *ubuntu* as a potential root for animal dignity, from philosopher Julius Kapembwa. Kapembwa unpacks the term and its meanings to argue against claims that African animal ethics are constrained by human exceptionalism. This is followed by Meera Baindur's analysis of the spiritual idea of *prana*, as life-force, in Indian thought. She presents the idea of *prana*-wringing, as understood by communities rather than philosophers, as a correlate of dignity. For Baindur, wringing another being's *prana* is to disturb their fundamental needs or character, from keeping pets to feeding the wrong food to a stray animal. *Prana*-wringing shares much in common with dignity violations as forms of denigration or as the denial or obstruction of the agency or flourishing of another being.

    Michael Nelson and Cristina Eisenberg offer a critical perspective on dignity as human exceptionalism and draw on both Ojibwe philosophy and the notion of intrinsic value from environmental ethics to suggest that dignity as honour can both unite separate approaches and strengthen their ethical role in the world. The section closes with Michael Reiss's analysis that while theological perspectives often make a special place in creation for humans, there's also considerable justification, both textually and spiritually, for extending dignity beyond *Homo sapiens*.

PRELUDE IV
Lead Me into Thy Nest
Nelson Bukamba

I have been privileged to live among non-human animals all my life. This began with our family dog Simba. Tragically, Simba died in a road accident. As the years passed, it became clear to me that if Simba hadn't crossed that road first (because he was always ahead of me), I would have been the one lying in the middle of the road. He was my guardian, and he always led the way.

The day Simba died, we couldn't find a veterinarian and I remember asking my dad why we couldn't take him to the nearest hospital. I could see the uncomfortable look on my dad's face. He told me: *because he is just an animal*. That day I started on my path to becoming a vet.

Over the years, as I went through veterinary school, I always looked out for unprivileged or neglected animal communities. Chimpanzees came my way. Chimpanzees are an endangered primate species that belong to the Great Ape family, together with orangutans, bonobos, gorillas, and humans. In Africa, chimpanzees face several threats including injuries from wire snares and mantraps planted by poachers for either bush meat or the pet trade. Traders prey on the young chimpanzees from trapped, defenceless mothers.

I was the only graduating wildlife veterinarian in ten years in my country. But my priority became chimpanzees, and a long and lonely path to save these special beings. Over the years, my daily encounters with the chimpanzees of Kibale National Park have been filled with special moments, full of emotions and physical drama. Their attentiveness to our presence – they have keen, sharp eyes – is sufficient for us to recognize their intelligence and awareness.

§

It is 4:00 am out here in the heart of Kibale National Park, and my alarm goes off. At exactly 4:30 am, I must head to the main camp with the rest of the field assistants and rangers straight into the forest. There, we silently observe the chimpanzees as they begin their day. Chimpanzees make nests at night using tree branches and leaves, a routine they learn repeatedly from their mothers and other members of the community. The first nest in a chimpanzee's life marks the first step into adulthood.

At dawn, they rise from their nest beds, one by one, with pant hoots and buttress bangs – signs of their appreciation for another day of life. Our day begins here too, as we monitor the routine health of the community until we see them off to sleep in their new nests in some other part of the forest.

Once fully grown up, chimpanzees look like gorillas but with a face that appears as if it has been smashed by a frying pan. Native to savanna woodlands, grassland-forest mosaics, and tropical moist

Figure 12 Wenka, a female individual I rescued from a snare wire in 2019 from Kibale National Park, credit Nelson Bukamba.

forests, from sea level to about three thousand metres in elevation, this group of primates spends its first years of life eating, sleeping, and travelling with its mother.

It's such a powerful bond. Jane Goodall writes of it, in her book *Visions of Caliban* (Goodall and Peterson, 2000), where she recounts the hours that she spent watching mother chimpanzees interacting with their infants. Seeing herself in them, as a mother, Goodall could appreciate the powerful instincts of a female chimpanzee with her infant, and the emotional needs of chimpanzee infants just like human children.

It is through such empathy that we can imagine the despair and feelings of abandonment that a young chimpanzee experiences when a poacher, urged on by the high-end wildlife pet trade, sneaks into the forest and cuts the bonds between the mother and the child. The mother is killed to access her baby, who will find itself the plaything of a wealthy human somewhere.

Just like humans, young chimpanzees have an intense relationship with their mothers characterized by both activities and emotions that facilitate the learning of various cultural and survival traits that are necessary before a chimpanzee can live alone successfully. They learn about hierarchy, who the bad guys are, and how to relate with the rest of the members of the community. They learn what to feed on, right from the bellies of their mothers and as they ride on their backs. It is during this long 'childhood' period, that chimpanzee adolescents learn to forage for wild figs, bird eggs, seeds, insects, and to hunt small mammals like white colobus monkeys. They learn to work around with sticks to extract ants hidden under the soil through tiny holes, knock down fruit from trees, and use leaves to wipe themselves clean. In short: all the lessons necessary for daily life.

When you get to appreciate the individuality and uniqueness of each chimpanzee, you understand the realities of who we are destroying or denigrating. A chain of actions from a life in the wild into the pet trade ends a generation, breaks the cultural bond between a mother and a baby chimpanzee. Many poachers kill and hunt out of necessity, but this is facilitated by a rich buyer who sees a long generation of chimpanzee lives as meaningless: only a toy for sale.

How do we decide which species or individuals deserve certain kinds of treatment, but not other kinds of treatment? Think about the injuries inflicted by snare wire. If it results in the loss of a hand or foot, or even just deformation of limbs, the chimpanzee's quality of life is affected. In Budongo forest, for example, it has been recorded that chimpanzees with snare injuries re-use nests more often possibly because it is more difficult for them to make new nests.

I had an open discussion with a village hunter who argued that if a chimp was that closely related to humans why can't they figure out how to remove the snares or act as a community to help a fellow remove them. He concluded that these are just 'animals'. This kind of speciesism implies that humans need not take animals' interests into our consideration because they lack intellectual or moral ability. Yet speciesism would be abhorrent if turned on us. So why do we impose it on other animals?

References

Goodall, J. and D. Peterson. (2000), *Visions of Caliban: On Chimpanzees and People*, Athens: The University of Georgia Press.

Chapter 9
Killing Dogs in Zambia: Prospects for *Ubuntu*
Julius Kapembwa

Domesticated dogs (*Canis lupus familiaris*) originated in southern East Asia some 33,000 years before dispersing to the rest of the world around 15,000 years ago (Wang *et al*., 2016). Ever since, dogs and humans have helped each other in many ways ranging from emotional companionship to saving each other's lives. The loyalty of a dog is rightly expressed by the dictum that dogs are 'man's best friend.'

Evidence from Stone Age paintings and reports of early explorers indicate dogs in Africa pre-date the arrival of Europeans on the continent (Baderoon, 2016). In Africa, dogs are used for hunting, protecting property and livestock, and companionship (McCrindle *et al*., 1999). However, dogs are sometimes killed in isolation or in mass-culling operations. When considering the killing of dogs in a developing country such as Zambia, the possibilities of animal dignity from the perspective of African animal ethics become visible.

Zambia has an estimated dog population ranging between one to two million (Munang'andu *et al*., 2011; Babaniyi *et al*., 2016) against a human population of over 19.6 million (Zambia Statistics Agency, 2022). Many households have dogs – ownership is as high as eighty-five per cent in the Nyimba district (Mulipukwa *et al*., 2017).

Dogs in Zambia, as elsewhere in Africa, are killed for various reasons. A few helpful distinctions can be made. The first distinction is between the killing by owners or community members and the killing by legally mandated government officials. Owners or members of the community may kill dogs that are very sick or exhibit what is deemed inappropriate behaviour. Inappropriate behaviours for dogs include excessive aggression towards humans and the eating of domestic poultry or eggs, while puppies may be killed as population control or sex preference (Czypryna, 2016). Owners or community members in Zambia kill dogs by stoning, hitting with a stick, axeing, strangulation or hanging (personal communications). These killings are perceived among community members with mixed feelings from outrage, indifference, to applause. As dogs are regarded as private property, what one does with their dog is entirely their business. Thus, an angry owner may freely kill a dog over 'theft' of meat in the house. While this may outrage some readers, it is of note that in the US, dogs can be killed for more trivial 'extra medical' reasons (Rollin, 2006: 298–9). These reasons include the dog no longer being cute, not able to learn some desired dog training, not matching the new house colour scheme, or the owner going on vacation.

Although dogs are consumed as food elsewhere in Africa, especially in West Africa (Gurumyen et al., 2020), Zambians do not traditionally eat dog meat; eating dog meat is taboo. However, there are anecdotes of dogs being stolen or killed for food by some members of the Chinese community. Moreover, despite the general Zambian visceral aversion to dog meat, there have been some reports of Zambians eating dog food under unfortunate circumstances. Some Zambians have been reported to kill dogs for food to avoid starvation (PANA, 2002); some have been forced to eat dog meat at work by their Chinese supervisors (*Lusaka Times*, 2014); while other Zambians have unsuspectingly been sold dog meat deceptively packaged as bushmeat (Mwenya, 2020).

Many Zambians react to Chinese eating dogs with disgust and racist remarks on social media networks such as Facebook. This perception of Chinese among Zambians originates in the dynamics that emerged in the 1960s and 1970s during the construction of the Tanzania–Zambia railway line by the Chinese. The perception is further entrenched by Zambian media reports of the annual dog meat festival in China. It is a reminder that our perceptions of the ethical treatment of other species are often profoundly entangled with intergroup and cultural prejudices or conflicts.

The second type of killing is by government officials or veterinary medical personnel, which can be categorized into two further types.

The first kind is euthanasia. Euthanasia means intentionally ending another's life using the least painful means to prevent prolonged irreversible suffering. In other words, the killing is for the sole benefit of the one being killed (Regan, 2004). Although euthanasia is not mentioned explicitly, the Prevention of Cruelty to Animals Act 245 of 1994 of the Laws of Zambia prescribes that if 'it would be cruel to keep the animal alive. . . the animal [should] be destroyed'. It is of note that the Veterinary Association of Zambia uses the term 'euthanasia' inconsistently. Their Code of Conduct and Ethics of 2014 uses the term appropriately. However, in their 2019 'Position Paper on the Control of Stray Dogs', they refer to all acts of killing stray dogs, regardless of their healthiness, as euthanasia. This confirms Tom Regan's worry of practitioners using euthanasia as a euphemism for killings that are not in the interests of the non-human animals.

Dogs sometimes donated by owners for use in training veterinarians are also said to be euthanized even when they are in good health (personal communication). Veterinarians primarily use euthasol to kill dogs, but there have been reports of the use of methylated spirit. This is injected into the heart of the dog, which results in the dog convulsing and frothing before it dies.[1]

In addition to euthanasia, the Control of Dogs Act, Cap 247, of the Laws of Zambia, provides for the killing of dogs to prevent the spread of diseases to humans or other non-human animals. First, dogs may be killed simply because they are unregistered. Any dogs above four months of age 'if found without a badge issued in respect of such dog, or without a collar bearing its owner's name and address, may be forthwith destroyed by any officer or by the owner or occupier of a farm on which such dog is found straying'. Further, registered or not, dogs may be killed if they are in poor health due to disease, severe injury, or some other poor physical state. Particularly, a dog known to be infected with rabies 'shall' be destroyed. Those suspected to have rabies may be either quarantined or killed.

Dogs invoke love but also fear and panic among Zambians. There were 14,818 reported dog bites in 2013 from 226 in 2004 which translates to 0.2 dog bites per 10,000 persons in 2004 to 4.24 dog bites per 10,000 persons in 2013 (Babaniyi *et al*., 2016). Dogs have recently killed people including a police officer, a septuagenarian woman, and an eight-year-old boy (*Lusaka Times*, 2012; Mwila, 2022;

Vaidyanathan, 2019). In the cases of the woman and child victims, many social media commentators condemned the owners for keeping dangerous exotic breeds and failing to secure them properly. In the case of the boy, the dog was killed.

By far the most known and feared disease from dogs to humans in Zambia is canine rabies. Rabies is endemic in Zambia (Kaneko, 2021). Dogs are the biggest reservoir of rabies and vector to humans.[2] The disease has an almost one hundred per cent mortality rate and is untreatable after onset of clinical signs. Rabies is very expensive to prevent or treat in a poor country such as Zambia in which fifty-four per cent of the population is poor, with forty per cent in extreme poverty (Central Statistical Office, 2016).

With this background, perhaps the public hysteria about dog bites and the ensuing shooting spree to cull dogs is understandable. And yet the culling of free-roaming dogs is ineffective for rabies control and may have undesirable unintended consequences (Morters *et al.*, 2013; Castillo-Neyra *et al.*, 2016). Thus, although the institutionalized hysteria that culminates in the mass killing of dogs may placate human fears, it does not mitigate rabies in any sustainable way.

From any perspective, it seems that the extensive killing of dogs in Zambia is an object lesson in the absence of animal dignity. But does that mean that the concept of non-human animal dignity in Zambia, or Africa more widely, is improbable?

Kai Horsthemke (2015) ascribes to African morality an unwavering anthropocentrism. On his view, in African moral thought, dogs are without any dignity as any moral treatment accorded to them can only be indirect duties supervening upon some direct duties to humans. Edwin Etieyibo (2017), however, argues that none of Horsthemke's premises – the hierarchy of being, or the slaughter of animals for rituals, for bushmeat, or for cures – entail the conclusion of an intractable anthropocentric African animal ethic. I agree with Etieyibo. Sacrifice is not necessarily coexistent with disrespect. For example, Christians do not believe Abraham's attempted offer of his son as sacrifice entailed Abraham denying the son had intrinsic value. It is possible to have a value system in which both death and respect coincide, no matter how anachronistic this appears. And so, to kill and offer a non-human animal as sacrifice does not necessarily preclude the belief that the animal has intrinsic value or moral status. My point, however, should not be taken as in any way supporting sacrifice of animals. It is simply that Horsthemke's argument that animal sacrifices in Africa entail lack of African appreciation of animal intrinsic value is flawed.

Similarly, a lower ontological status of non-human animals does not necessarily translate into a lower moral status, let alone the absence of moral status. The ontological ranking may be based on factual aspects which, as we know from the is-ought fallacy, do not imply any value judgements. Therefore, despite the ontic hierarchy that puts humans above non-human animals, along with the various human exploitations of non-human animals, there is still room to conclude that non-human animals can have dignity from an African perspective.

Ubuntu is a good African philosophical candidate. *Ubuntu* moral theory in African philosophy has received intense scholarship in the past two decades. It has been applied to many *human* activities and institutions. The core of *ubuntu* theory stresses character and harmonious relations with others (Mweshi, 2019). According to *ubuntu*, one's personhood is premised on communion with others and through a dialogical relationship to the community. However, sometimes the element of communalism is overemphasized and thus the concept of *ubuntu* is impoverished. When this happens, *ubuntu* can easily be misinterpreted as ignoring or even abrogating individuality or as endorsing human exceptionalism. However, any further discussion of *ubuntu* is beyond the needs of this chapter. Instead, I will delve into the concept as discussed in the context of non-human animal ethics.

Renowned *ubuntu* philosopher, Thaddeus Metz, argues that non-human animals have a moral status, even if it is assumed to be lower than that of humans. Appealing to the notion of *ubuntu* (which translates roughly as 'humanness'), Metz (2017) argues that moral status is a function of a being's capacity to commune with others. For Metz, therefore, moral status comes in degrees, with a being possessing it 'to the extent to which it is the kind of thing that can be party to a relationship in which there is communion, understood in terms of identifying with others and exhibiting solidarity with them'. The 'communal' in *ubuntu*, Metz elaborates, encompasses the ability to love and be loved by others (Metz, 2017:166–70). If Metz is right, then African animal ethics, contra Horsthemke, is not straightforwardly anthropocentric. Given Metz's theory, dogs can have a moral status by dint of their capacity to commune with others, but not to the extent that this capacity equals that of humans. Consequently, according to this philosophy, whenever there is a forced trade-off between the interests of a dog and of a human, the human's interest should prevail by default.

However, this African animal ethics as presented by Metz is subject to some objections. First, Metz's stipulation of communing that is essential for moral status is dubious or question-begging. Why should being capable of 'relating communally with *characteristic human beings*' be the only moral status-conferring sort? Many non-human animals commune among themselves, some analogous to human communing. They exhibit a repertoire of emotions, an intricate labyrinth of social relations and a normative dimension as well (see Rowlands, 2012; Bekoff and Pierce, 2009; Moss and Colbeck, 1992). Furthermore, domesticated non-human animals like dogs possess agency and engage in extensive communing with humans, loving and being loved, and undertake cooperative tasks with humans (Pearson, 2013). On this basis alone, they are good candidates for citizenship (Donaldson and Kymlicka, 2011).

However, if we use human communing as the standard for non-human animals as well, it is not surprising that they end up with a lower moral status. Although Metz closely associates human moral status with human dignity, he seems to exclude non-human animals as he understands humans having dignity as meaning humans 'are good for their own sake *to a superlative degree*'. At best, dignity would also come in degrees with dogs possessing lower dignity than humans. Metz's argument for moral status reflects a play on the human–animal dualism; a denial of our intrinsic animal nature that so often ends in, or rationalizes, denigrating and abusing non-human animals (Challenger, 2021).

Second, taking human communing as a necessary condition for dignity poses a further challenge for humans who cannot yet commune, are unable to commune from birth or have lost their ability to commune due to age or some illness or medical condition that prevents two-way communing. However, African communities recognize the dignity of such humans and isolate them as especially in need of care, love, and support from the community. For example, it is anathema for an African family or community to consign old people to a care home placed among strangers. Even through palliative care, they remain valued community members until their death. Moral dignity, as contrasted with social status dignity, does not come in degrees in Africa. Every human possesses dignity equally and may lose it only through egregious violation of social norms or mores but not by unfortunate inability for reciprocal communing. Thus, human communing is a rather weak candidate for that which confers moral status or dignity.

Third, Metz thinks our intuition that we are required to pick a human over a dog in forced trade-offs is a point in favour of his African animal ethics theory. However, such an intuition cannot be seen as an innocent arbiter between theories. It could be a widely shared intuition in some societies that in hard cases, a white person's interests should prevail over a black person's interests. Our intuitions can be explained more simply as an implicit bias that reflects prevailing attitudes – racist, sexist, speciesist. A sound moral theory could bring up some counterintuitive implications such as treating equally similar interests, for a dog or for a human.

The intuition to sacrifice the non-human animal for the human has a further limitation. In Africa, as in Europe, many dogs are treated as bona fide family members. Many humans routinely care as much for these 'fur babies' – as dogs are commonly referred to in LAWS WhatsApp groups to which I belong – as they would for humans where their interests are the same.[3] Many who live with dogs can choose to save their dog's life over a human. Thus, rather than corroborating Metz's theory of graded moral status, the hard choice may reflect the special positive duties or attachments a person has towards other beings, dog or human.

Metz admits *ubuntu* does not encapsulate the entirety of morality. However, I think the concept has been under-analysed by limiting it to human communal relationalism. *Ubuntu* is much more than that. Both Danford Chibvongodze and John Mweshi contend that *ubuntu* or African ethics seamlessly extends to non-human animals and the natural environment (Chibvongodze, 2016; Mweshi 2019). In my language, Bemba, '*Uyu muuntu!*' goes beyond 'This is a human being' or 'This is a person'. It is moral praise – an attribution of practical wisdom and moral excellence. Practical wisdom and moral excellence are comprehensive, and they stress virtuous character in its totality, transcending human-to-human relations. A *muntu* proper respects not only humans but non-human animals as well. The Bembas, the largest ethnic grouping in Zambia, say *Ukuteeka imbwa, mano* (keeping a dog well, is wisdom). No matter how good a person is to fellow humans, if they do not respect dogs and attend to their interests, then they are not wise and are less human for it. It is through this ethic that even after a dog has aged and can no longer hunt, for example, many Zambians would treat her with care into old age. That many Zambians keep dogs for no apparent reason than love points to the intuition that dogs are fellow and companionable creatures.

So how to make sense of the killing of dogs? The neglect that many dogs suffer can be explained in part by the high poverty rates in rural areas and high population density sections of urban areas rather than to a belief that dogs lack dignity or moral status. Similarly, the shooting by local councils of free-roaming dogs and 'euthanasia' of otherwise treatable dogs may be due to economic challenges to implementing the humane dog population and rabies control programmes recommended by the World Health Organisation.

However, the proliferation of non-human animal welfare organizations around Zambia points to increasing appreciation of non-human ethics. Some members of the Lusaka Animal Welfare Society 'drive through town every day to rescue animals in need. . . . They come across the most shocking cases.'[4] Very sick dogs are taken to qualified veterinarians where they are euthanized. Corpses of dogs or cats that are victims of roadkill are picked up and given a dignified burial. Hence, amidst the gloom of isolated or institutionalized mass killing of dogs, there is hope as some groups mobilize to ensure dignity for dogs.

In conclusion, while some philosophers argue that Africa is fundamentally anthropocentric or that African morality recognizes diminished moral status for non-human animals, I argue that *ubuntu* theory and practice in contemporary Zambia offers hope for the full recognition of dignity for dogs.

Notes

[1] The informant is a lecturer and researcher in veterinary medicine at the University of Zambia. He reported this incident of witnessing the use of methylated spirit to euthanize a dog in a rural district of Zambia and attributed this to lack of resources.

[2] See WHO, 'Expert Consultation on Rabies Third Report' Geneva, 2018.

[3] LAWS = Lusaka Animal Welfare Society.

4 A female member of LAWS who at the time of communication was fostering two dogs awaiting their adoption into a 'caring and loving' family.

References

Babaniyi, O., et al. (2016), 'Epidemiological characteristics of rabies in Zambia: A retrospective study (2004–2013)', *Clinical Epidemiology and Global Health* 4(2): 83–88.

Baderoon, G. (2016), 'Animal likenesses', *Journal of African Cultural Studies* 29(3): 345–361.

Bekoff, M. and J. Pierce. (2009), *Wild Justice: The Moral Lives of Animals*, Chicago: The University of Chicago Press.

Castillo-Neyra, R., M. Z. Levy, and C. Náquira. (2016), 'Efecto del sacrificio de perros vagabundos en el control de la rabia canina', *Revista Peruana de Medicina Experimental y Salud Pública* 33(4): 772.

Central Statistical Office. (2016), '2015 Living Conditions Monitoring Survey Report', Lusaka: Central Statistical Office.

Challenger, M. (2021), *How to Be Human: What It Means to Be Human*, London: Canongate.

Chibvongodze, D. (2016), 'Ubuntu is not only about the human! An analysis of the role of African philosophy and ethics in environment management', *Journal of Human Ecology* 53(2): 157–166.

Czupryna, A. (2016), 'Ecology and demography of free-roaming domestic dogs in rural villages near Serengeti National Park in Tanzania', *PLoS ONE* 11(11): e0167092.

Donaldson, S. and W. Kymlicka. (2011), *Zoopolis: A Political Theory of Animal Rights*, Oxford: Oxford University Press.

Etieyibo, E. (2017), 'Anthropocentrism, African metaphysical worldview, and animal practices: A reply to Kai Horsthemke', *Journal of Animal Ethics* 7(2): 145–162.

Gurumyen, B., O. Akanle, Y. P. Yikwabs, and T. S. Nomishan. (2020), 'Zootherapy: The use of dog meat for traditional African medicine In Kanke Local Government Area, Plateau State, Nigeria', *Journal of Tourism and Heritage Studies* 9(2): 1–14.

Horsthemke, K. (2015), *Animals and African Ethics*, London: Palgrave Macmillan.

Kaneko, C. (2021), 'Domestic dog demographics and estimates of canine vaccination coverage in a rural area of Zambia for the elimination of rabies', *PLOS Neglected Tropical Diseases* 15(4).

Lusaka Times. (2012), 6 dogs kill Lusaka cop, *Lusaka Times*, 16 April 2012. Available from https://www.lusakatimes.com/2012/04/16/6-dogs-kill-lusaka-cop/.

Lusaka Times. (2014), Shamenda appalled by reports of Chinese firm forcing Zambian workers to eat dog meat, *Lusaka Times*, 13 May 2014. Available from https://www.lusakatimes.com/2014/05/13/shamenda-appalled-reports-chinese-firm-forcing-zambian-workers-eat-dog-meat/.

McCrindle, C., J. Gallant, S. T. Cornelius, and H. S. Schoeman. (1999), 'Changing roles of dogs in urban African society: A south African perspective', *Anthrozoos* 12(3): 157–161.

Metz, T. (2017), 'How to Ground Animal Rights on African Values: Reply to Horsthemke', *Journal of Animal Ethics* 7(2): 163–174.

Morters, M., O. Restif, K. Hampson, S. Cleaveland, J. L. N. Wood, and A. J. K. Conlan. (2013), 'Evidence-based control of canine rabies: A critical review of population density reduction', *Journal of Animal Ecology* 82(1): 6–14.

Moss, C. and M. Colbeck. (1992), *Echo of the Elephants: The Story of an Elephant Family*. New York: William Morrow and Company.

Munang'andu, H., A. S. Mweene, V. Siamudaala, J. B. Muma, and W. Matandiko. (2011), 'Rabies status in Zambia for the period 1985–2004', *Zoonoses and Public Health* 58(1): 21–27.

Mulipukwa, C., B. Mudenda, and A. R. Mbewe. (2017), 'Insights and efforts to control rabies in Zambia: Evaluation of determinants and barriers to dog vaccination in Nyimba district', *PLoS Neglected Tropical Diseases* 11(10).

Mwenya, J. 2020. Kabwe dog meat seller on the run, *News Diggers!* Lusaka. Available at https://diggers.news/local/2020/04/01/kabwe-dog-meat-seller-on-the-run/#:~:text=A%20KABWE%20man%20is%20on,that%20it%20was%20game%20meat.

Mweshi, J. (2019), 'The African emphasis on harmonious relations: Implications for environmental ethics and justice', in M. Chemhuru (ed.), *African Environmental Ethics: A Critical Reader*, Cham: Springer.

Mwila, P. (2022), Gruesome details of dog attack revealed, *Zambia Daily Mail*, 4 June 2022. Available from http://www.daily-mail.co.zm/gruesome-details-of-dog-attack-revealed/.

PANA. (2002), 'Hungry Zambians eat dog as famine deepens', 4 October 2002. Available at https://reliefweb.int/report/zambia/hungry-zambians-eat-dog-famine-deepens.

Pearson, C. (2013), 'Dogs, history, and agency', *History and Theory* 52(4): 128–145.

Regan, T. (2004), *The Case for Animal Rights*, updated edn, Oakland: University of California Press.

Rollin, B. (2006), *Animal Rights and Human Morality*, 3rd edn, New York: Prometheus.

Rowlands, M. (2012), *Can Animals Be Moral?*, Oxford: Oxford University Press.

Vaidyanathan, V. (2019), 3 dogs kill 8-year-old boy after escaping home, shot dead by police, *International Business Times*, 16 July 2019. Available from https://www.ibtimes.com/3-dogs-kill-8-year-old-boy-after-escaping-home-shot-dead-police-2806833.

Wang, G., *et al*. (2016), 'Out of southern East Asia: The natural history of domestic dogs across the world', *Cell Research* 26(1): 21–33.

World Health Organization. (2018). 'WHO expert consultation on rabies: Third report', Geneva: World Health Organization. Available from https://apps.who.int/iris/handle/10665/272364. License: CC BY-NC-SA 3.0 IGO.

Zambia Statistics Agency. (2022), '2022 census of population and housing: Preliminary report', Lusaka: Zambia Statistics Agency.

Chapter 10

Let All Beings Be Happy: Dignity and *Prana*, the Vital Force in Indian Thought

Meera Baindur

Popular comics and cartoons often represent the Indian cow as having the free run of the roads in India, while people, automobiles and other means of transport surrender to its supremacy and right on the road.[1] This is not a mere stereotype, for even as I drive to work every day a few cows embark on their leisurely morning journey on the narrow roads and I sometimes find myself at the head of a long queue of vehicles waiting to cross this herd. It is of note that nobody honks or shouts at me for waiting or slowing down to let the animals have right of way.

The understanding of dignity is bound by a two-way relationship between the human and animal (technically a non-human animal). Discussions on animal dignity often involve the various discourses around animals' rights and the flourishing of a non-human other. This way of recognizing dignity may depend on the expression of a special and mutual relationship between human beings and animals. Second, this may also depend on the philosophical and ethical principle of acknowledging the intrinsic value of a non-human being.

Figure 13 Bull in Varanasi, India, credit Jo-Anne McArthur / We Animals Media.

The first-described foundation of grounds for animal dignity can be seen in our behaviour toward domesticated animals, which emerge through deeply personal and working relationships between humans and their non-human companions. On the other hand, the second foundation depends on ethical principles derived from the conceptualization of the non-human world and from recognizing the intrinsic value or the moral standing of Nature.

In what follows, I explore the grounds for dignity within Indian intellectual and cultural traditions. I rely on the language used to describe such a relationship and the oral transmission of norms to support my understanding and speculate on some of these notions that can be extended to serve as a better understanding of human and non-human relationships and behaviours that would be appropriate to Indian cultures.

Prana

A prayer in the ancient texts of India goes like this:

> *Let all be happy, let all beings be free of disease, let all perceive good things, let no being experience sorrow.*

When the prayer talks about 'all beings being happy' it refers to the flourishing of all beings, including the non-humans and the environment. The prayer offers us the possibility of what dignity means for Indian cultural traditions – it is fundamentally associated with a living condition, a life of peace, free from sorrow. Unlike 'happiness' that is achieved by satisfying desire, this peace and joy refers to the continuity of an uninterrupted existence in the world. Culturally, it is seen that when humans and non-humans cohabit in an environment, dignity is afforded to both organisms as well as non-living forms such as rocks, trees, rivers, or mountains. This inclusive view of the non-human not only protects animals from wanton abuse but also provides an incentive to protect their habitats as essential parts of their life-world and their existence.

The Indian intellectual traditions propose a vital force that is based on the perceptual quality of life, rather than on life as a property that is defined as a response to stimulus. Life is given as a 'condition of being' by the word *prana*, which can be translated loosely as life-force. The idea of *prana* is not linked to the idea of sentience alone; rather, sentience is seen as an effect of the presence of a strong *prana*. *Prana* is present everywhere, its expression finding different scales of intensity, from the most intense in supernatural beings to the least in inanimate rocks and minerals.

Prana is also conceptualized as the loom on which the warp and the weft of the universe are woven, entangling all beings – the non-human and the human – and associated with their role in the universe. *Prana* holds together the form *and* function of being. One of the Upanishads equates *prana* with absolute self, who is seen as the form of Brahman, the unitary self in Indian philosophy:

> This immense, unborn self is none other than the one consisting of perception here among the vital functions (*prana*). There, in that

space within the heart, he lies – the controller of all, the lord of all, the ruler of all.

(Olivelle, 1998, trans. *Brhadaranyaka Upanisad*, verse 4.4.22)

The belief that *prana* is embodied in the form of all beings makes all beings sacred and, by extension, the manifestation of life sacred. Metaphysically speaking, the *prana* is seen as a manifestation of the absolute (or the supreme being in some theistic traditions) and a form of primordial creative nature in others. This system of belief is called 'Panentheism', where the divine permeates and at the same time transcends the creation as its overlord (Mumme, 2000: 138). Though the original Vedic beliefs are not commonly followed by people, the same kind of conceptualization continues to exist in modern practices of the living theistic tradition of devotion and worship of gods and goddesses, still widely practised in India.[2] This gives rise to a popular adage in Hindi: *Kan-kan may basa Ram!* (The lord Ram lives in every particle).

Prana thus becomes a creative constituent that is a necessary and sufficient condition not only for life but for existence itself. By invoking *prana* as a broader category of a world infused with the potential to express life, dignity is afforded to the non-human as part of a broader notion of existence. If something *is*, it deserves both acknowledgement and dignity.

By this logic, the model human being's behaviour is to practise non-injury towards all beings. The belief that informs ethical values is designated by the word '*sraddha*'. It is used in Sanskrit to represent sincerity and authenticity. To have *sraddha* is also to have faith, because to treat something with dignity, requires one to believe in the presence of *prana* or its manifestation.

The first verse of instruction in the Isa Upanishad states:

This whole world is to be dwelt in by the Lord, whatever living being there is in the world. So, you should eat what has been abandoned; do not covet anyone's wealth.

(trans. Olivelle, 1998: 407)

Citing an earlier work in his translation, Olivelle notes that this as an injunction not to kill living beings for food:

. . . some take this to mean that one can eat, or more generally enjoy or use, what has been abandoned by the Lord, namely, what is without life or is dead.

(Olivelle, 1998: 612)

This nonviolence is also seen as a mental attitude, not just abstinence from physical harm to another being:

The observances of non-injury (*ahimsā*, etc.) also have internal or mental (*ādhyātmika*) aspects. For example, non-injury is not only the act of not killing an embodied being but also the absence of aversion or hatred.[3]

(Larson and Bhattacharya, 2016: 565)

Thus, the idea of dignity in India is linked to the preservation of that which holds life. Furthermore, due to the granting of beingness to all creation, the habitat also becomes a part of an animal's life-world – it 'holds' life. Elsewhere I have argued about how the habitats are viewed as Nature – beings, whose bodies are diffused in nature (Baindur, 2015: 194). I have argued that the concept of 'shelter' and 'sheltered' creates a gradation of the intensity of violence, where habitat destruction both renders an animal homeless and submits them to an undignified existence:

. . . human destruction of nature is morally reprehensible. This is a 'restraint' kind of ethics wherein humans intentionally should not cause harm to other shelterers. The destruction of the 'beings' such as those that provide shelter to many more beings (ecologically one could call them habitat-beings) is a grade worse than say killing an animal for food.

(Baindur, 2015: 194)

This idea of extending respect and acknowledgment to non-humans beyond sentient to sapient and environmental beings follows from the conceptualization of the vital force, *prana*. *Prana* is viewed as omnipresent. The shelter that habitat provides is understood as infused with divine life. And, accordingly, a recognition of *prana* requires us to acknowledge animals as beings beyond their utilitarian value:

Just as we do not view the parts of our home as economic resource to be sold, similarly we do not treat the cosmic nature – *prakṛti* – as a commodity.

(Rao and Seshagiri, 2000: 37)

In practice, the sacred text-based ideas of *prana* are not philosophically analysed or considered critically by publics, but the concept of *prana* is nonetheless used in everyday language and associated with many rituals and practices. In local languages of South India, a common expression for the complaint 'so and so is causing me a lot of pain and not letting me alone' is 'wringing my *prana*'. This phrase is a marker of an affront to dignity. Sometimes the synonym for *prana*-wringing is '*Jiva-himse*', violence to a life-form. Violence thus gets associated with disturbing *prana* (not just the act of injury or killing) and is discouraged. Most traditional values also discourage wanton violence against animals and insects. As in most cultures, for instance, hunting for food is a sacred act, but hunting and killing for pleasure is seen as sinful.

'Not wringing *prana* / causing *himsa*' as dignity

It is easy to identify examples of animal worship or animal stewardship and relatedness to special charismatic or sacred animals within a culture and lay claim to an appealing idea of animal dignity. This means that the worship of the cow or the observation that a goddess rides a tiger as a mount could be considered an instantiation of a non-human receiving cultural sanction and dignity. However, establishing whether a ritual or cultural norm locates on an idea of dignity requires both experiential and anecdotal evidence.

In my own lived experience in a traditional south Indian family, I have observed that when people in India acknowledge the presence of different animals in their habitat (from insects to snakes), they neither seek the total eradication of animal life around them nor to create friendships or personal relationships with them. As a young child, when I would try to feed and befriend stray kittens, the elders in my family would say 'Don't wring its *prana*, it has to learn to hunt and survive.'

Though my action seemed morally right to me as a child, my elders viewed this as an affront to the dignity of the animal's own right to hunt.

Kicking a stone out of place in the garden to look at the insects under it was also met with stern warning. 'Don't disturb the life of *being*.' Pets were discouraged. There were useful animals – the dog for guarding, the horse for riding, the cow for milk – but there was no 'pawrenting'. We loved animals as our duty and not as our passion.[4] Of course, we shared spaces with other beings, but personal emotional involvement was not encouraged.

In this traditional Indian perspective, the act of domestication is a transfer of the duty of shelter from nature to the human. The animal becomes dependent on a human for its survival and loses its original independent nature.[5] This can be understood as a dissolution of dignity. In the web of creation, every being has its place and role; interfering with the natural order is a moral failure. This is notably different from Western conceptualizations of nature. As Rolston notes:

> According to holders of the humanistic perspective, humans can have no duties to rocks, rivers, or ecosystems, and almost none to birds or bears; humans have serious duties only to each other, with nature often instrumental in such duties; the environment is the wrong kind of primary target for an ethic; nature is a means, not an end in itself; nothing there counts morally; and nature has no intrinsic value.
> (Rolston, 1999: 410)

On the other hand, in Indian traditions, we find evidence to suggest that maintaining the order of the universe, known as '*Dharma*', is morally positive. To accord dignity is to respect nature's order (known as *Rṛa*) and its practice of moral obligations (*Dharma*). As an example, Mumme refers to a sacred text that insists moral good (*dharma*) is supporting that which sustains nature:

> The Narayaniya section of the Mahabharata especially important to Vaisnavas, says: *Dharma* [from the root *dhr* 'to sustain'] is so called on account of its capacity for sustaining [the world]. On account of *dharma*, creatures (*praja*) are sustained separately in their respective stations. Whatever sustains that is proper; that indeed is *dharma*.
> (Mumme, 2000: 146)

During a field trip to Bandipur wildlife sanctuary in Southern India, I met some villagers who were not upset with monkeys raiding their granary store. 'They also have to eat, they don't destroy our standing crop, they wait for us to harvest and then tax our grain,' said a farmer. Such wild animal–human relatedness derives from a kind of active tolerance on the part of humans – cohabitation rather than co-dependency. Communities, particularly in rural or suburban areas, have a sort of neighbourhood ethics with respect to wild animals that is conferred by co-habitation, or *Sahacara* (co-foraging/moving).

Sahacara, the path to a *prana*-sharing dwelling

The primary support of life is food, and the provisioning of food for all beings holds a very important place in moral action in India. Traditionally, consumption of food for living is given by the Sanskrit word '*cara*' – a process of gathering and eating food. Zimmermann refers to this as interaction with the environment. He remarks:

> *Cara* is perfect example of a word with a double reference: to nature and to man. The objective or spatial reference – the environment – is incorporated within the subjective or practical reference – the environment regarded as a source of the means of subsistence.
>
> (Zimmermann, 1999: 21).

When animals and humans share the same *cara*-place, there is a congenial relatedness of cohabiting a space, an agreement of tolerance and co-existence where each being occupies its role in nature. A human would not wantonly walk in front of a tiger and nor would they deliberately kill the animal unless they enter his village to hunt. Neither would a person poison the carcass of a tiger kill. As such, poachers seldom find support in rural communities as they have broken the pact of dignity. At the same time people who want to pet the tigers and feed them would also find little support from the villagers. Every being is allowed the dignity to eat and find its sustenance on its own terms.

Another feature of the *cara*-place is the importance given to procreation. Hunting of pregnant animals or even animals who are in the act of mating is regarded as reprehensible. Creating life is sacred.[6]

Such instructions derive their ecological wisdom from both lived experience of wild species and a shared understanding of dignity as non-interference. Dignity, as practised by such villagers, is not about direct compassion or care or establishing a special relationship with the other. Instead, I argue, this kind of rooted, community-led notion of dignity is an acknowledgment of the other animal's capacity and a willingness to let the being exist without exercising the right to power.

In some form or other, all philosophical and cultural systems believe in a primal life-giving constituent of creation that is the source of life and existence. The practice of *sahacara* provides a foundation for dignity located on practices indigenous to India. The relationship to other animal beings of the villagers that practice *sahacara* is functional but not utilitarian. Functional relationships respond to environmental habitat cues and natural knowledge derived from proximity and co-existence with other species.

To offer a closing anecdote, when a leopard killed a shepherd's dogs in the Himalayas, the shepherd said to me, 'I am very sad, but it is fate. Two brave souls fought and one of them was the victor, that is god's will. I left the meat in the jungle for the leopard. We don't consume dog meat. Let that poor creature have its fill of its kill.' This is a form of dignity in practice. It is a dignity that respects food and cohabitation. A dignity that is embodied by the adage in the local Hindi language, *Sab kuch apne sthan par rahene do* (Let everything be in its place in its world).

Notes

1 A notable example is an episode 'Homer Goes to India' of the popular serial cartoon Simpsons, Homer visits a stereotyped India and is forced to deal with a cow (that seems to be a bull?) with a judgmental 'native' crowd watching with disapproval.

2 To an outsider the number of gods and divinities may seem to be overwhelmingly diverse and incommensurable with the idea of unity, but it is common belief in these traditions to believe that all gods are but

names and forms of one supreme deity. The Vedic corpus refers to this deity as Brahman or Prana, but later sectarian devotional traditions equate their own particular deity such as Krishna or Kali and so on as the supreme.

3 Translated with notes from the original text, Yogarahasya, by the authors.
4 There are now actual debates by ethicists on why we should not keep animals as pets, which make sense from what I was taught.
5 Similar arguments are found in the debates between the pros and cons of conservation of wild species in zoos and in natural wildlife sanctuary.
6 As an aside, embryos are seen as embodied living beings after the 90th day of pregnancy. Before that the body is unoccupied particularly if the soul is morally good. Wicked souls may suffer through the entire nine months, the first few months being spent in a limbless vegetative state.

References

Baindur, M. (2015), 'Nature in Indian philosophy and cultural traditions', in P. Bilimoria (ed.), *Sophia Studies in Cross-Cultural Philosophy of Traditions and Cultures*, New Delhi: Springer, 1–211.
Larson, G. and R. S. Bhattacharya. (2016), *Encyclopaedia of Indian Philosophies (Vol. 12): Yoga: India's Philosophy of Meditation:* V. XII, New Delhi: Motilal Banarsidass.
Mumme, P. Y. (2000), 'The potential contribution of Śrivaiṣṇavism', in L. E. Nelson (ed.), *Purifying the Earthly Body of God: Religion and Ecology in Hindu India*, New Delhi: D K Printworld, 133–163.
Olivelle, P. (1998), *The Early Upanisads: Annotated Text and Translation*, Oxford: Oxford University Press.
Rao, K. and L. Seshagiri. (2000), 'The Five Great Elements' in C. K. Chapple and M. E. Tucker (eds.), *Hinduism and Ecology: The Intersection of Earth, Sky, and Water*, New Delhi: Oxford University Press, 23–37.
Rolston, H. (1999), 'Respect for life: Counting what Singer finds of no account', in D. Jamieson (ed.), *Peter Singer and His Critics*, Oxford: Blackwell.
Zimmerman, F. (1999) *The Jungle and The Aroma of Meats: An Ecological Theme in Hindu Medicine*, New Delhi: Motilal Banarsidass Publishers.

Chapter 11
Two-Eyed Seeing: Animal Dignity through Indigenous and Western Lenses

Cristina Eisenberg and Michael Paul Nelson

Our central question is this: can we make sense of the notion that human animals ought to grant dignity to non-human animals? At a minimum, to be granted dignity is to be deemed worthy of respect. And to be deemed worthy of respect is to be acknowledged to be of direct moral standing – to count, to matter, to be considered valuable beyond one's mere use or instrumental value. Hence, the granting of dignity is a moral matter – it comes with moral consideration. Beyond direct moral standing, to be granted dignity is to be worthy of a place of honour. So, is there a case to be made for the direct moral standing of, or even a place of honour for, non-human animals? We believe that there are, in fact, many reasonable cases to be made for such positions (and few to be made in opposition).

Notice first how we are presenting this notion of dignity. We consider dignity as something that is granted or acknowledged. We can act in a dignified manner, but dignity and the respect it evokes is bestowed.

That is, to grant (or to refuse to grant) another human or non-human being dignity is to make a worldview choice, a choice about how you construct and think about the world around you. The place of animals in the worlds humans create, or in our diverse worldviews, varies tremendously. Some human cultures have no problem with the concept of animal dignity, respect, direct moral standing, or even recognizing that non-human animals are worthy of a place of honour. Some human cultures – including the dominant Western colonial worldview – struggle mightily with this idea, even finding it threatening. Once again, the place of animals is, therefore, a choice. Indeed, how we construct (or reconstruct) our worldview is a human choice.

Another way to phrase our central question is to ask: should humans from cultures not already inclined to do so (what we call 'morally exclusive cultures'), choose to grant dignity to non-human animals? Not only do we suggest there is a case to be made for the dignity of non-human animals as worthy of both respect and a place of honour, but we also further suggest that the failure to dignify the world will ultimately undermine the morally exclusive cultures that promote such exclusivity. Hence, the granting of dignity to animals and the world is not only a choice we all *can* make but also a moral imperative if we are to survive and thrive as a species. This danger becomes apparent when we contrast moral exclusivity with the moral inclusivity that is foundational to Indigenous worldviews.

Two approaches to animal dignity

The granting or acknowledgement of animal dignity is not entirely novel to humans. We briefly explore two systems of thought – one Indigenous and one Western – that deem animals as worthy of respect.

An Indigenous perspective

The following is an Indigenous story from the Ojibwa people who live in the Upper Great Lakes region of the United States. This is our redacted version of their story about the relationship between wolves and humans, which we respectfully share.

Learning the world from Ma'iingan

In the creation story of the Ojibwa people, Ma'iingan, the wolf, is a great teacher; a Kinomaagan. The Ojibwa people learned about the world from the wolf. The instruction included woodcraft: the names of the plants, the trees, and the other animals. Most importantly it was the wolf who taught the people the lessons about Mother Earth herself: her moods both raucous and tender, the ebb and flow of her processes, and the majestic romp through life and death as predator, and ultimately, as prey.

When Ma'iingan's grand tutorial had ended, the Great Spirit announced that we humans and our Kinomaagan, the wolf, were to walk separate paths. These paths were rarely to cross. We and the wolf became estranged siblings – the wolf the elder and wiser older brother, guide and mentor – both departed from home, meeting only in fleeting moments, or not at all. And so the affirmation has come to pass and we encounter Ma'iingan in whispers and shadows on edges of dawn and dusk.

At the same time the Great Spirit also entwined our fates. The Great Spirit foretold that the Ojibwa and Ma'iingan would both be misunderstood and persecuted in their time. But the Great Spirit warned that if the wolf's demise came to pass then the end of wild Nature would be marked. The end of wild Nature would mean that the Ojibwa would pass from existence and from loneliness of spirit. The end of the Ojibwa would mark the beginning of the end of the human race. For humans have been given something powerful by the Great Spirit: the medicine, the knowledge of how to live with Nature. The loss of Ma'iingan demonstrates the loss of this vital wisdom. For as goes the wolf, so go the people.

In the Ojibwa story Ma'iingan, the wolf, is mentor, teacher, life-lesson guide, elder, and family member. So when our paths do cross, the Ojibwa people believe that we humans, we non-wolves, are meant always to recall with humility and respect the central role that brother-wolf played in our beginning. And we are to behave accordingly.

In this story, the wolf holds a place of honour as a teacher. The wolf teaches humans how to live in the world. The wolf is wiser, older, and a mentor for humans. The fates of humans and wolves are entwined such that to protect wolves is to protect humans and to harm wolves is to harm the Ojibwe prospect for survival.

Figure 14 Wolf up close, credit Istock.

Other Ojibwa stories – much like stories from all Native American tribes – portray animals as occupying either dignified roles in Ojibwa culture or as kin to the Ojibwa. In the Ojibwa culture, animals occupy a place of direct moral standing and a place of honour. In Indigenous cultures in general, animals are universally seen as teachers, and often, thereby, as superior to humans. Indeed, many North American Tribal Nations have creation stories that portray animals welcoming humans into the world and teaching humans how to survive and live rightly. In other Indigenous worldview structures, animals are viewed as kin, part of the larger collective family, often occupying special familial roles such as brother, mother, grandmother, or grandfather.

It is of note that, according to Baraga's *A Dictionary of the Ojibwa Language* (1992), there is no word in the Ojibwa language for dignity and no discussion about what it is in the world that is worthy of dignity either. Frederic Baraga was a Slovenian missionary priest who studied the Ojibwe language in the first half of the nineteenth century. However, the absence of a direct linguistic correlate does not presuppose the absence of a recognizable concept or practice that can root modern notions of dignity in Indigenous philosophy.

The word 'respect' is in Baraga's dictionary, however. That word is '*Manaaji'idiwin*', and it means to go easy on, to spare, to honour, to respect. It is an animate verb and transitive – in other words, it's reciprocal: we and the world respect one another. Moreover, respect is one of the Ojibwa seven grandfather teachings, describing how to rightly live in the world. Those teachings apply to 'all my relations', to all beings of the world. Such a meaning inspires restraint and reciprocity, which means seeing life as a gift, taking only what is needed, acknowledging that one is morally obligated to reciprocate the gift, and doing so with humility and respect. From *Manaaji'idiwin* we can grasp an approach to non-human dignity from an Indigenous worldview. If the starting assumption is the idea that all the world is worthy of dignity, we are gifted the idea that we ought to respect the world and all of its beings.

From the Indigenous perspective, therefore, it is possible to create moral systems granting animals dignity, whether we use that word or not. A critic might suggest, however, that the notion of non-human animal dignity would contradict some core values of the dominant Western intellectual tradition. Contrary to this assertion, however, philosophical and ethical work over the past fifty years demonstrates this is not the case.

A Western parallel

The parallel concept that can ground non-human animal dignity in the Western worldview comes from the field of environmental ethics and is the notion of intrinsic value (see Soulé, 1985; Callicott, 1986; Naess, 1986; Rolston, 1999; Batavia and Nelson, 2017). To recognize or acknowledge dignity is to acknowledge intrinsic value (i.e., value beyond use value or utility), and to subsequently grant direct moral standing to those holding that value. Beginning in the early 1970s, some Western philosophers engaged more seriously and systematically with questions about the intrinsic value of nature. Since then, a wide variety of arguments have been offered supporting the idea of animal dignity and the intrinsic value and direct moral standing of the non-human world. These arguments typically come in one of two forms.

First, arguments concluding that other animals merit intrinsic value and direct moral standing appeal to the consistent application of some quality that we humans already believe is relevant and intrinsic-value-bestowing in the human realm. Maybe that quality is sentience (the ability to experience pleasure and pain), being the experiencing subject of a life, or simply being alive. Whatever the quality, a commitment to consistency implies that we are obligated to apply it consistently to all those beings possessing said quality. Since non-human animals are also sentient experiencing subjects of a life, and alive, they too merit intrinsic value and direct moral standing. Of course, different qualities would create slightly different moral communities since arguably not all animals possess all these qualities.

Second, sometimes arguments work to portray animals as part of our larger biotic community – something like the kin notion in Indigenous belief structures. Aldo Leopold's 'Land Ethic' ([1949] 2020) is perhaps the most notable argument of this kind. Leopold argues that contrary to the dominant Western narrative, we humans are 'plain members and citizens of the biotic community,' enlarging the boundaries of our sense of community, and implying that community membership requires us to grant intrinsic value and direct moral standing to the community and its members, including non-human animals. Specifically, for Leopold, 'A thing is right when it tends to preserve the integrity, stability, and beauty of the biotic community. It is wrong when it does otherwise' (Leopold, [1949] 2020: 224). These arguments often appeal to a variety of Western sciences (most notably ecology, evolutionary theory, quantum theory, etc.) to inspire and ground this enlarged view of community.

The granting of intrinsic value, dignity, respect, direct moral standing to the non-human world has practical purchase as well. Essentially, such an attribution shifts the burden of proof on to those who would callously mistreat animals or other morally relevant parts of our world. This is tantamount to a system where nature is innocent until proven guilty rather than guilty until proven innocent.

These moral inclusive Western approaches run contrary to more traditional Western ideas that relegate the non-human world to, at best, of value for what they provide humans (or certain humans). Even seemingly enlightened Western ideas like 'sustained-yield', which are premised upon the realization that human well-being is dependent on so-called 'natural capital', are reflective of the worldview lying at the root of the life-altering environmental challenges – from droughts to the climate migration – we now face. From both an Indigenous perspective and a morally inclusive Western perspective, anthropocentrism (human-centeredness) is a hazardous, even deadly paradigm.

Dignity: An adaptive choice

The question is this: what in the world should we acknowledge as possessing of dignity and worthy of respect? Note the weight of such a question. The cognitive apparatus of humans confers on us an amazing power, the power to grant moral standing, the ability to live in a world imbued with dignity and respect or to live in a morally impoverished world. The ideas and stories we use to frame and justify our actions are choices. So, what choice should we make?

In the face of our climate crisis, humans will need to develop new technologies, new schemes to manage so-called 'natural resources', and we will need to create new social and political structures as well. But we will need to be adaptive in another sense also. We suggest that what is broken in the dominant Western worldview are the most fundamental assumptions that justify the exploitative and extractive status quo. These assumptions include often unexamined ideas about what humans are, what the world is, and what an appropriate human/nature *relationship* looks like.

Again, it is important to acknowledge that our worldview is a choice. A few hundred years ago, Western society chose to adopt a worldview that portrayed the world as purely material and mechanistic, without sacredness or intrinsic value, valuable only for use by humans, unremarkable, ownable. This worldview was based on scientific knowledge that enabled us to exploit natural resources within a capitalistic model. We also chose to believe that humans were distinct from that world – distinct as in separate, special, superior.

Worldviews that ran counter to this, such as Indigenous worldviews, were viewed as both mistaken and dangerous – exemplified in the North American Residential School system which tried to force Indigenous children to abandon their cultural and religious traditions and base their lifeways on a capitalistic relationship with nature.

However, what has emerged within the dominant Western tradition in the past hundred years or so are the elements of a new worldview. This, we believe, can be understood as a great convergence of mutually reinforcing knowledge. These knowledge foundations include ecological science, evolutionary theory, quantum theory, Indigenous wisdom, and lived experience. Each contributes powerful evidence that the rest of the living world is both more dynamic, more complex, and more entangled than the narrow determinations of human exceptionalism claim. As such, the strand of Western thinking that justifies destructive human actions solely for economic gain or for simplified notions of progress is not only too small, but also wrong and indefensible. It has led us to unbridled consumption of natural resources, bringing us to the point of requiring the newly recognized legal concept of *ecocide*.[1]

This converging worldview emphasizes that new properties and entities evolve or emerge from the interdependencies and interactions of natural systems, not from their matter alone. Wildflowers or consciousness or beauty, for example, are not snapped together from particles of matter like so many LEGO® bricks. Rather, they emerge over long expanses of time from the evolving organization of systems. As systems become more complex and interactive, they organize themselves into new patterns, new life forms, and new realities. The interrelationships between non-human beings and humans are myriad and extraordinarily complex – so complex that we are still developing the statistical analysis tools to glimpse the strength of these relationships. As an example, the work done in Western science on wolves in places like Yellowstone and Isle Royale has found that wolves can touch just about everything in a food web, and with their presence create healthier, more resilient ecosystems.

Seven decades ago, Aldo Leopold intuited this from his observations, long before scientists had the tools (e.g., GPS collars for animals, multivariate statistical analysis methods) to measure and analyse these relationships. But his ideas about the value of wolves to humanity and about wolves as our teachers were nothing new. The Ojibwa, and many other tribes in places as far-flung as Mongolia, Ecuador and Africa, knew and respected these relationships and built entire cultures around animal teachers. Their knowledge was empirical too – derived from direct, lived experience alongside these animals. For example, in Mongolia the Indigenous horsemen learned to hunt by watching wolves hunt. Wolves led them to game during times of drought. And Mongolian Indigenous hunters established hunting routes that paralleled the routes wolves used to ambush prey.

This new worldview braids together Traditional Ecological Knowledge (TEK) with the best of Western science. TEK is defined as knowledge and practices passed from generation to generation informed by cultural memories, sensitivity to change, and values that include reciprocity.

This new worldview looks to the past to re-imagine a more sustainable world in which human and non-human animals don't just co-exist, but they sustain one another. At its core, this is reciprocity.

In this re-imagined worldview, also known as Two-Eyed Seeing, humans are members of the community of beings. We share the urgency of life, shaped by our cultural, ecological, and physical relationships. We share a common fate as well. Animals are our teachers. And if we listen, honour, and dignify them, they will teach us what we need to survive. There is no hierarchy of value in such a world; the value assigned to human beings is distributed throughout the world. If all beings are worthy, then all count in the calculation of what is morally permissible – and what is not. *A'ho*.[2]

Notes

1 A legal definition of ecocide was drafted in 2021. See https://www.stopecocide.earth/legal-definition
2 *A'ho* is a term used by many North American Indigenous peoples as a form of thanks.

References

Baraga, F. (1992), *A Dictionary of the Ojibwa Language*, St. Paul: Minnesota Historical Society Press.
Batavia, C. and M. P. Nelson. (2017), 'For goodness sake! What is intrinsic value and why should we care?', *Biological Conservation* 209: 366–376.
Callicott, J. B. (1986), 'On the intrinsic value of nonhuman species', in B. Norton (ed), *The Preservation of Species: The Value of Biological Diversity*, Princeton, NJ: Princeton University Press.
Leopold, A. ([1949] 2020), *A Sand County Almanac*, New York: Oxford University Press.
Naess, A. (1986), 'Intrinsic value: Will the defenders of nature please rise?', in M. Soulé (ed.), *Conservation Biology: The Science of Scarcity and Diversity*, Sunderland: Sinauer.
Rolston, H. (1999), 'Respect for life: Counting what Singer finds of no account', in D. Jamieson (ed.), *Peter Singer and His Critics*, Oxford: Blackwell.
Soulé, M. (1985), 'What is conservation biology?', *Bioscience* 35, 727–734.

Chapter 12
Dignity in Non-Humans: A Theological Perspective

Michael J. Reiss

My mother-in-law, Doreen, died shortly before the start of the COVID-19 pandemic. She had had Alzheimer's for about ten years and spent the last six years of her life in a specialist Alzheimer care home unable to recognize me for the last three years and her one child, Jenny, to whom I am married, for the last two.

The care home, as good care homes do, tried their best to help Doreen maintain her sense of dignity, even after this was not, I suspect, of conscious importance to her. Each day, for instance, even if she gave the appearance, as she usually did, of simply wanting to stay in bed, they would ensure that Doreen got up, got dressed in day clothes and spent some time out of her room.

When she died, the prepaid funeral plan that she had was, by coincidence, with Dignity Funeral Directors, who did a good job at both the funeral service itself (where I was the officiating minister) and at the internment of her ashes, with those of her husband, some eighteen months later.

I mention all this because I suspect any of us would have done the same. There simply seems something appropriate about treating someone with dignity even if, because of dementia or other circumstances, they may not appreciate it – and those who are being buried or cremated certainly don't appreciate the care that family members, friends and other put in and the respect that they manifest.

And yet, there has been a long tradition in many of the world's religions for doubting that it makes sense to talk of non-humans, however aware and mentally alert they are, possessing dignity.

Religious understandings about dignity in non-humans

Most religions privilege humans over the rest of creation. So, in Judaism, Christianity and Sufism (within Islam), humans are created in the image and likeness of God – *imago Dei* (Takeshita, 1982; Robinson, 2011; Rabie-Boshoff and Buitendag, 2021). Despite the importance of this concept, it features infrequently in scripture – occurring only three times, for instance, in the Jewish scriptures. As Rabie-Boshoff and Buitendag (2021) point out, its importance, despite its scriptural scarcity, seems precisely to be to do with the fact that it is taken as a means of distinguishing humans from non-humans and in a way that aligns humanity with the creator. Furthermore, we can note that other claims about the distinctiveness of humans – that non-humans can't use tools, lack genuine intelligence, do not have feelings, lack self-awareness, aesthetic awareness and a moral sense and so on – can and have been empirically investigated with findings that weaken the distinction between all the other animal species on Earth and ourselves (understood as members of the species *Homo sapiens*). The claim that we are made *imago Dei* is different. We can *try* to explain what it means in scientific language but those with the appropriate religious faith can always fall back on scripture.

However, there have been substantial moves within the Abrahamic faiths to come to a deeper understanding of the purpose of God's non-human creation. In part such moves have resulted from greater awareness of ecological considerations (Page, 1996). The net result of such thinking has been to soften the binary distinction between humans and the rest of creation. For a start, theologians nowadays are more likely to insist that there is much that humans can learn from other creatures. Re-readings of the scriptures have revealed how much they say about the natural world that previous generations seemed hardly to notice, for example: 'Go to the ant, O sluggard; consider her ways, and be wise. Without having any chief, officer or ruler, she prepares her food in summer, and gathers her sustenance in harvest' (*Proverbs* 6:6–8); 'Consider the ravens: they neither sow nor reap, they have neither storehouse nor barn, and yet God feeds them. Of how much more value are you than the birds!' (*Luke* 12:24); 'And your Lord inspired the bee, saying, "Take you habitations in the mountains and in the trees and in what they erect. Then, eat of all fruits, and follow the ways of your Lord made easy (for you)." There comes forth from their bellies, a drink of varying colour wherein is healing for people. Verily, in this is indeed a sign for people who think.' (*Qur'an* 16:68–69).

Furthermore, there is a danger of reading too much into *imago Dei*. By far the greater emphasis in the Abrahamic religions is of the distance between God and all of creation. Of course, God cares for and sustains creation, but God created it and there is therefore an ontological distinction *between* God and the created order that is of a different kind to the distinctions that exist *within* the created order.

Despite all this, other religions can generally be characterized as being more positive about animals than the Abrahamic ones. Several Asian ones, in particular Buddhism, Hinduism and Jainism, ascribe dignity to animals (Chapple, 2014). At first sight it might be thought that this claim does not sit well with the fact that Hinduism (best considered as an aggregate of the beliefs and practices of ancient Indian cultures and traditions) sees a hierarchy among living creatures with humans at the top. The position of each kind of animal within this hierarchy is revealed by *karma* (actions and their consequences) so that good *karma* is rewarded by reincarnation further up the hierarchy and bad *karma* by the opposite. However, the sacred texts of Hinduism, for instance in the *Rig Veda* and the *Atharva Veda*, praise those who show sensitivity toward animals (Caruana, 2020).

Perhaps more significantly, the idea that there is a clear hierarchy with non-humans below humans below the gods is troubled by the fact that reincarnation occurs among the gods who may appear as animals. Krishna is one of the most widely revered of all Hindu deities and is seen as the divine cowherd (Simoons *et al.*, 1981). The festival of Gopashtami, which falls in the early autumn, commemorates the occasion when Krishna, along with his brother, first took his father's herds of cattle to graze in the forests of Vrindaban in Uttar Pradesh. At this time, cattle are given a rest from work, are washed, decorated, fed special foods, and worshipped. Indeed, cows are worshipped on many other occasions. To walk three times round a cow just before or while it is giving birth is equivalent to a very lengthy pilgrimage, some would say to walking around all India.

There are many accounts in Hindu literature of how caring for a cow, its presence or even the sight of it brings good fortune and drives away evil or protects against it. Dust in the hoofprints of a cow is an ingredient in native medicines; dust kicked up by cows may be applied to a person's forehead, put on a newly born infant as protection against the evil eye, and sprinkled on a bride and groom (Simoons *et al.*, 1981). Of particular relevance in purification are the five products of the cow (milk, curd, ghee, urine and dung): 'These products . . . play a significant role for orthodox Hindus in gaining and maintaining the state of ritual purity they so greatly desire.' (Simoons *et al.*, 1981: 130). The reverence accorded to Indian cows has led to the establishment of cow shelters (*gaushalas*); here aged, infertile, diseased, rescued and abandoned cows are sheltered for the rest of their life, until they die of natural causes (Sharma *et al.*, 2019). There are thought to be some 3,000–4,000 cow shelters, caring for 600,000 or more cows (Kennedy *et al.*, 2018).

Buddhism retains from Hinduism the hierarchical view of beings and the idea of reincarnation (Caruana, 2020). Animals are regarded as sentient, while the doctrine of rebirth means that there isn't the ontological distance between them and humans that we see in the Abrahamic religions. Nevertheless, rebirth as an animal is not to be desired; Buddhists often portray the life of animals, wild as well as domesticated, as one that is filled with fear and suffering. Furthermore, Barstow, writing of the moral status of animals within the Tibetan tradition, points out that while animals are sentient, they are less intelligent than humans. Accordingly, he concludes:

> This lack of intelligence means that animals are assumed to be incapable of practising religion, meaning that they are incapable of alleviating their suffering on anything more than a temporary, worldly level. Nevertheless, despite their stupidity relative to humans, the Tibetan tradition also makes clear that animals have rich inner lives. They feel physical pain, of course, but also emotions such as fear, love, and desire.
>
> (Barstow, 2019: 1)

In Japanese Buddhism, too, animals are considered sentient but of lesser mental capacity than humans. They are therefore seen as 'spiritually hindered beings' (Ambros, 2014: 256). While Buddhism is often portrayed in the West as being 'pro-animal', the reality is more complex. In Japanese Buddhism, Ambros concludes that:

> premodern Japanese Buddhism displayed, as did Buddhism in general, a high degree of ambivalence toward animals by presuming a fundamental kinship between humans and other animals while also taking for granted that nonhuman animals occupied a subhuman status. Animals were regarded as living, sentient beings and ignoble beasts, as having superhuman powers yet being karmically hindered, as paragons of gratitude and beings culpable of evil deeds, as the bestowers of reward and punishment as well as embodiments of attachment, ignorance, and pollution.
> (Ambros, 2014: 259)

Even though there are only some six million Jains, their position with regard to animals is such that it warrants discussion here. One of Jainism's principal tenets is the idea of *ahimsa* (non-violence), so that virtually all Jains are vegetarians. As in Buddhism, there is a hierarchy of living things and a cycle of rebirth, from which humans need to be liberated:

> It is the strictest religion as regards avoiding harm to animals. All living things are meant to help one another. Killing is not allowed, even in self-defense. Going further than Hinduism and Buddhism, Jainism considers nonviolence the highest moral duty . . . One important prayer includes a plea for forgiveness from all living beings. The idea of *Jiva* corresponds somewhat to what Western thinkers call consciousness or soul but Jainism sees *Jiva* as present everywhere, in gods, humans, animals, plants, hell beings, and even in inert matter.
> (Caruana, 2020: 9)

Mention of *jiva* leads into the growing interest in some theological circles of the possibility of panpsychism (Leidenhag, 2019). Long seen as a core belief within Vedanta (Deutsch, [1969] 1973), the spiritual foundation of Hinduism, panpsychists see mentality as fully natural, as fundamental to the universe, but not reducible to the physical. The growing interest in panpsychism is partly due to increasing explorations of the relevance of quantum theory to theology. While there are a range of views about this (Saunders, 2002; Leidenhag, 2019), at the very least such remarkable, yet well-established, physical phenomena as quantum entanglement ('spooky action at a distance' – to cite Einstein), in which, in certain circumstances, measurements on one particle (e.g., to determine its spin) *instantaneously* cause changes in one or more other, distant particles, raise questions about our understanding of the fundamentals of our universe (including the nature of causation and of time). There are competing interpretations among physicists as to what is going on, but one feature of particular interest is that this seems like evidence for deep connections between entities in a way that is at least consonant with theological understandings of the universe that see something mysterious shared between all entities. Such phenomena as quantum entanglement give some support to the notion, as expressed in the Upanishads, that Brahma (ultimate reality) is pure consciousness (Deutsch, [1969] 1973).

The overall conclusion is that humans may not be as distinct from the rest of the cosmos as we generally presume. There is an inherent worth to all entities, a notion that is not far from that of ascribing dignity to all entities. Even in the Christian tradition, there are instances that hint at the worth and dignity of all of creation, not just of animals. One thinks of St Francis of Assisi's *Canticle of Brother Sun and Sister Moon*, with such passages as:

> Praised be You my Lord with all Your creatures,
> especially Sir Brother Sun,
> Who is the day through whom You give us light.
> And he is beautiful and radiant with great splendour,
> Of You Most High, he bears the likeness.
>
> (St Francis of Assisi, n.d.)

Concluding thoughts

In Orwell's *Animal Farm*, Napoleon, the pig, famously changes the rule 'All animals are equal' to 'All animals are equal but some are more equal than others.' Some religious traditions see humans as special but not

Figure 15 Polar Bear at Zoo, credit Library of Congress, www.loc.gov/item/2016820238/.

as separate from non-humans. Aristotle saw plants as having souls with the powers of nutrition, growth and reproduction, animals as having souls with the additional powers of perception and locomotion, and humans as having a rational soul thanks to our powers of reason and thought. He did not use the term dignity in regard to non-humans but I suspect he would have seen every organism as having a dignity appropriate to its nature (its form). We see this when we regard a majestic tree or the grace of some animals. Conversely, there are times when we recognize how the natural dignity of an animal has been damaged.

This understanding is not entirely dissimilar from Gerald Manley Hopkins's concept of 'inscape', the intrinsic form or essence of a thing. For Hopkins, every being in the universe 'selves' (enacts) its identity (Greenblatt et al., 2006). A more prosaic version is to talk of the distinctive 'thingness' of things, the 'pigness' of a pig, for instance. It is this that makes behaviour appropriate in one species – think of a big cat hunting prey – that we would consider inappropriate in another.

It is also worth mentioning a longstanding strand of thought in which we fail to understand what it is like to be an animal. In mainstream philosophy this view is perhaps most famously put by Nagel (1974) in his article 'What is it like to be a bat?'. The thinking here is that a bat's mind is so different from ours that we cannot really conceive of what a bat's life is like, let alone what it is thinking, except at a somewhat superficial level. That being the case, we are likely to underestimate bats, and other species, with regard to their capabilities, including their moral capabilities (cf. Peña-Guzmán, 2022).

More fancifully, in some people's eyes, is the poet Malcolm Guite's account of visiting the grave of Charles Williams:

> I HAD a curious experience in a graveyard last week. On my way to the University Church to preach a sermon at the conference's closing service, I thought that I would visit the churchyard of Holy Cross, and pay my respects to Charles Williams, who is buried there.
>
> . . .
>
> The churchyard of Holy Cross is wonderfully wild and overgrown, a haven for wild flowers, bees, and insects. Not many people seem to visit it, and, wandering on the paths there, which are so tangled with long grass and nettles, I wondered whether I could find his gravestone; for the paths seemed to wind in ways that I couldn't remember. The place was quiet, deserted, and still. Just as I began to feel that I might never find the spot, there was a movement at my feet, and a beautiful black cat appeared, purring and rubbing itself round my legs; then it turned and walked away. I followed, and it led me straight to Williams's grave, where it perched on a stone and asked for more fuss as its reward, purring all the time.
>
> . . .
>
> I left the churchyard and went to preach my sermon in the pulpit from which Lewis had preached his wonderful sermon 'The weight of Glory'. At the reception afterwards, I mentioned to the composer J. A. C. Redford . . . that I had visited Williams's grave. Before I could tell him anything more, he said: 'You know, years ago I had a strange, almost a mystical, experience there. I somehow got lost in the tangled paths and couldn't find the grave, and then, from out of the undergrowth, there stepped a beautiful red fox, which looked at me,

turned around, and trotted down the path that led me straight to Williams's grave.'

(Guite, 2022)

Before the Axial Age (from around the eighth to the third century BCE, a time when religions formalized and the first scriptures were probably written), religions were probably far more open to animistic and shamanistic thought, experiences, and practices than many of the world's organized religions are nowadays (Dunbar, 2022). Animism is the belief that all objects, not only animals but also non-living entities and places, perhaps even words, have a spiritual essence. Given the current unprecedented ecological crisis and the disengagement from nature that many people feel, it is perhaps unsurprising that animism is making something of a comeback – see for example, Harvey's (2017) *Animism: Respecting the Living World*. Related to animism is shamanism, religious practices that entail a shaman acting as an intermediary between this world and the spirit world, often through altered states of consciousness. David Abram (2011) in his aptly titled *Becoming Animal* discusses from a Western perspective what it is like to be a shaman. It is increasingly common for people to live with a less strict dividing line between human and non-human animals, a feature that makes it easier for us to recognize their inherent dignity and worth.

References

Abram, D. (2011), *Becoming Animal: An Earthly Cosmology*, New York: Vintage Books.

Ambros, B. (2014), 'Animals in Japanese Buddhism: The third path of existence', *Religion Compass* 8(8), 251–263.

Barstow, G. (2019), 'On the moral standing of animals in Tibetan Buddhism', *Études Mongoles et Sibériennes, Centrasiatiques et Tibétaines* 50.

Caruana, L. (2020), 'Different religions, different animal ethics', *Animal Frontiers* 10(1), 8–14.

Chapple, C. K. (2014). 'Nonhuman animals and the question of rights from an Asian perspective', in N. Dalan and C. Taylor (eds.), *Asian Perspectives on Animal Ethics: Rethinking the Nonhuman*, London: Routledge, 148–168.

Deutsch, E. ([1969] 1973), *Advaita Vedanta: A Philosophical Reconstruction*, Honolulu: University of Hawaii Press.

Dunbar, R. (2022), *How Religion Evolved and Why It Endures*, London: Penguin Random House.
Greenblatt, S., *et al.* (eds) (2006), 'Gerard Manley Hopkins', in *The Norton Anthology of English Literature*, 8th edn, vol. 2. New York: W. W. Norton & Co.
Guite, M. (2022), 'Poet's corner', *Church Times*, 12 August.
Harvey, G. (2017), *Animism: Respecting the Living World*, 2nd edn, London: C. Hurst & Co.
Kennedy, U., A. Sharma, and C. J. Phillips. (2018), 'The sheltering of unwanted cattle, experiences in India and implications for cattle industries elsewhere', *Animals* 8(5), 64.
Leidenhag, J. (2019), 'The revival of panpsychism and its relevance for the science-religion dialogue', *Theology and Science* 17(1), 90–106.
Nagel, T. (1974), 'What is it like to be a bat?', *The Philosophical Review* 83(4), 435–450.
Page, R. (1996), *God and the Web of Creation*, London: SCM.
Peña-Guzmán, D. M. (2022), *When Animals Dream: The Hidden World of Animal Consciousness*, Princeton, NJ: Princeton University Press.
Rabie-Boshoff, A. C., and J. Buitendag. (2021), '*Imago Dei*: We are but dust and shadow', *HTS Theological Studies* 77(3), 1–8.
Robinson, D. (2011), *Understanding the "imago Dei": The thought of Barth, von Balthasar and Moltmann*, Farnham: Ashgate.
Saunders, N. (2002), *Divine Action and Modern Science*, Cambridge: Cambridge University Press.
Sharma, A., U. Kennedy, C. Schuetze, and C. J. Phillips. (2019), 'The welfare of cows in Indian shelters', *Animals* 9(4), 172.
Simoons, F. J., F. I. Simoons, and D. O. Lodrick. (1981), 'Background to understanding the cattle situation of India: The sacred cow concept in Hindu religion and folk culture', *Zeitschrift Für Ethnologie* (H. 1/2), 121–137.
St Francis of Assisi (n.d.). *Canticle of Brother Sun and Sister Moon*. Available from: https://ignatiansolidarity.net/blog/2015/06/04/canticle-of-brother-sun-and-sister-moon-of-st-francis-of-assisi/.
Takeshita, M. (1982), 'The *Homo imago Dei* motif and the anthropocentric metaphysics of Ibn 'Arabi in the Insha' al-Dawa'ir', *Orient* 18, 111–128.

PART FOUR

Dignity in Practice: *What Work Can Animal Dignity Do?*

Summary

Once the concept of animal dignity has been examined and clarified (including sensitivity to and recognition of cultural variations), and the grounds given, the final step is to consider the practical applications of the concept of animal dignity. What follows if we recognize animal dignity, and what forms might such recognition take both in philosophy, policy, education, science, and law?

This section opens with a poem by Craig Santos Perez. Perez speaks to the wider historical conditions in which we find ourselves today, amid the extinction crisis and climate change. Many of the chapters touch on the harms that come to those species that we profit from, but others point to the human exceptionalism that has justified widespread disruption to the living world such that many species face huge losses to their communities or even species extinctions.

We turn next to a select section from Martha Nussbaum's recently published volume *Justice for Animals: Our Collective Responsibility* (2023). Nussbaum argues for the necessity of moving from a recognition of animal dignity to a formal constitution that enshrines animal dignity and the duties we owe to non-human animals by virtue of their unique capabilities. One should refer to her book for the arguments in full. Her proposal has elements in common with some Indigenous Peoples-led initiatives, particularly the Haudenosaunee confederacy, the 'Great Binding Law of Peace', 'in which foreign nations and individuals enjoy liberty, respect and worthiness protected by the rule of law' (Wein, 2020).

Legal scholars Visa Kurki and Eva Bernet Kempers offer complementary but importantly distinct reflections on the ways that animal dignity could manifest in law. Neuroscientist Lori Marino details the practical ways that animal dignity could be applied with respect to species in captivity, especially whales and dolphins. Veterinarian and anthrozoologist, Samantha Hurn reflects on the relationship between dignity and aesthetics, regarding disabilities (both of humans and non-humans alike). She suggests that animal welfare policies grounded in dignity recognition require us first to challenge extant human assumptions about the health and beauty of other species.

Scientists and ethicists, Barbara Smuts, Christine Webb, Becca Franks, and Monica Gagliano take us into the waters to consider the dignity of fishes. They argue that a recognition of dignity in scientific practice could strengthen the justifications for studies and, potentially, the quality of the outputs.

Finally, biologist David George Haskell writes of his own experiences both as student and teacher of biology and presents his recommendations for how recognition of animal dignity could transform the ways science and education are conducted.

References

Nussbaum, M. (2023), *Justice for Animals: Our Collective Responsibility*, New York: Simon & Schuster.

Wein, T. (2020). 'A review of the literature on dignity in international development', *The Dignity Project*, 17. Available online: https://dignityproject.net/ (accessed 25 January 2023).

PRELUDE V
The Last Safe Habitat
Craig Santos Perez

for the Kauaiʻi ʻŌʻō, whose song was last heard in 1987

I don't want our daughter to know
that Hawaiʻi is the bird extinction capital
of the world. I don't want her to walk
around the island feeling haunted
by tree roots buried under concrete.
I don't want her to fear the invasive
predators who slither, pounce,
bite, swallow, disease, and multiply.
I don't want her to see paintings
and photographs of birds she'll never
witness in the wild. I don't want her to
imagine their bones in dark museum
drawers. I don't want her to hear
their voice recordings on the internet.
I don't want her to memorize and recite
the names of 77 lost species and subspecies.
I don't want her to draw a timeline
with the years each was 'first collected'

---

* 'The Last Safe Habitat' by Craig Santos Perez, in *Habitat Threshold*, Omnidawn Publishing, 2020. Used by permission of the author.

and 'last sighted.' I don't want her to learn
about the Kauaʻi ʻŌʻō, who was observed
atop a flowering ʻŌhiʻa tree, calling
for a mate, day after day, season after
season, because he didn't know he was
the last of his kind –
    until one day, he disappeared,
forever, into a nest of avian silence.
I don't want our daughter to calculate
how many miles of fencing is needed
to protect the endangered birds
that remain. I don't want her to realize
the most serious causes of extinction
can't be fenced out. I want to convince her
that extinction is not the end. I want
to convince her that extinction is
just a migration to the last safe habitat
on earth. I want to convince her
that our winged relatives have arrived
safely to their destination: a wondrous
island with a climate we can never
change, and a rainforest fertile
with seeds and song.

> 'What is lost when a species, an evolutionary
> lineage, a way of life, passes from the world? What
> does this loss mean within the particular
> multispecies community in which it occurs: a
> community of humans and nonhumans, of the
> living and the dead?'
> (Thom Van Dooren, *Flight Ways: Life and Loss at
> the Edge of Extinction*, 2014)

Chapter 13
Extending the Capabilities Approach to Non-Human Animals

Martha Nussbaum

Human beings are vulnerable sentient animals, each trying to achieve a good life amid dangers and obstacles. Justice is about promoting the opportunity of each to flourish in accordance with the person's own choice, through the use of laws that both enable and restrain. People are often used as tools, but the Capabilities Approach (hereafter CA)[1] holds that a nation is minimally just only when each person is treated as an end in some very important areas of life, their dignity respected. In thinking about what to put on the list, I have inevitably thought about opportunities that we can expect a large number of people to hold dear, and I have suggested that we focus on those that seem intuitively to be inherent in the idea of a life worthy of human dignity. But because the ends are opportunities, people with minority choices are also protected, in areas of central importance: thus the free exercise of religion protects both Roman Catholics, who are numerous, and members of small religions – as well as atheists and people who are indifferent to religion.

This chapter by Martha Nussbaum is adapted from a section of her recently published volume *Justice for Animals: Our Collective Responsibility* (2023), reproduced by permission of Simon & Schuster.

Why on earth would such an approach to the lives of other animals not be appropriate, for similar reasons? They too are vulnerable sentient animals. They too live amid a staggering, and today an increasing, number of dangers and obstacles, many of them of our making. They too have an inherent dignity that inspires respect and wonder. The fact that the dignity of a dolphin or an elephant is not precisely the same as human dignity – and that the dignity of an elephant is different from that of a dolphin – does not mean that there is not dignity there, that vague property that means, basically, deserving of end-like treatment rather than means-like use. Christine Korsgaard (2018) was correct in her argument that the pursuit of valued goals by an animal, all by itself, entitles the striving animal to end-like treatment: it has a dignity, not just a price. We see that dignity intuitively when we watch dolphins swimming freely through the water in social groupings, echolocating their way around obstacles and leaping for joy; when we see a group of elephants caring communally for their young and attempting to rear them in safety despite the ubiquity of man-made threats. Our sense of wonder is an epistemic faculty oriented to dignity: it says to us 'this is not just some rubbish, something I can use any way I like. This is a being who must be treated as an end.' Why, then, should we think we are more important than they are, more deserving of basic legal protection?

A characteristic form of life

Animals, like humans, have, each of them, a form of life that involves a set of important goals toward which they strive. For now let's think of this form of life as a species form. In thinking about human beings, we thought about some things that are especially important for human beings trying to live. We can do the same thing for each type of animal, if we learn enough and look hard enough. Each animal is a teleological system directed toward a set of good ends centring around survival, reproduction, and, in most cases, social interaction. What the CA thinks in the human case is that those strivings should not be thwarted. And (agreeing with Korsgaard) that it is arrogant, presumptuous, groundless, and just plain selfish to say that we matter more than they do. Each form of life is different. But each one is the right one for that type of being. If a magpie flourishes, it will be in the way characteristic of the life of that bird species. Being more like a human would not be good or pertinent for a magpie. We humans are similar to magpies, dolphins, and elephants in groping toward survival and flourishing in a mostly hostile world; we differ in the specific nature of the goods we seek.

The CA is basically about giving striving beings a decent chance to flourish. That is how it views the role of law and government. Humans will have to take the lead in making the laws and establishing the institutions of government, but there is no reason why humans should do this only *for* and *about* other humans. There is no good reason to say that only some sentient[2] creatures matter. Each matters in its own way. The metric of likeness to humans makes no sense from the point of view of a horse or a whale. Nor is it useful for a fair-minded lawmaker, trying to help sentient creatures have a shot at living decent lives of the sort they seek.

Nor is there any good reason why only humans should participate actively in legislation and institution-building. Animals do not speak human language, but they have a wide range of language-like ways of communicating about their situation, and if we humans happen to be in the driver's seat politically, it should be our responsibility to attend to those voices, to figure out how animals are doing and what obstacles they face. We already do this for human beings who have disabilities that prevent them from participating in political life *in the usual way*: we give them guardians or 'collaborators'[3] to whom they express their situation and who become adept readers of their needs. We should never say that non-verbal children are *passive citizens* or non-participants in political life: they actively express themselves in many ways, and it is our responsibility to translate that into political action. Also, most ordinary citizens do not understand their legal rights and could not represent themselves in court or perform many of the other tasks of citizenship without representation. So too, I claim, with non-human animals.

At this point we must ask whether direct, non-representational, participation in politics is intrinsically valuable, or only instrumentally valuable. This is a debated point by users of the CA. I myself think it is instrumentally valuable: the important thing is being able to influence the conditions that govern one's own life by one's own agency. But this doesn't mean that every human citizen has to go to court, or organize political projects, or, even, vote – so long as there is someone who represents the person's demands in courts and legislatures, and votes on that person's behalf (as I have urged for people with severe cognitive disabilities). With animals I think the solution need not and should not involve a proxy vote for every animal in every election. This would quickly become absurd. Rather, duly qualified animal 'collaborators' should be charged with making policy on the animals' behalf and bringing challenges to unjust arrangements in the courts.

In attending to animal voices as quasi-guardians and listeners, we will not focus only on pleasure and pain. The reductive Benthamite way of thinking about the good of a living thing seems wrong for non-human creatures. It has undeniable power because currently humans cause so much unnecessary pain to non-human creatures, and simply eliminating that would be great progress. But we need a map of the goal that is adequate to the complexity of animal lives. For other animals, as for us, avoiding pain is not all that matters. Social relationships, kinship, reproduction, free movement, play and enjoyment, all these matter to most animals, and as we understand each specific form of life more adequately, we can make the list more complete.

To get the pertinent issues on the table, we need to listen to many stories of animal lives, told by experts who have lived closely with a certain type of animal and studied those animals over long periods of time – looking at shared goals, internal diversity, and prevalent problems and obstacles. We would consider the stories about abused and neglected companion animals. These stories give us ideas about how law needs to promote the flourishing of companion animals, preventing cruelty, promoting nutrition, and, more generally, conveying models of reciprocity, respect, and friendship. We would consider the stories scientists who have lived with wild animals tell about the animals with whom they work, and about the obstacles to their flourishing – seeking both expertise and diversity in our sources, and attending to ways in which different experts emphasize different points. This task, so exhilarating and so urgent, is potentially unending, as new knowledge turns up, and problems and circumstances change. That, after all, is also true of our study of the situation of humans in different parts of the world. The task is long, but with companion animals we have been working this way for a long time, holding public hearings and constructing humane laws. So we know it can be done.

A virtual constitution

In the human case, the CA supplies a template for constitution-making. The list has both content and a tentative threshold for each item. A nation aiming at minimal justice can consult it, and also consult its own particular environment and history, and frame its own list with more locally specific accounts of each of the major capabilities on the list. For two reasons this approach to the other animals is not possible at present. First, the other animals often roam across national borders, or occupy regions of air and sea that are not the property of a single nation; so a national constitution is not sufficient to protect migratory species. Second, there is not anything like sufficient political will in most of the nations of the world to enact any such protections any time soon.

The ideal outcome would be for all the nations of the world (listening astutely to the demands of animals and those who most knowledgeably represent them) to agree to a legally enforceable constitution for the various animal species, each with its own list of capabilities to be protected, and each supplied with a threshold level beneath which non-protection becomes injustice. Animals would then be protected no matter where they are, just as whales are (inadequately) protected all over the world by the IWC (International Whaling Commission). This constitution could then be supplemented by more specific nation-based laws for animals living within a given national jurisdiction, in a way tailored to those specific contexts. However, we know that humanity's halting steps toward international accountability for human injustice have not been terribly successful. Even in the human case, our best hope is with the laws of individual nations. If that is so for humans, it is far more so for animals. I will later discuss the role of international treaties and conventions, but for the most part, for the foreseeable future, animals must be protected by the laws of nations, states, and localities. That does not mean, however, that there is no use in having an international map of destination.

Right now, therefore, the CA aims to supply a *virtual constitution* to which nations, states, and regions may look in trying to improve (or newly frame) their animal-protective laws. It is my hope that over time this virtual constitution can increasingly become the object of a Rawlsian political 'overlapping consensus', both within each nation and across national boundaries. This will take time and work; so too does the task of framing and protecting human rights. Still, this flexible approach permits nations to stride boldly ahead without waiting to get a global consensus. The basic goal is that all animals would have the opportunity to live lives compatible with their dignity and striving, up to a reasonable threshold level of protection.

This virtual constitution, like the human version of the CA, is political and not metaphysical. Because its aim is to secure, over time, an overlapping consensus among all the fair-minded comprehensive doctrines of value, it will not make contentious metaphysical claims, and it will not cover every issue. Animal capabilities are not held to have intrinsic value and claims of intrinsic value are not denied either. My hope is that support for animal capabilities can come from many directions: from religious views that believe in human superiority for religious and metaphysical reasons, but are still willing to extend fair terms of cooperation to animals and to support their capabilities; from ecocentric views that really believe that ecosystems, not individuals, should be the primary focus of concern, but are willing, politically, to support animal capabilities as one crucial element in helping ecosystems to flourish; from Buddhist views that similarly deny the salience of the individual, but still recommend fair treatment of animal lives; from views like Korsgaard's, that remain agnostic about claims of intrinsic value; and from views like my own, which (ethically, though not in my political theory) thinks of animal lives as having intrinsic value.

Lists and lives

Ideally we should learn enough to make a separate list for each type of creature, putting on the list the things that matter most when it comes to survival and flourishing. The list is really made by the animals themselves, as they express their deepest concerns while they try to live. The people who can be trusted to record the unheard voices of animals are people who have lived with a given type of animal for years and with love and sensitivity, for example Barbara Smuts with baboons, Joyce Poole and Cynthia Moss with elephants, Luke Rendell and Hal Whitehead with whales, Peter Godfrey-Smith with octopuses, Frans de Waal with chimpanzees and bonobos, Janet Mann and Thomas White with dolphins. Ideally there should be a group of such people for each species, because any individual is fallible. These 'collaborators' and listeners should know individual animals within the species in all their variety, and should be able to tell many – about what obstacles each creature faces, and what interventions prove helpful.

One remarkable example of the basis for such a list is the elephant Ethogram recently compiled by Joyce Poole and her fellow-workers for the African savannah elephant. This remarkable database incorporates all our knowledge to date about the elephant form of life (for that species): communication, movement, and all characteristic activities.[4] Studying the ethogram, friends of elephants can then suggest the capabilities that seem most central, most important to protect.

My idea means a huge number of different lists, based on many different ethograms. However, I believe that if we focus on the large general rubrics of the CA list for humans, it offers good guidance as a starting point in virtually all cases. That should come as no surprise, since the CA list captures, in effect, the shared terrain of vulnerable, striving animality that each species inhabits in its own way. All strive for life; for health; for bodily integrity; for the opportunity to use whatever senses, imagination, and thought are characteristic for that kind of creature. Practical reason sounds, at first, too human to be a good guide: but really it isn't. All creatures want the opportunity to make some key choices about how their lives will go, to be the makers of plans and choices. Affiliation is crucial for all animals, though its types vary greatly. All seek to relate well to the world of nature around them, and this usually includes members of other species. Play and fun are not peculiar to humans, as researchers increasingly understand, but key aspects of animal sociability. And all animals seek types of control over their material and social environment. If there are other large rubrics pertinent to animal lives that the human list omits, I can't think of them now, but would be totally open to expanding the large rubrics of the list, if any should be convincingly brought forward.

People might worry that such a list is bound to be anthropomorphic, verging on some of the errors of the 'so like us' approach. I understand this charge, but think it mistaken. The list was made up not by thinking of what is distinctively human, but by thinking in very general terms about animality – allowing for significant variations at the specific level, but insisting that at a general level we can find a common pattern. However, we must always be on our guard against obtuseness or self-privileging perception.

Sometimes the lists we frame will include items within the finer rubrics of the human list that appear at first blush not to matter to the lives of animals. Consider 'freedom of association' and 'freedom of speech.' What are most zoos but means of denying freedom of association to animals? As for speech, animals express what they need and want in their own ways, often very sophisticated. Even under formal US law, freedom of speech pertains to many forms of expressive activity, not just to words on paper. Why then should this legal category not include the ways animals speak? It certainly could, if only animals had legal standing in the first place.[5] It's not that they don't speak, it's that we humans usually don't listen. Animals are not free to speak, however, when their complaints are ignored, when information about conditions in the factory farming industry are systematically screened from public view, when even human allies of the afflicted pigs and chickens are prevented by 'ag-gag' laws (laws restricting reporting) from describing those conditions. Freedom of speech is hugely pertinent to animals, and it is important for exactly the reasons John Stuart Mill, a defender of animal rights, gave when he defended free speech in *On Liberty*: free speech gives information we need to make our society better; it challenges complacency and smugness; it brings forward unfashionable positions that deserve, indeed require, a hearing.

And what about 'freedom of the press' and 'political participation'? Animals do not write newspaper articles, but the free circulation of information about their predicament is a crucial part of their good, in this world where humans dominate all animal lives. In *Poverty and Famines*, Amartya Sen argued that a free press is an essential ingredient of staving off (human) famine, because there must be information out there to goad people into political action. I would extend Sen's point: correct information about all the dire predicaments of animals today – habitat loss, torture in the meat industry, poaching, the filling of the seas with plastics – all of this information must get out there if action preventing terrible animal suffering is ever to be taken. To be sure the articles and books and films will have to be made by humans. But they matter for and in the lives of the animals whose voices of complaint they record and whose intolerable conditions they display.

Much the same is true of political participation. Most animals, though often political enough within their own species group, have little interest in political participation in the human-dominated world, and are unaware of elections, assemblies, and offices. Nonetheless, what happens there matters hugely for them. In the human-dominated world, politics determines the rights and privileges of all denizens of a given place, and makes crucial decisions about matters of welfare, habitat, and so forth. So it matters that animals have a political say, which means, I believe, legal standing (the right to go to court as the plaintiff of an action) and some type of legal representation. Right now we allow surrogate representation for humans with cognitive disabilities, so the proposal involves nothing terribly surprising. Creatures who live in a place should have a say in how they live.

It might appear that it is only because we humans dominate the world and have created a lot of trouble for animals that freedom of the press and political participation matter for them. One would think this way if one thought that the world of nature without human interference is idyllic, or wonderful, or peaceable, or in some way good for animals. I do not think this. Even without our damaging interference, there would still be famines, floods, and other forms of climate disaster. I therefore think that even without our own bad behaviour, we have strong reasons to make sure that the news of their predicaments gets out and that their voices have a say in how they live.

At the level of the concrete rubrics of the list, however, there will also be much divergence, and we should always be open to surprise and learning: thus each kind of animal has its own form of social organization, and even of sense-perception. Only painstaking and loving study will show what should be said.

Notes

1 To read the Capabilities Approach in full see Nussbaum (2011).
2 Sentience defined by Nussbaum as 'the ability to feel, to have a subjective perspective on the world – and is a necessary basis for being a subject of justice.'
3 This word is frequently preferred in the disability-rights literature, as more suggestive of joint activity than the word 'guardian.'
4 https://www.elephantvoices.org/elephant-ethogram.html. For a brief description, see https://www.nytimes.com/2021/06/04/science/african-elephants-ethogram-behavior-poole.html.
5 See Nussbaum (2018).

References

Korsgaard, C. (2018), *Fellow Creatures: Our Obligations to the Other Animals*, Oxford: Oxford University Press.

Mill, S. ([1859] 2010), *On Liberty*, London: Penguin.

Nussbaum, M. (2011), *Creating Capabilities: The Human Development Approach*, Cambridge, MA: Harvard University Press.

Nussbaum, M. (2018), 'Why freedom of speech is an important right and why animals should have it', *Denver Law Review* 95: 843–856.

Nussbaum, M. (2023), *Justice for Animals: Our Collective Responsibility*, New York: Simon & Schuster.

Sen, A. (1983), *Poverty and Famines: An Essay on Entitlement and Deprivation*, New York: Oxford University Press.

Chapter 14
Beyond Animal Welfare: Respecting Animal Dignity in Continental Law

Eva Bernet Kempers

When Switzerland recognized the dignity of animals in its Animal Protection Act in 2008, a debate erupted over the question of whether it made sense to extend the legal application of dignity to non-human beings (Bolliger, 2016; Schindler, 2013). Opinions on the matter were divided. On the one hand, the concept of 'human dignity' in international human rights law had been introduced to distinguish the human species from other species on the basis of a metaphysical quality, which made the extension to animals seem contrary to the very purpose of the concept for the law (Heeger, 2015: 141–5).

On the other hand, theorists recognize that there is nothing inherent in the notion of dignity that prevents its application to other animals (Etinson, 2020; Meyer, 2001). Animal dignity can, for example, exist in law as a more general form of dignity – the dignity of living beings – next to human dignity as a species-specific version, as the Swiss example demonstrates (Balzer et al., 2000). In fact, a growing number of scholars suggests that the concept may be well-suited to address some of the current problems in the legal approach towards animals (Lansink, 2019; Vining, 2013: 573). But what does respect for dignity, as applied to animals, require from law?

The current legal approach towards animals in continental Europe is based in animal welfarism. The starting point is that humans may use animals for all kinds of reasons, but their suffering should be minimized. The animal welfarist approach is pathocentric: it is all about the ability to feel pain. Animals matter because they feel pain and also to the degree that they feel pain. Their interest to exist without pain is weighed against the human interests to use them in ways that may result in pain. This balancing exercise culminates in a primary norm: the prevention of unnecessary suffering (Francione, 2004: 108–43). To determine the amount of suffering that is 'necessary', animals are classified into use categories (Robertson, 2015). What 'necessary suffering' constitutes for an animal used in experiments is not the same as what it means for an animal kept as a companion. Therefore, one and the same animal (a pig, for instance), may be addressed by different standards of protection, depending on its use-classification (Kotzmann and Nip, 2020; Kymlicka, 2017).

However, it must be noted that there is no upper limit to the suffering that can be caused: if the human interest is strong enough, animal interests are easily weighed away. Furthermore, the legitimacy of animal use itself is never tested (Francione and Garner, 2010). It is assumed that humans can use animals for all kinds of purposes as long as the amount of suffering is minimized.

The animal welfarist assumptions that inform the existing legal paradigm have some implications for the legal existence of animals in continental Europe (and potentially elsewhere). Since 'animal welfare' is an objective of public interest (protected because humans attach value to it, just like, for instance, the environment) the law remains blind to individual animals and their specific interests. Animals are merely objects of law; they can be owned by humans just as tables and lamps – only humans and companies can be subjects of rights.

Animals' legal status thus has more in common with inanimate objects than with human beings; their individuality and interests remain legally invisible and irrelevant. This also means that, when animal protections are breached, animals are not considered the victims of crime (Flynn and Hall, 2017). No one can claim compensation on their behalf, nor initiate a legal case against the wrongdoer. Crimes of animal abuse are victimless crimes; they are, at most, crimes against society as a whole (Whitfort, 2019). The law does not actually 'see' animals; it only sees objects in which humans vest interests through their property rights. Animal welfarism thus means that animals are protected to some degree, but only via the interests that humans have in them. The law remains essentially anthropocentric, taking human beings as a starting point (Deckha, 2013).

Due to its anthropocentric nature, the legal approach towards animals thus gives rise to several inconsistencies and incoherencies about the interpretation and application of the laws. Already for decades, animal advocates strive to improve the laws addressing animals, emphasizing the immorality of their status as property (Francione, 1995). According to many of these advocates, the existing incoherencies and inconsistencies would be solved if we would just change animals' legal status to that of the legal person with rights.

Proponents of this view, such as Steven Wise and his Non-human Rights Project, initiate cases 'in the name of animals' in court, arguing that they are persons too (Wise, 2010). Making an analogy with slavery some centuries ago, the Non-human Rights Project files *habeas corpus proceedings* that aim to convince judges that animals' status as property should be abolished. Animals such as chimpanzees and elephants possess the required capacities to be recognized as persons: they have self-awareness, recognize themselves in a mirror, and have practical autonomy (Wise, 2004). The idea is that, as soon as their personhood is recognized, the liberation of all animals from human instrumentalization and oppression will follow. Animals will hold fundamental rights to be free, to live their own lives according to their own agency. All we have to do is to put down our speciesist glasses and accept that animals have too much in common with humans to be excluded from the personhood category.

Despite the fact that animal legal personhood is built on strong arguments, the successes of the Non-human Rights project remain limited (Staker, 2017). The argument for animal legal personhood encounters practical as well as theoretical opposition. First, the conviction that animals should be legal persons with fundamental rights (leading to the abolition of most, if not all, animal uses) is shared by only a small minority. Many people, legal scholars included, remain resistant to the idea of extending the border of personhood to other animals. There are fears that such extension would cause a large degree of legal uncertainty: that animals might claim all kinds of human rights; that humans would no longer be able to use animals in any way; or that non-human animal personhood may diminish the strength of the legal personhood of humans (Cupp, 2016).

Aside from these objections, there is also a growing resistance to the logic underlying the central argument that animals should be persons. This resistance originates in the concern that 'personhood' is an equally anthropocentric assumption (Deckha, 2021). Personhood rights-based approaches assume that only animals that are sufficiently like humans and possess human-like cognitive abilities (such as chimpanzees, elephants, and dolphins) may be included in the category of persons (Bryant, 2007). This so-called similarity-argument leads to a hierarchal way of thinking in which value is measured by the degree to which a being is 'like' the paradigmatic human, working 'to institute, maintain and reproduce an entire world that rotates around the privilege of those most fully associated with "the human", a grouping that has never included the entire human species and that has only ever included the tiniest fragments of the animal world' (Calarco, 2015: 64). The argument for recognizing animals as legal persons may seem revolutionary but is not so, as it does not challenge the anthropocentric infrastructure of law in any way but simply moves animals from one side to the other (Favre, 2020).

The question is therefore whether animal dignity can provide an alternative starting point for a legal approach towards animals that also overcomes the binary way of thinking about animals as either persons or things, which stood central in animal law until now (Francione, 2004). To answer this question, we need to have an idea of what animal dignity, as a moral concept, entails. Martha Nussbaum has greatly shaped our understanding of animal dignity in her version of the Capabilities Approach (Nussbaum, 2007). Featuring as the basis for this approach, the concept of dignity forms the ground for a being's claim to justice. Instead of the Kantian view of dignity as contingent on the ability to act rationally, Nussbaum argues that dignity is rooted in our vulnerability, our mortality and animality. Non-human animals, too, have dignity by virtue of their vulnerability as living creatures; their flourishing aims may be compromised by the harmful agency of another being (Nussbaum,

2007). Animal dignity then consists of two aspects. First, it represents the intrinsic value of animals derived from the fact that they strive for their own good. Second, it represents the idea that in the context of our human society, all beings that strive for their own good have an entitlement towards the state to reach a minimum standard of capabilities to flourish, as a matter of justice (Fulfer, 2013).

Even though the capabilities theory, as elaborated by Nussbaum, is essentially a political theory, we can infer what the legal implications of animal dignity would be. Respecting the dignity of other animals would require that these aspects – the intrinsic value of animals as individuals and the entitlement to a minimum level of capabilities to flourish – be safeguarded throughout the legal realm.

Consequently, I propose to define the minimum core of dignity for law as a normative claim with three elements; the law needs to a) respect intrinsic value b) safeguard capabilities to flourish c) ensure visibility as individuals with independent interests throughout the legal system (Bernet Kempers, 2020). This means that the state needs to ensure that animals' intrinsic value is respected in every interaction with them, implying a prohibition of those practices that treat animals as mere things; a minimum standard of flourishing should be ensured by the legislator; and animals' specific interests as individuals should be rendered visible and relevant to the judiciary and executive branch, requiring differentiation between animals and inanimate things that are only the objects of rights.

Ensuring respect for animal dignity, then, is not about changing animals' legal status from thing to person. Instead, the concept can feature as a normative guideline with which to reshape the law to ensure that it supports animals' capabilities to live dignified lives. As a legal principle, animal dignity requires something from legislatures, courts, and executors of law. It requires respecting animals' value as the beings they are, as a kind of their species as well as a unique individual, and to take them into account for their own sakes. Animal dignity does not start from a use-classification based on human interests in animals, but from the idea that animals live their own species-specific lives, they have their own good and their flourishing matters for legal decision-making at all levels. Such an approach goes beyond pathocentric animal protection by taking more than the suffering of animals into account, requiring the active facilitation of animals' capabilities to flourish (Bolliger, 2016). Laws addressing animals are no longer motivated by the aim to protect humans' commitment to animal welfare as a public interest, but rather by the inherent aim to protect animals' interest in flourishing, just as the law protects and safeguards the flourishing aims of humans. Animal dignity encapsulates the idea that taking animals into account is not a matter that depends on the opinions of human beings who value those animals that are similar to them, but rather a matter of justice that the law needs to respect as just.

The principle of animal dignity would not threaten or alter the existing legal concept of human dignity in any way (Sitter-Liver, 2009). Rather, following Martha Nussbaum's conception of dignity, we should understand human dignity as a species-specific version of a more general form of dignity. At its very minimum, dignity codifies the intrinsic worth of living beings – the idea that those who live have their own objectives to flourish, which should be considered in any legal decision. They have intrinsic legal relevance. This more general form we could conceptualize as 'the dignity of living beings' (Jaber, 2000), of which various types exist. Human dignity is about what constitutes a dignified life for a member of the human species; horse dignity is about what constitutes a dignified life for a horse; duck dignity is about what constitutes a dignified life for a duck (Etinson, 2020). Animal dignity is thus an umbrella term; its precise legal implications may differ according to the individual involved (Michel, 2012). Some species may have an interest in liberty that should lead to a fundamental right to be free; other species may have an interest in owning the territories in which they live; other species may need access to swimming water in order to flourish in their species-specific way (Reed, 2016). There is no need to prove the similarity to humans to determine what an animal needs to live a life with dignity.

Some traces of animal dignity can be found in positive law already. To an increasing extent, animal protection acts are being substantiated by the aim to protect animals as intrinsically valuable beings, no longer needing anthropocentric legitimation. Except for the negative protection against unnecessary suffering, a positive duty to care for an animal's wellbeing in line with its species-specific needs has been implemented (Blattner, 2019). In some cases, the laws even literally aim to protect the dignity or intrinsic value of animals.[1] A growing number of jurisdictions have included animals in their Constitution (among others: Switzerland,

Germany, Luxembourg, and Italy), meaning that 'the lived experiences of animals themselves are now recognized as constitutionally significant' (Eisen, 2018: 922). Furthermore, animals and their interests are increasingly taken into account by legal decision-makers in other fields of law, for instance family law and property law (Bernet Kempers, 2021).

A large number of continental European jurisdictions have added a provision to their Civil Code that distinguishes animals from legal things, defining animals as 'living creatures' that have 'biological needs', making clear that animals do not equal other forms of property: the rights of the owner may be limited by the intrinsic value of animals.[2] These developments may be regarded as fragmentary evidence for a growing respect for animal dignity as a general principle of continental law. It is up to legal scholars to clarify how this principle should be further implemented.

Both animal welfarism and personhood provide very narrow accounts in law of what is important in animal lives: rationality and intelligence or pleasure and the avoidance of pain. Martha Nussbaum has shown us that both these approaches fail to consider the many differentials and complex lives that animals lead. In light, thereof, I have suggested that it is time to leave behind the debate on whether the animal can be a legal person based on the similarity to humans and foreground the concept of 'animal dignity'. Rather than seeing the person–thing division as a binary distinction in which animals need to take either side, it is time to recognize that essentializing legal personhood to apply it to animals (insofar as they are *like* humans) is in itself an anthropocentric effort. The focus then shifts from establishing similarity and personhood to determining those obligations that ensure the flourishing of humans and other animals into the future. It is in this transition that the concept of animal dignity could play an important role, opening up the legal realm for the diversity of modes of existence by reshaping the relationships between humans and animals in a way that ensures respect for animals as intrinsically valuable beings.

Notes

1   Such as the Dutch Animal Protection Act [Wet van 19 mei 2011, houdende een integraal kader voor regels over gehouden dieren en daaraan

gerelateerde onderwerpen], which recognizes the 'intrinsic value' of animals in article 1.3.

2 Austria, §285a ABGB Allgemeines bürgerliches Gesetzbuch since 1988; Germany, §90a BGB Bürgerliches Gesetzbuch since 1990; Switzerland, Art. 641a ZGB Zivilgesetzbuch, since 2002; Moldova Art. 458 CC Codul Civil since 2002; Czech Republic, Art. 494 OZ Ob▨anský Zákoník; since 2012, France, Art. 515-14 CC Code Civil since 2015; The Netherlands, Art. 3:2a BW Burgerlijk Wetboek since 2016; Belgium, Art. 3.38-39 BW Burgerlijk Wetboek since 2021; Spain, Art. 333bis CC Código Civil since 2022. A similar provision exists in some non-European civil law jurisdictions such as Quebec, section 898.1 CC Civil Code since 2015.

References

Balzer, P., K. P. Rippe, and P. Schaber. (2000), 'Two concepts of dignity for humans and non-human organisms in the context of genetic engineering', *Journal of Agricultural and Environmental Ethics* 13(1–2), 7–27.
Bernet Kempers, E. (2020), 'Animal dignity and the law: potential, problems and possible implications', *Liverpool Law Review* 41(2), 173–199.
Bernet Kempers, E. (2021), 'Neither persons nor things: The changing status of animals in private law', *European Review of Private Law* 29(1), 39–70.
Blattner, C. E. (2019), 'The recognition of animal sentience by the law', *Journal of Animal Ethics* 9(2), 121.
Bolliger, G. (2016), *Legal Protection of Animal Dignity in Switzerland: Status Quo and Future Perspectives*, Zürich: Schulthess Juristische Medien AG.
Bryant, T. L. (2007), 'Similarity or difference as a basis for justice: Must animals be like humans to be legally protected from humans?', *Law and Contemporary Problems* 70(1), 207–254.
Calarco, M. (2015), *Thinking through Animals*, Stanford, CA: Stanford University Press.
Cupp, R. L. (2016), 'Focusing on human responsibility rather than legal personhood for non-human animals', *Pace Environmental Law Review* 33, 517.
Deckha, M. (2013), 'Initiating a non-anthropocentric jurisprudence: The rule of law and animal vulnerability under a property paradigm', *Alberta Law Review* 50(4), 783–814.
Deckha, M. (2021), *Animals as Legal Beings: Contesting Anthropocentric Legal Orders*, Toronto: University of Toronto Press.
Eisen, J. (2018), 'Animals in the constitutional state', *International Journal of Constitutional Law* 15(4), 909–954.
Etinson, A. (2020), 'What's so special about human dignity?' *Philosophy and Public Affairs* 48(4), 353–381.

Favre, B. (2020), 'Is there a need for a new, an ecological, understanding of legal animal rights?', *Journal of Human Rights and the Environment* 11(2), 297–319.
Flynn, M., and M. Hall. (2017), 'The case for a victimology of non-human animal harms', *Contemporary Justice Review: Issues in Criminal, Social, and Restorative Justice* 20(3), 299–318.
Francione, G. (1995), *Animals, Property, and the Law: Ethics and Action*, Philadelphia: Temple University Press.
Francione, G. (2004), 'Animals – property or persons?' in M. C. Nussbaum and C. R. Sunstein (eds.), *Animal Rights: Current Debates and New Directions*, New York: Oxford University Press.
Francione, G., and R. Garner. (2010), *The Animal Rights Debate: Abolition or Regulation?* New York: Columbia University Press.
Fulfer, K. (2013), 'The capabilities approach to justice and the flourishing of nonsentient life', *Ethics and the Environment* 18(1), 19–42.
Heeger, R. (2015), 'Dignity only for humans? A controversy', in M. Düwell, J. Braarvig, R. Brownsword, and D. Mieth (eds.), *The Cambridge Handbook of Human Dignity: Interdisciplinary Perspectives*, Cambridge: Cambridge University Press.
Jaber, D. (2000), 'Human dignity and the dignity of creatures', *Journal of Agricultural and Environmental Ethics* 13(1–2), 29–42.
Kotzmann, J., and G. Nip. (2020), 'Bringing animal protection legislation into line with its purported purposes: A proposal for equality amongst non-human animals', *Pace Environmental Law Review* 37(247).
Kymlicka, W. (2017), 'Social membership: Animal law beyond the property/personhood impasse', *Dalhousie Law Journal* 40, 123–155.
Lansink, A. (2019), 'Technological innovation and animal law: Does dignity do the trick?', *European Journal of Risk Regulation* 10(1), 80–93.
Meyer, M. (2001), 'The simple dignity of sentient life: Speciesism and human dignity', *Journal of Social Philosophy* 32(2), 115–126.
Michel, M. (2012), 'Die Würde der Kreatur und die Würde des Tieres im schweizerischen Recht : – Eine Standortbestimmung anlässlich der bundesgerichtlichen Rechtsprechung', *Natur Und Recht* 34(2), 102.
Nussbaum, M. C. (2007), *Frontiers of Justice*. Cambridge, MA: Harvard University Press
Reed, E. L. (2016), 'Animal dignity', *Animal Law* 23, 1–64.
Robertson, I. (2015), *Animals, Welfare and the Law*, London: Routledge.
Schindler, S. (2013), 'The animal's dignity in Swiss Animal Welfare Legislation: Challenges and opportunities', *European Journal of Pharmaceutics and Biopharmaceutics* 84(2), 251–254.
Sitter-Liver, B. (2009), 'Würde der Kreatur versus Menschenwürde?', *Journal für Verbraucherschutz Und Lebensmittelsicherheit* 4(3), 313–323.
Staker, A. (2017), 'Should chimpanzees have standing? The case for pursuing legal personhood for non-human animals', *Transnational Environmental Law* 6(3), 485–507.

Vining, J. (2013), 'Dignity as perception: Recognition of the human individual and the individual animal in legal thought', in C. McCrudden (ed.), *Understanding Human Dignity*, New York: Oxford University Press.

Whitfort, A. (2019), 'Wildlife crime and animal victims: Improving access to environmental justice in Hong Kong', *Journal of International Wildlife Law and Policy* 22(3), 203–230.

Wise, S. M. (2004), 'Animal rights, one step at a time', in M. C. Nussbaum and C. R. Sunstein (eds.), *Animal Rights: Current Debates and New Directions*, New York: Oxford University Press.

Wise, S. M. (2010), 'Legal personhood and the non-human rights project', *Animal Law* 17, 1–12.

Chapter 15
Animal Dignity as More-Than-Welfarism
Visa A. J. Kurki

Dignity is a difficult and multifaceted concept. I will in this chapter attempt to make sense of how animal dignity could be understood in legal contexts, mostly within Europe. My overall claim is that animal dignity is often invoked to express and plug gaps in the ideology of legal welfarism. However, whereas philosophers often understand animal dignity as a radical concept that could fundamentally remake how we treat – or should treat – animals, the concept is typically much less radical in law.

Countries that have animal protection laws typically base these laws on the ideology of welfarism. According to welfarism, we can exploit animals and treat them as property, as long as they are treated 'humanely', and certain animal welfare standards are met. One can, in fact, detect two branches, or layers, of what is today called welfarism. The older branch deals with animal cruelty: egregious acts of violence committed toward animals by individual human beings. The newer branch deals with how animals should be treated in farming, when kept as pets and so on. It is thus more focused on regulating practices rather than on preventing individual acts of cruelty toward animals.

Welfarism is quite limited in many ways, and its limitations may run counter to how many people think animals should be treated. First, as already mentioned, welfarism allows for the exploitation of animals.

Second, given that welfarism is focused on the welfare of animals, it does not prohibit acts that express disrespect toward animals, unless they also affect the animal's welfare by, for instance, causing pain to the animals. Consider questions such as the following: Should we treat dead animals' bodies with respect? May we dress animals in funny and demeaning costumes? According to welfarism, these questions are reduced to questions of animal welfare: Dead animals' bodies can no longer feel pain or pleasure, so there is no need to treat them with respect. On the other hand, treating living animals in demeaning ways can only be problematic if it causes pain to the animals, or in some other way affects their welfare negatively.

From the point of view of moral philosophy, the idea of dignity is radically different from the precepts of welfarism. In the philosophy of Immanuel Kant, for instance, entities that have dignity have inherent value, and should never be treated merely as means. The idea that animals have dignity but that we can still relatively freely exploit them would sound ridiculous to many moral philosophers. However, this is not how the idea of dignity has worked in law – so far. Instead, animal dignity can be understood as 'welfarism+', or 'more-than-welfarism'. The introduction of animal dignity into law does not mean a fundamental change regarding how we think about animals. Rather, it can be understood as 'plugging the gaps' of welfarism – at least to some extent.

Plugging the gaps

Animal dignity now figures in the legal systems of a number of European countries. The most prominent example is Switzerland, whose federal constitution protects the dignity of living beings (Swiss Constitution, Article 120). However, this introduction of dignity has not fundamentally changed the structure of Swiss animal protection legislation. Rather, welfarism is still the main rule, with dignity adding an additional element. I would argue that this additional element can be summarized in terms of respect.

The notion of animal dignity in Switzerland is fleshed out in its Animal Welfare Act. In its Article 3(a), the notion of dignity is defined as follows:

dignity means the inherent worth of the animal that must be respected when dealing with it. If any strain imposed on the animal cannot be justified by overriding interests, this constitutes a disregard for the animal's dignity. Strain is deemed to be present in particular if pain, suffering or harm is inflicted on the animal, if it is exposed to anxiety or humiliation, if there is major interference with its appearance or its abilities or if it is excessively instrumentalised[.]

Dignity is here understood as the inherent worth of the animal, and its implications operationalized using the notion of strain. Animals can be strained in various ways: not only by causing pain, suffering or harm, but also by disrespecting them in various ways – by humiliating them, interfering with their appearance or abilities, or excessively instrumentalizing them. However, strain can be justified by overriding interests, so this provision does not mean that animals could never be harmed, humiliated or instrumentalized, or that one could not interfere with their appearance or abilities.

What we can see here is that legal animal dignity does not – at least yet – constitute a turn away from welfarism or its fundamental principles. Rather, dignity-based animal law augments welfarist animal law by the notion of respect: we should not only minimize unnecessary animal suffering, but also show (a modicum of) respect toward them.

The notion of respect is perhaps no less elusive than the notion of dignity. I would argue that it can take at least four different forms: non-instrumentalization, egalitarianism, flourishing, and sanctity. All of these four aspects are interrelated and difficult to completely detach from each other.

First, non-instrumentalization means the prohibition of using others merely as means to one's own purposes. This aspect of dignity is most prominently associated with the philosophy of Immanuel Kant, and has received prominence in, for instance, modern human rights law: a central idea underlying human rights is that no-one should be used merely as a means. However, this standard is watered down in the Swiss Animal Welfare Act, as is typical of dignity in animal law: rather than prohibiting the treatment of animals merely as means, the provision classifies excessive instrumentalization as strain. Hence, instrumentalization is still the acceptable point of departure, even if it may be prohibited in certain cases. In fact, Lena Hehemann has argued that the prohibition of excessive instrumentalization can be understood as the sacrosanct core of the Swiss notion of animal dignity (Hehemann, 2018).

Egalitarianism refers to hierarchies and social structures. One aspect of dignity has to do with the lack of such hierarchies. Jeremy Waldron has in his famous account of dignity argued that human dignity can be understood as the high rank of everyone. Inspired by the work of Gregory Vlastos, Waldron invokes the notion of 'an aristocratic society that has just one rank (and a pretty high rank at that) for all of us' (Waldron and Dan-Cohen, 2012: 34). The Swiss Animal Welfare Act classifies animal humiliation as strain; this can be understood as exhibiting the egalitarianist aspect of dignity. However, as it stands, animal dignity under Swiss law is still clearly hierarchical: whereas the idea of human dignity can be understood as entailing only one rank for every human being, animals still clearly rank below humans. Rather, one might say that animals should not be relegated to the very bottom of the social ladder. Instead of removing ranks, animal dignity (in its current form) reduces the distance between the different ranks.

Third, flourishing refers to a state of being that an entity has when it enjoys certain capabilities that are central for that kind of being. Martha Nussbaum lists life, bodily health, bodily integrity and practical reason among central human capabilities. Given that Nussbaum is a contributor to this book, I do not address her views in great detail. However, I should note that Nussbaum understands her capabilities approach in species-specific terms: one's dignity, and the list of capabilities that one should have, are determined based on one's species (Nussbaum, 2006: 347). This aspect of dignity can be seen in the Swiss Animal Welfare Act's listing of 'major interference with [an animal's] appearance or its abilities' as one type of strain. The formulation can be seen as implicitly employing a species-specific approach: by interfering with an animal's appearance or abilities, we are meddling with their species-specific capabilities and features.

Finally, sanctity is perhaps the most elusive of the four, and the least palatable for our modern secular culture. (If the religious terminology here is too much, essence-respect or inviolability may serve as alternative labels.) I am here inspired by Ronald Dworkin's treatment of abortion and euthanasia, where he notes that one argument against these practices is that they may deny or offend the sanctity of human life (Dworkin, 1993: 24). This is a 'detached' argument, meaning that it is not based on the rights or interests of, say, the foetus, but rather on some more 'objective' considerations: there is something inherently good in respecting human life. A similar, detached aspect of animal dignity can be discerned in Article 120 of Switzerland's constitution:

> Art. 120 Non-human gene technology
> 1. Human beings and their environment shall be protected against the misuse of gene technology.
> 2. The Confederation shall legislate on the use of reproductive and genetic material from animals, plants and other organisms. In doing so, it shall take account of the dignity of living beings as well as the safety of human beings, animals and the environment, and shall protect the genetic diversity of animal and plant species.

This 'dignity of living beings' applies not only to animals but even to plants. It is, I submit, difficult to explain the value basis of such a broad understanding of dignity exhaustively using only the notions of non-instrumentalization, egalitarianism and flourishing. One issue here has to do with something that philosophers call the non-identity problem: If we plan to alter a living animal in some way, we can say that we are turning it into something different. However, if we modify the genetic material of some animal species, and then create a new animal individual using that genetic material, we have not changed any individual animal into something that it is not. A calf that has been genetically engineered not to have horns has never been a calf with horns. Hence, it is difficult to say that we would have, for instance, harmed the calf by 'removing' its horns. Rather, there seems to also be a 'detached' element involved here: the use of reproductive and genetic material from animals and other organisms appears problematic, even if such use would not wrong any animal or other organism.

Hence, discussions of legal animal dignity can be understood as being constituted by (at least) four aspects. However, it should be mentioned that these aspects are not mutually exclusive in any way. For instance, egalitarianism can be seen as reinforcing non-instrumentalization as well: if we treat someone as having a high rank, we will probably avoid instrumentalizing them as well.

Figure 16 Calf suckling concrete, credit Gabriela Penela / We Animals Media.

Finally

Animal dignity in law is a multifarious idea. One may, indeed, even ask whether it is one idea, or rather many ideas combined under one label. At any rate, as it stands, the notion of legal animal dignity can be understood as more-than-welfarism: as expanding the scope of animal protection law to cover things that welfarism does not cover. As such, dignity-based animal law may also depart from certain fundamental assumptions of welfarism. For instance, welfarism is sentiocentric, meaning that it protects only sentient beings: beings that can suffer and experience welfare. On the other hand, dignity-based animal law can, for instance, prohibit humiliating acts toward animals, regardless of whether the humiliation affects them directly in any way. Hence, dignity-based animal law could also be used to protect animals that are not sentient.

The future of animal dignity in law is difficult to predict. On one hand, a number of European countries have adopted legislation that makes reference to dignity or to the idea of respect for animals. However, at the same time, welfarism is still clearly the prevalent ideology. Furthermore, dignity is not the only new legislative trend of the recent decades. Some other examples include legislation declaring that animals are 'not things' or that they are sentient beings. Finally, some scholars are highly critical of using dignity as a basis for animal law (e.g., Pietrzykowski, 2021).

Whether dignity-based animal law will become 'the new welfarism' – the paradigmatic way of approaching the legal protection of animals – remains to be seen. However, dignity has clearly already established its own niche in the ecosystem of animal law.

References

Animal Welfare Act (Switzerland) of 16 December 2005 (Status as of 1 January 2022).
Dworkin, R. (1993), *Life's Dominion: An Argument About Abortion, Euthanasia, and Individual Freedom*, New York: Knopf.
Federal Constitution of the Swiss Confederation of 18 April 1999 (Status as of 13 February 2022), article 120.
Hehemann, L. (2018), 'The Protection of the Dignity of Laboratory Animals in Switzerland: Different Procedures? Different Standards?' *Global Journal of Animal Law* 6(1): 2–27.
Nussbaum, M. (2006), *Frontiers of Justice*, Cambridge, MA: Belknap Press of Harvard University Press.
Pietrzykowski, T. (2021), 'Against dignity: An argument for a non-metaphysical foundation of animal law', *Archiwum Filozofii Prawa i Filozofii Społecznej* 27(2): 69–82.
Waldron, J. and M. Dan-Cohen. (2012), *Dignity, Rank and Rights*, Oxford: Oxford University Press.

Chapter 16
Dignity: A Concept for All Species
Lori Marino

Defining dignity

When we ponder dignity as a concept in general, and then what it means for other animals, we are faced with the fact that there is a certain ineffable quality to it. You know it when you encounter it, but it might best be considered a fuzzy concept. A fuzzy concept defies a precise consensual definition, and its meaning is best understood in context (Markusen, 2003). The lack of clear-cut characteristics does not, however, diminish the weight of its meaning or its value. Most complex concepts, like personhood, virtue, mental health, intelligence, etc., have varying degrees of fuzziness to them.

Another compatible way to think about the notion of dignity is as a Roschian concept (Rosch, 1973). Roschian concepts are mental constructions typically used to categorize entities with unclear boundaries organized around a hypothetical prototype. A simple example of a Roschian concept is that of a bird. We know a bird when we see it and some birds, like robins, have all or almost all the characteristics of the concept (flight, a beak, feathers, etc.) and are, therefore, prototypical. Others, like penguins, have some of those characteristics and are farther from a prototypical bird. Again, the absence of fixed criterial features predisposes Roschian concepts to deliberation and debate but does not negate their scientific, ethical, and moral weight. Fuzzy and Roschian concepts do not relieve us of the responsibility to understand and come to terms with what they mean in nature.

The concept of dignity has traditionally been reserved for humans and is thought to be inherent in all human beings whether that is true or not. Gruen (2014: 231–47) has made the interesting point that dignity appears to be a relational concept. In other words, dignity is not just a characteristic of an individual but is a concept that has normative implications for how whole groups (human and non-human) are viewed and treated. Standard definitions of dignity acknowledge that dignity has been understood *both* as intrinsic to an individual and also as something that *others* see an individual as possessing. The relational concept also means that how we treat others reflects our own dignity or lack thereof. By this definition, dignity is, therefore, a bidirectional concept. If you take it away from someone you lose your own. I will return to this idea in the conclusion.

§

Dignity is inextricably linked to such concepts as rights, autonomy, personhood, and respectability. Thus, for many, the question of non-human animal dignity amounts to whether other animals possess these characteristics. But we should avoid making the mistake that not acknowledging the rights or personhood of other animals reflects anything more than our own ideas about human exceptionalism. A human being placed in a situation where they cannot exercise their autonomy doesn't lose his/her dignity. Their dignity is simply not respected under those circumstances. The same argument can be made for other animals. Simply because we do not treat other animals with respect or recognize their rights doesn't mean they are devoid of rights or dignity. Their dignity is just not respected.

Dignity does not exist in a vacuum nor is it simply an abstract concept. Whether we view someone as having dignity or not can make a significant difference in how we treat that individual. Of course, viewing someone as having dignity does not guarantee treatment in accordance with it. But arguably, if one is not seen as having dignity then there may be fewer limits on the range of ways one can be mistreated. Recognition of dignity has actual consequences for how others are treated, and this is nowhere clearer than in how we relate to and behave towards other animals. Most ways of treating humans are interrogated quite seriously in terms of whether human dignity is upheld. The Geneva Convention, the Helsinki Declaration, the Nuremburg Code, and the Belmont Report are all examples. But there are no equivalent protections for non-human animals. Therefore, the range of ways we can exploit, and harm other animals goes far beyond that accepted for humans.

Arguably, the question of whether other animals have dignity (while granting wholesale dignity to all members of our own species) seems ironic given our human propensity to mistreat each other, other animals, and the rest of nature. Perhaps we should be asking whether humans have as much dignity as non-human animals. For now, the critical question is whether there are ways to understand dignity across species and in forms and practices that uphold the force of its meaning for both humans and non-humans alike. In other words, can the same protections that exist for humans be brought into existence for non-human animals? Is there a nonspeciesist definition of dignity?

Non-human animal dignity

Despite the lack of a precise definition for dignity in human and non-human animals the concept includes certain precepts. First, dignity is a property of an individual and not an aggregate. Second, dignity does not require that the holder have a concept of dignity. Third, dignity is based on species characteristics, that is, the ability to live as a member of one's species (Nussbaum, 2011). Fourth, dignity has to do with rights, not welfare.

Dignity is arguably only upheld by philosophical and legal approaches that respect these four tenets. This leaves out approaches like Utilitarianism, which may be useful under some circumstances but glosses over individual needs and worth in favour of aggregate calculations (Singer, 1998). The concept of dignity also dispenses with notions about moral value being based on a social contract of any kind given that children, who arguably cannot understand the concept of dignity fully, are still afforded recognition of their own dignity. And, importantly, dignity has to do with rights – not welfare – and the ability to live as a member of one's species.

Classic welfarism inherently denies dignity because it places any individual subject squarely at the mercy of human interests. If an individual is treated as a means to an end, then that individual's dignity is being ignored. Settings such as research laboratories, zoos and marine parks, factory farms, circuses are all dignity-negating situations because, independent of welfare, individuals in these circumstances cannot live as a member of their own species (Marino, 2016). A gazelle being killed by a lion on an African savanna is not, at the time, enjoying a high level of welfare in the traditional sense but she is living as a gazelle. Gazelles have a *right* to do that. Therefore, notions of 'justice' in nature imposed by protecting prey species like gazelles from predatory species deny the dignity of all the animals involved (Nussbaum, 2004). This is not to say that all the ways other animals are harmed by human activity within the context of their own lives is moral or ethical, but here I am making a point about the concept of dignity specifically.

Zoos and marine parks: Examples of dignity negation

Nussbaum (2006) argues that dignity is determined by species-specific characteristics, which determine what a member of that species needs to flourish as a member of that species. When a non-human being is prevented from acting in a way typical of his/her species, dignity is being violated. Certainly, captivity is problematic for dignity and while some conditions of captivity, e.g., sanctuaries, are aimed at promoting dignity, zoos and other entertainment venues hold non-human beings captive in ways that are arguably inherently dignity-negating (Marino and White, 2022: 275–95).

To varying degrees, non-human beings living on display in a zoo or marine park are prevented from the natural expression of species-specific capabilities by virtue of being forced to live in an artificial environment that is largely designed to meet the needs of humans. For naturally wide-ranging large animals, for instance, space is insufficient in a zoo compared with a natural setting and prevents movements across changing locations (Clubb and Mason, 2007). Opportunities for problem-solving and meeting the challenges of a complex dynamic

Figure 17 Orca, credit Jo-Anne McArthur / We Animals Media.

environment are severely restricted as well. Even the act of eating, for many confined animals, e.g., captive dolphins and whales, is made into a monotonous task where absolutely no physical or cognitive processing is necessary.

It is difficult to imagine that anyone seeing an orca – one of the world's top predators begging for food with mouth open at the side of a tank while a dead fish is thrown in – is engaged in a dignified act. And, for highly socially complex animals, living with a small artificial collection of other individuals in a tank or in an enclosed display severely hinders the ability to express normal social and emotional capacities. There is no doubt that zoos and marine parks severely limit the ability of other animals to live as members of their respective species. That is why zoos and other such facilities implement environmental enrichment. Indeed, enrichment was first recognized as essential by the zoo and marine park industry precisely because of the animals' observed difficulties in coping with the incongruity between artificial and natural environments (Swaisgood and Shepherdson, 2005).

Zoos and marine parks negate dignity by not only preventing species-specific behaviours in impoverished environments that lack sufficient complexity – i.e., withholding important parts of life – but also by imposing unwanted encounters onto the individual. In other words, in many entertainment facilities, there is not much to do that is satisfying on a species-specific level and, to add to that, often quite a bit to do that is aversive and unavoidable. Some animals in zoos or marine parks, especially dolphins, elephants, and wild baby animals, are forced to endure human interaction and touch. Swim-with-the-dolphin programmes, dolphin shows involving tricks with trainers, petting pools, elephant rides, and photography with baby tigers are all examples of dignity-negating activities some animals are forced to endure in zoos and marine parks. Under these circumstances, they are forced to cope with violations of personal space and physical touch by a member of another species in a way wholly unnatural to their species. And this kind of imposition also extends to animals on display who are not part of an interaction programme.

Randy Malamud (1998) has written extensively on the issue of the human gaze at animals in zoos and marine parks and its societal effects. He has argued that when visitors come to see animals on display it is a form of voyeurism that not only demeans the dignity of the animals but those who engage in it. Wild animals, if afforded the opportunity, tend to shy away from being in view of human beings, but in a zoo they are forced to be looked upon. Gruen argues that: 'Thinking of animals as things to be looked at and believing that doing so makes for an enjoyable weekend outing, precludes seeing animals as having dignity' (2014: 242). Philosopher Ralph Acampora (2008) likens looking at animals in zoos to a pornographic gaze. Human gawking is inherently a dignity-denying activity on all fronts.

Promoting non-human dignity through sanctuaries

Given that our species engages in such widespread disrespect for the dignity of non-human beings in entertainment facilities, factory farms, laboratories, and so many other domains, what can be done that will do the work of moral repair? Is restitution possible? If not, how can we realistically move towards the promotion of non-human dignity?

One concrete way to make amends to those animals kept confined in zoos and marine parks is to put into place alternatives that exemplify an act of (albeit imperfect) dignity promotion in the form of authentic sanctuaries. Sanctuaries are necessary because most captive animals in zoos and marine parks cannot be safely introduced to a wild setting. The majority are captive-born and have no natal group or territory to return to let alone the skills to survive 'in the wild'. But the reality of sanctuaries being captive facilities should not deter efforts to create them to mend our relationship with captive wild animals when we can. While sanctuaries are still captive environments, they differ from zoos and marine parks in important ways. Authentic sanctuaries prioritize the residents' well-being and autonomy over any other goals. They combine necessary human care with an environment that most closely resembles one to which the residents are adapted. There are no performances, no up-close visitors, no unnecessary experimentation, no unnecessary human contact, no impositions other than what is needed to monitor and maintain the health and safety of the residents.

There are, of course, also limitations that cannot be reasonably overcome. In authentic sanctuaries there is no breeding, space is not unlimited, and the residents are still often fed by humans. In this sense sanctuaries are not full restitution to the other animals, but they do play a critically important role in morally repairing our relationship to them. They are an authentic attempt to do better by them and there is every reason to accept the proposition – based on scientific first principles and empirical evidence – that other animals *do* experience a better life in sanctuaries than in zoos and other entertainment facilities.

By their very existence, sanctuaries serve to educate others about why we should not be exploiting other animals for entertainment in zoos and marine parks. The stories that can be told about the residents can be faithful to the lived experience of these individuals uncorrupted by the need to encourage ticket sales or push mythologies about 'ambassadorships' saving endangered species. Finally, unlike zoos and marine parks, sanctuaries are a necessary step towards completely phasing out captivity for entertainment. Sanctuaries seek to put themselves out of business eventually. Given the harsh abuse of being confined to entertainment facilities, authentic sanctuaries, especially for wild animals, are the most realistic way we can make amends and begin changing societal norms so that these abuses are a thing of the past.

Respecting the dignity of non-human animals and regaining our own

In summary, in addition to the tangible problems associated with being forced to live in impoverished physical and social environments, animals in zoos and marine parks endure human touch and gaze. Because of these conditions they are not treated with dignity. They are prevented from exercising choice and expressing their autonomy, their right to privacy, and their right to develop important species-specific skills necessary to engage in the world appropriately.

In returning to the bidirectional aspect of dignity, by treating other animals as a means to an end in entertainment facilities like zoos and marine parks we diminish our own dignity. All efforts, like sanctuaries and other concrete ways of protecting the rights of other animals, are the only paths towards moral repair. Wild animals in tanks or on display (and in other exploitative situations) suffer tremendously at our hands but never lose their inherent dignity. It is the human species – the species that refuses to acknowledge the rights of other animals – that is in dire need of regaining its own.

References

Acampora, R. (2008), 'Zoos and eyes: Contesting captivity and seeking successor practices', in S. Armstrong and R. Bozer (eds.), *The Animal Ethics Reader*, 2nd edn, New York: Routledge, 501–506.

Clubb, R. and G. Mason. (2007), 'Natural behavioural biology as a risk factor in carnivore welfare: How analysing species differences could help zoos improve enclosures', *Applied Animal Behavior Science* 102: 303–328.

Gruen, L. (2014), 'Dignity, captivity, and an ethics of sight', in L. Gruen (ed.), *The Ethics of Captivity*, New York: Oxford University Press.

Malamud, R. (1998), *Reading Zoos: Representations of Animals and Captivity*, New York: New York University Press.

Markusen, A. (2003), 'Fuzzy concepts, scanty evidence, policy distance: The case for rigour and policy relevance in critical regional studies', *Regional Studies* 37(6–7): 701–717.

Marino, L. (2016), 'Why animal welfarism continues to fail', *Animal Sentience* 1(7): 5.

Marino, L. and T. White. (2022), 'Cetacean personhood, rights, and flourishing', in G. Notarbartolo di Sciara and B. Würsig (eds.), *Marine Mammals: The Evolving Human Factor*, Switzerland: Springer Nature.

Morgan, K. and C. Tromborg. (2007), 'Sources of stress in captivity', *Applied Animal Behavior Science* 102: 262–302.

Nussbaum, M. (2004), 'Beyond "compassion and humanity": Justice for non-human animals', in C. Sundstein and M Nussbaum (eds.), *Animal Rights: Current Debates and New Directions*, Oxford: Oxford University Press.

Nussbaum, M. (2006), 'The moral status of animals', *Chronicle of Higher Education* 52(22): B6–B8.

Nussbaum, M. (2011), 'The capabilities approach and animal entitlements', in T. Beauchamp and R. Frey (eds.), *Oxford Handbook of Animal Ethics*, Oxford: Oxford University Press.

Rosch, E. (1973), 'Natural categories', *Cognitive Psychology* 4: 328–350.

Rosen, M. (2012), *Dignity: Its History and Meaning*, Cambridge, MA: Harvard University Press.

Singer, P. (1998), 'A utilitarian defense of animal liberation', in L. P. Pojman and P. Pojman (eds.), *Environmental Ethics: Readings in Theory and Application*, Boston, MA: Cengage Learning, 96–105.

Swaisgood, R. and D. Shepherdson. (2005), 'Scientific approaches to enrichment and stereotypies in zoo animals: What's been done and where should we go next?' *Zoo Biology* 24: 499–518.

Chapter 17
Four Legs Good, Three Legs Bad? The Aesthetics of Animal Dignity

Samantha Hurn

Introducing Moon

Moon is a 23-year-old Arab mare who joined my family in 2003 after I sustained numerous head, neck, and back injuries following a disabling fall from another horse while conducting fieldwork for my PhD. I entered a deep depression after being discharged from hospital and struggled to motivate myself to engage in the physical therapy needed to walk again. Moon was offered to me by a neighbour to incentivize my recovery and rehabilitation.

After helping me to regain mobility and confidence, Moon had a successful county-level showing career, where she was judged according to her conformity to the aesthetic ideals expected of her breed. She also carried me tirelessly and enthusiastically during my doctoral fieldwork as I conducted research on foxhunting and hill farming (see Hurn 2008). However, as I haven't ridden her since 2012, she has lived her own life at liberty or, as one of my interlocuters opined, as a 'field ornament'. This term denotes the widespread objectification of horses as aesthetic commodities whose function is to be ridden and has implications for their dignity as we shall see.

As Moon has aged, she has experienced several injuries and illnesses which have left her disabled too. These include a deformed forelimb catalysed by a kick from another horse, which has left her permanently unsound or lame. Her hind knee joint dislocates or locks periodically, also because of a kick from another horse. And she has Pituitary Pars Intermedia Dysfunction (PPID), commonly referred to as equine Cushing's disease, an incurable condition that typically affects aged horses and causes erratic and excessive hormone production. Each time a vet comes to take her blood sample and sees Moon, they query her quality of life (and the expense of treating a horse who cannot be ridden) and suggest euthanasia as an appropriate course of action.

Yet, despite her physical disabilities, Moon is still arguably 'healthy'. Krahn *et al.* (2021: 2) argue that health has come to be recognized as a continuum as opposed to a static state. They suggest that health is 'the dynamic balance of physical, mental, social, and existential well-being in adapting to conditions of life and the environment' (2021: 1). Moon has successfully adapted to her conditions and is, for the most part, able to balance her physical, mental and social well-being, aided by her human caregivers, the other members of her herd (who accommodate her mood swings), and a supportive environment. For example, she currently lives on a large piece of land belonging to a neighbour, which is classed as a Site of Special Scientific Interest (SSSI) due to the range of flora and fauna, and the diverse habitat which incorporates wildflower meadow, along with some rougher scrub grazing, woodland and stream. Here she is truly at liberty, as one side of the meadow backs onto open moorland and there is no need to stable her. For Moon, being stabled results in what might be interpreted as existential discomfort and compromised welfare.

Ethologist Marian Stamp Dawkins suggests that an accessible and helpful definition of welfare needs to be concerned with 'what the animal wants' (2021: 8). Dawkins gives the example of a trapped bird fluttering against the bars of a cage. This individual clearly wants to be released, and so to continue to contain them negatively impacts on their welfare. Of course, there may be instances when confinement or other action taken that is not something the animal wants may be in that individual's best interest (keeping an injured bird contained to enable healing, for example). But for the current purposes, acknowledging that other animals have a personal stake in their own welfare and are able to

Figure 18 Moon, credit Samantha Hurn.

express their 'wants' is key. When Moon is stabled, her compromised welfare is expressed in the exhibition of stereotypies such as box walking, hyper vigilance (staring into the distance and calling frantically), barging at the stable door, inappetence, and loose stools. In such a situation, Moon clearly wants to be outside, appears concerned by her change in environment, and is unable to adapt.

In response to her disabilities, Moon has developed her own stumbling and irregular gait, which, according to normative equestrian ideals is ugly, ungainly, and unsound. To my mind, however, it is beautiful, as is her uneven musculature, which has developed over the years as she compensates for her disabilities by using her 'good' legs to support her. Moon can engage in all 'normal' equine behaviours to varying degrees – she can move through all the gaits, including gallop when the mood or circumstance takes her. She can lay down, roll, get up again, groom herself and the other horses, graze, and drink. But she cannot easily navigate over some of the obstacles within her field such as fallen trees, steep riverbanks, or very uneven ground. While she limps and occasionally falls in the field, her disabilities don't seem to bother her. But in 'allowing' Moon to exist in such a manner, am I compromising her dignity?

Dignity

The *Cambridge Dictionary* (n.d.) provides two definitions for dignity, the first of which is 'calm, serious, and controlled behaviour that makes people respect you', which certainly doesn't apply to Moon. Her behaviour is often erratic, she is highly strung and impulsive. However, the second definition acknowledges 'the importance and value that a person has, that makes other people respect them or makes them respect themselves.' Whether the other horses in her small herd 'respect' Moon is difficult to assess. They certainly respond to her aggressive outburst with little or no retaliation. They also engage in mutual grooming practices, which suggest they at least regard her with some affection. When it comes to humans, her size and bulk demands respect for her potential to cause bodily harm. But as noted at the outset, respect for her integrity, importance and inherent value is a source of conflict between her human caregivers, and the professionals (especially veterinarians and farriers) who provide specialist care and for whom her disability is problematic.

Much extant literature equates dignity with humanity, perpetuating the status quo of human exceptionalism – a means of differentiating humans from other animals by way of discrimination that serves to limit the rights and freedoms of other animals. This has implications for some humans as well as other animals, as Meyer explains:

> The concept of human dignity purports to safeguard human lives equally, but in fact, because it grounds human inviolability in the violability of animal lives, it exposes and endangers those human beings whose racialized, gendered, and embodied differences have been historically constructed through animality.
>
> (Meyer, 2020: 205).

The term dignity has been dismissed by some bioethicists, with Macklin for example stating 'Dignity is a useless concept in medical ethics and can be eliminated without any loss of content' (2003: 1419–20). Macklin argues that 'respect for persons' is more precise and therefore preferable. However, Hauskeller (2011: 54) presents two objections to Macklin's stance. First, 'respect for persons' fails to articulate why persons are to be respected or to clarify what differentiates persons from non-persons, and second, as an ethical principle 'respect for persons' lacks the scope and nuance of dignity. Hauskeller argues that in contemporary bioethics, 'respect for persons' is synonymous with respect for autonomy, which implies that those lacking in autonomy or with diminished autonomy are less deserving of respect. While Hauskeller is writing about human embryos, the distinction has relevance to the current discussion of animal disability. Hauskeller proposes *bonitas* as a more inclusive alternative. He argues that while dignity might indeed be something to be respected, *bonitas* invites responses of awe – an 'immediate value experience' grounded in emotional affect (2011: 56). Contrary to dignity and respect, which are attributed to others based on certain pre-determined traits or characteristics (such as being human, or having autonomy), awe is an emotional, affective response that arises from experience or encounter with the awe-inspiring being or entity. Such a line of argument resonates with anthropological discussions of personhood as something that can be perceived and then known about another through embodied experiences and interactions with the 'person'.

Perceiving personhood, perceiving dignity?

An embodied approach to dignity therefore might help to challenge the exceptionalism of human dignity. Anthropologists Tim Ingold and Gili Palsson (2013) argue that individuals experience the world as both biological and social beings. First, the way they encounter and experience the world is mediated, limited, or facilitated by their biological form – for example, their species, and their genetic heritage, or their disability. But individuals don't just experience and understand the world as a result of their biological selves. Social interactions with others and the fusion or entanglement of biological and social selves result in a relational process that Ingold and Palsson term 'biosocial becomings'. Anthropologists Vivieros de Castro (2004) and Eduardo Kohn (2007) argue that individuals perceive the personhood of others through their subjective and relational states, which will vary between species as well as between individuals. Each will operate under the influence of a particular ontology as well as biological form, which enables them to relate to other beings as persons, while adhering to species-specific norms, behaviours, and preferences.

Such positions resonate with claims that while other animals may not have human dignity, they nonetheless possess their own versions of these characteristics which are in many cases, equivalent (Etinson, 2020; Gruen, 2014). As Gruen notes, Martha Nussbaum (2006) argues 'that the properties that are typical of proper species functioning, that allow an individual animal to live a characteristic life as a member of its species, should be respected' as species-specific animal dignity (Gruen, 2014: 236).

Over the course of my research into the care of and attitudes towards disabled animals, I have begun to wonder whether there is a risk that the argument presented by Nussbaum and others in defence of animal dignity could in fact be used to undermine the dignity of *individual* animals who, by dint of their age or disability, are not necessarily able to 'live a characteristic life' of a member of the species to which they belong.

Moon can do pretty much everything the other horses in her herd can do with some limitations and adjustment (e.g., daily drugs to manage her pain and other symptoms), but she can't be used for human ends as she can't be ridden. Because of this, she does not 'live a characteristic life' as a member of the (domesticated) species to which she belongs. But does this mean that she is less dignified than her able-bodied conspecifics? Or that by intervening and removing the barriers that she experiences as a disabled individual, her dignity is undermined?

Gruen (2014) argues that when humans make other animals behave in certain ways that, following Nussbaum, are not species-specific (Gruen gives the example of animals wearing costumes and performing in a circus) their dignity is being compromised. Gruen states that 'when animals are forced to be something other than what [and I would add who] they are [. . .] this is disrespectful and their "animal dignity" is being denied' (2014: 235). Previously I have argued that forcing other animals to wear clothes (even something as seemingly benign or in their interests as horses wearing rugs [coats] during inclement weather) can constitute a disrespectful act (Hurn, 2011). But this is perhaps only in cases where it is done for human benefit rather than out of respect or concern for the animal's interests and inherent value. So, rugging and clipping a horse to keep them clean and readily accessible for riding at the rider's convenience is very different to rugging a horse because they are old, ill and unable to thermoregulate. The way humans go about engaging with horses often has the potential to undermine equine dignity, but it depends on the individuals involved, and the context.

Further, Gruen argues that dignity, like personhood, is a relational concept. An individual (regardless of species) might be accorded dignity on the basis of how they are perceived within their social context, and whether or not the behaviour of that individual is deemed 'worthy of respect'. The act of riding itself is not necessarily dignity denying but can be if the way it is enacted (e.g., using whips or spurs to force horses to do things they'd rather not) can undermine dignity. Gruen argues that this way of conceiving of dignity helps us understand why dignity is often invoked in situations where it has been denied – when individuals are treated in a disrespectful manner, their value has not been recognized and in the process, the offender also loses 'some of their own worth as a moral agent' (Gruen, 2014: 234).

Overcoming aesthetic anxiety

In human medicine, disability was traditionally viewed as a pathology to be overcome or eradicated. As Taylor (2011: 193–4) has argued, this 'medical model' of disability sees disability as a 'deviance' and positions 'the disabled body as working incorrectly, as being unhealthy and abnormal, as in need of cure'.

However, following civil rights movements in the 1970s, a shift was made to what is termed the 'social model' of disability. This approach argues it is society that disables human individuals, and not their physical or mental differences. In other words, the construct of disability is imposed on individuals by powerful social systems and institutions such as government, healthcare providers and legislature. Consequently, the social model of disability advocates supporting disabled individuals, enabling them to surmount the barriers they encounter, including pain and other symptoms, but also helping them overcome social and ideological obstacles, such as how medical professionals, caregivers and employers, perceive and treat their disabilities.

Much writing about disabled humans has highlighted that when encountering physical disabilities, nondisabled people can experience existential, affective and aesthetic anxieties – in other words, nondisabled observers can feel uncomfortable around disabled bodies (e.g., Harris, 2019). It has been argued that this is because of the stigmatized and objectifying ways in which disabled bodies are viewed and associated with negative states of being such as ill-health and deficiency. In the process, the dignity of the disabled individual is compromised.

Animal caregivers and members of the veterinary profession in particular have much to gain from embracing the social model of disability. To do this, they need to re-evaluate the aesthetics of dignity and come to perceive disabled individuals as awe-inspiring with the potential to flourish when given the right support to overcome obstacles to their health and wellbeing. Admittedly not all companion animal guardians will be willing or able to provide the care, resources, or environments necessary for their disabled or elderly pets to thrive, and not all disabled individuals will be able to cope with their conditions sufficiently for pleasure to outweigh their suffering. Nonetheless, more nuanced approaches to treating disabled and elderly animals are needed, which recognize them as dignified individuals, who, with appropriate care and support, can flourish and enjoy intrinsically valuable lives worth living.

References

Cambridge Dictionary. (No date). Available from https://dictionary.cambridge.org/dictionary/english/dignity.

Dawkins, M. S. (2021), *The Science of Animal Welfare: Understanding What Animals Want*, Oxford: Oxford University Press.

Etinson, A. (2020), 'What's so special about human dignity?', *Philosophy & Public Affairs* 48(4), 353–381.

Gruen, L. (ed). (2014), *The Ethics of Captivity*, Oxford: Oxford University Press.

Gruen, L. (2021), *Ethics and Animals: An Introduction*. Cambridge: Cambridge University Press.
Harris, J. E. (2019), 'The aesthetics of disability', *Columbia Law Review* 119(4), 895–972.
Hauskeller, M. (2011). 'Believing in the dignity of human embryos', *Human Reproduction & Genetic Ethics* 17(1), 53–65.
Hurn, S. (2008), 'The "Cardinauts" of the Western coast of Wales: Exchanging and exhibiting horses in the pursuit of fame', *Journal of Material Culture* 13(3), 335–355.
Hurn, S. (2011), 'Dressing down: Clothing animals, disguising animality?', *Civilisations. Revue internationale d'anthropologie et de sciences humaines* 59(2), 109–124.
Hurn, S. (2012), *Humans and Other Animals: Cross-Cultural Perspectives on Human-Animal Interactions*. London: Pluto Press.
Ingold, T. and G. Palsson. (eds.) (2013). *Biosocial Becomings: Integrating Social and Biological Anthropology*. Cambridge: Cambridge University Press.
Kohn, E. (2007), 'How dogs dream: Amazonian natures and the politics of transspecies engagement', *American Ethnologist* 34(1), 3–24.
Krahn, G. L., A. Robinson, A. J. Murray, S. M. Havercamp, S. Havercamp, R. Andridge, L. E. Arnold, J. Barnhill, S. Bodle, E. Boerner, and A. Bonardi. (2021), 'It's time to reconsider how we define health: Perspective from disability and chronic condition', *Disability and Health Journal* 14(4), 101129.
Macklin, R. (2003), 'Dignity is a useless concept', *British Medical Journal* 327(7429): 1419–1420.
Meyer, E. (2020), 'The recursive violence of anthropological exceptionalism: Toward the ecological transformation of dignity', *Journal of Religion & Society* (Suppl) 21, 203–225.
Nussbaum, M. (2006), *Frontiers of Justice: Disability, Nationality, Species Membership*, Cambridge, MA: Belknap Press.
Taylor, S. (2011), 'Beasts of burden: Disability studies and animal rights', *Qui Parle: Critical Humanities and Social Sciences* 19(2), 191–222.
Viveiros de Castro, E. B. (2004), 'Exchanging perspectives: The transformation of objects into subjects in Amerindian ontologies', *Common Knowledge* 10(3), 463–484.

Chapter 18
Looking Up to Animals and Other Beings: What the Fishes Taught Us

Becca Franks, Christine Webb, Monica Gagliano, and Barbara Smuts

Imagine: Strolling through a public garden, you come upon a water-lily pond and within it, notice a koi fish swimming toward you. They wave their radiant pectoral fins in your direction, waving and staring up at you before swimming away . . . And then, they circle back. Pausing while gazing up at you, they wave again. How do you respond? In the interest of fish dignity, what is the best way to respond?

The world is filled with koi (*Cyprinus rubrofuscus*) and many other fishes held within human-dominated spaces. Humans are now in closer contact with fishes and on a broader scale than ever before. Recent estimates suggest that humans directly control the lives of roughly *one hundred billion* fishes, the vast majority of whom are in some sort of farming operation (Franks *et al.*, 2021).[1] For the fishes in these systems, daily life entails crowding, social discord, vastly diminished choices, suboptimal water conditions, parasite infestations, and ultimately, inevitably, slaughter. The predominant form of human–fish relations is not a promising realm to contemplate the possibility and power of fish dignity.

Instead let us return to the shimmering individual from the water-lily pond. What if a koi, a silver-bodied, obsidian-flecked, medium-sized individual waved at you from a water-lily pond . . . What is the meaning of this behaviour? How should you think about this encounter? In the interest of fish dignity, what is the right way to think about it?

Before formulating your response, it may seem logical to begin by asking whether it is possible for a fish to experience dignity. Verifying the reality of fish dignity may even seem to be a necessary precondition, especially given that a vocal few persist in questioning whether a fish can feel anything at all. Alternatively, even if you take it for granted that fishes can feel some things, entering dignity into the equation may strike you as an *at best* second-order priority, speculative and impressionistic, a far cry from the urgent and tragic issues of the day.

Importantly, however, the question of this chapter is not whether fishes may have the ability or inclination to feel dignified. Rather, our concern is with what changes in *us*, in our knowledge systems, our relationships, our actions and worldviews when we seek to respect and acknowledge fish dignity instead of dismissing or denying its existence. This line of inquiry does not depend on certitude in a fish's capacities, preferences, or feelings. The nature of fishes' watery experience can remain an outstanding, fluid mystery while we explore the consequences of living in a world in which it is considered appropriate and good to treat fishes with dignity *vs.* living in a world in which treating fishes with dignity is considered nonsensical, silly, or even reckless. In more scientifically precise language, this is a chapter about how null hypotheses regarding fish dignity may influence the way we think about, probe, relate to, see, conceive of, and treat fishes – and, thereby, perhaps, much of the rest of the animate world.

Accordingly, we follow the tradition of emphasizing dignity's relational nature. Dignity is used to describe the inherent worth and worthiness of an entity, but dignity is also a matter of standing in society and the respect and attendant justice that a society then affords certain groups (Nussbaum, 2005: 299–320). As Lori Gruen writes in her seminal chapter on animal dignity, the 'relational conception of dignity brings into focus both the being who is dignified and the individual or community who value the dignified in the right ways' (Gruen, 2014: 231–47).

With this relational take on dignity in mind, we begin with a brief history of the relationship between humans and fishes, exploring how the dominant culture came to such a distorted and degraded view of that relationship. We then consider how fish dignity may be a potent if unexpected corrective, a beacon to help us productively and justly reorient ourselves within the 'entangled bank' that Charles Darwin invoked to describe our shared world.

Humans and fishes through time (we are fish)

For terrestrial-bound human beings, aquatic beings are physically hard to access and even harder to observe well, a circumstance of geophysics that is arguably evident throughout human history. Consider, for instance, the wealth of cave paintings from around the world, some of which date back at least 40,000 years. Of the multitude of animal forms depicted, fishes are so rarely rendered that the few examples of fish imagery that do exist are famous for being exceptions to the rule.[2] Similarly, domestication of the first fish species likely occurred a mere 2,000 years ago, well over ten thousand years after the domestication of the first terrestrial animals (Harland, 2019). What is more, in addition to temporal separation on a historical scale, humans are temporally separated from fishes on the scale of an individual's lifetime, with most humans (though certainly not all[3]) spending effectively zero per cent of their time in close contact with free-living fishes.

With a history and present characterized by an utter lack of experience with fish lives, a rational response to fishes might be one of receptivity. We know very little and have much to learn – in such cases, the fishes themselves could be looked to as our best teachers. And yet, more often than not, the opposite is true. We look down on fishes. In a physical sense, this dynamic is unavoidable, water being heavier than air. Within mainstream media, legal systems around the globe, and in modern science, fishes are also conceptually looked down upon – regularly referred to as primitive, inferior to humans and many other animals, and not worthy of equal protection or serious consideration. Their inferior status is evident even in arguments designed to grant them greater moral standing: Fishes, but not other vertebrates, are repeatedly asked, in increasingly elaborate experimental designs, to prove that they can feel pain.

It may be worth pausing here to note that having one's sentience – one's ability to feel – questioned is not a dignified existence. The mere fact that humans ask such questions of fishes reveals the extent to which fish dignity is outside the mainline scope of how we conceptualize our relation to them.

From an evolutionary perspective, however, the relationship between humans and modern fishes is not one of superior-to-inferior, modern-to-primitive. Our last common ancestor with modern fishes lived over five hundred million years ago. Five hundred million years is a mind-boggling amount of evolutionary separation; five hundred million years ago, there were no trees, no grasses, no flowering plants, no polar ice caps, and a less oxygenated atmosphere above arid landmasses all in the southern hemisphere. The vast bulk of biodiversity was in the oceans, but the creatures swimming in those Palaeozoic waters bear little to no resemblance to the fishes of today.

Since that time, some of the most important evolutionary events have been the appearance of the first ray-finned fishes and the swim bladder. These adaptations were so successful that of the more than *thirty thousand* species of fish alive today, the majority are Actinopterygii (ray-finned fishes) with swim bladders. A modern fish would look back on the Palaeozoic creatures and, just like we would, see a far distant relative, not themselves.

Not all modern fishes are Actinopterygii, however – including the impressive Elasmobranchii lineage that includes our present-day giant oceanic manta rays (*Mobula birostris*), whale sharks (*Rhincodon typus*), and great whites (*Carcharodon carcharias*). The last common ancestor between the Actinopterygii and the Elasmobranchii is older still than the last common ancestor between the Actinopterygii and humans – back even farther in time, with an even less familiar creature at its origin.

To account for all modern fishes in a single evolutionary group, you would need to lop off the branch at this primordial node. In so doing, you would end up with a very large branch of animals indeed, and one that, perhaps surprisingly, also includes hamsters, hawks, and humans (to name a few). Evolution nestles modern humans among the modern fishes so inescapably that no evolutionarily justifiable cut can cleave off all the beings we call fishes from ourselves. What's more, from the perspective of an Actinopterygii, *Homo sapiens* belong to the more primitive, lobe-finned line, not the distinguished ray-finned line.

Thus, as we use it, the word and concept 'fish' represents a paraphyletic set – a grouping that artificially includes some species and excludes others. These dynamics form the basis for Lulu Miller's (2020) book *Why Fish Don't Exist*, which extends the observation that 'fish' is not a biologically meaningful group to the logical conclusion that there is no such thing as 'a fish'. In a straightforward sense, this conclusion is as illuminating as it is irrefutable. Processing these same facts from a slightly different angle, however, can bring us to a complementary perspective: We can accept that fish exist, but only if we admit that humans are another species of fish. For the sake of scientific consistency, if a shark is a fish, then you too, dear reader, are some kind of fish.

From this updated perspective, the past several hundred million years have gone like this: some fish lineages have been flourishing and diversifying in the oceans, some fish lineages have been flourishing and diversifying in newly forming bodies of freshwater on the continents, and some fish lineages have been flourishing and diversifying on dry land. Then, one day not so long ago, some members of a land-locked-fish species suddenly invaded the aquatic-fish species' world on an industrialized scale, decimating ecosystems, exterminating entire populations, and poisoning the water, wreaking such global havoc that the extinction rate is now on track to match that of the asteroid that killed the dinosaurs (Penn and Deutsch, 2022).

The 'Great Chain of Being' or *scala naturae* inherited from ancient Greek thinking instructs us to see this history differently: Rather than human-fish hitting the planet like an asteroid, it casts humans as near-god-like creatures interacting in due course with the rest of creation. The *scala naturae* (translated as 'ladder of nature') places humans at the top – the pinnacle of life on earth, surpassed only by angels and gods in the cosmos. Fish are near the bottom of the animal kingdom, which encourages humans to look down on them, if they deign to look at all. For, the *scala naturae* is not just an epistemological ordering of the world; it carries moral weight, with those at the top embodying the greatest worth and those below diminishing swiftly to moral irrelevancy.

Outwardly, the *scala naturae* is rejected as unscientific mythology – as indicated above, the evolutionary relationships between modern species are astonishingly complex and are anything but a well-behaved, sequential hierarchy. Yet the *scala naturae* remains deeply rooted and influential, especially within Western thought. Throughout popular media and even in biology textbooks and high-profile scientific articles, ladder-like structures dominate phylogenetic representations, with humans at the implied top and other taxa ordered neatly below (Baum et al., 2005: 979–81).

The problem with this imagery is not that it portrays human uniqueness. Humans are undoubtedly unique, in many ways. The problem with the *scala naturae* thinking is that it portrays human uniqueness as *the pinnacle* of uniqueness, a distortion that obscures the distinctiveness of other species and conflates our own specific way of being unique with superiority. It broadcasts the sham that humans are neatly separable from all other forms of life. Beyond factual inaccuracies, the *scala naturae* thus flatters us into believing that humans have domination over life on earth and fools us into thinking that it is possible to extract indefinitely and without consequence from the very system of which we are part.

To reach any kind of embodied understanding of something closer to our true position, we must replace the *scala naturae* with more accurate visual imagery. Instead of a ladder, we need a branching, intertwining, bushy mesh with the human-fish as one (unique) node among many (unique) nodes, in a web of beings.

Teachings of the fishes: Why fish dignity? Why now?

Modern fish-humans are not only in a mesh, we are also in a mess – an epochal mess of our own making. The Anthropocene, which began roughly 100 years ago (give or take a few decades), is marked in the geological record by soil alterations, radiation, species extinctions, a wealth of pollutants from industrialization, spiking CO_2 from burning fossil fuels, ocean acidification, plastics, coral bleaching, and a massive proliferation of chicken bones. As Timothy Morton and Dominic Boyer write in their recent book, *hyposubjects on becoming human*, 'the road to our present condition is paved with mastery of things, people and creatures and with weird faith in our species' alleged ability to always know more and better' (Morton and Boyer (2021: 14). Under the spell of human exceptionalism and superiority, we are consuming the earth and its inhabitants to an indefensible degree.

Is retreating into the status quo a logical response to the problems posed by the Anthropocene? Many appear to think so. In *Under a White Sky: The Nature of the Future*, Elizabeth Kolbert provides a litany of ever more absurd attempts to predict, manage, direct, control and dominate natural systems, oftentimes in the name of saving them – reversing and electrifying rivers, introducing novel species to deal with species who are deemed undesirable, seeking compounds to add to our atmosphere in an effort to block our sun.

The fishes offer an alternative. The fishes teach us that we are one of them and that we are embedded within a network of relationships with other beings. From this position, it is possible to look around (not down) and see other creatures and other entities as grand, mysterious, playful, and powerful in their own right. From the enmeshed position, it is possible to seek out the inherent dignity of those other beings. Hovering above, in contrast, it is only possible to question, interrogate, doubt, or deny the dignity of those below.

Thus the act of seeking fish dignity can be an antidote to human exceptionalism. It necessitates abdicating our imaginary throne as a

Figure 19 Koi fish swimming, credit Wirestock.

precondition to engagement. Building fish dignity into our premises – instead of ignoring it or getting to it as a second-order outcome, or treating it as a bizarre object of inquiry – prepares us for empathy, for prioritizing the feelings and experiences of others and, crucially, for responding with justice. Ladder-thinking, in contrast, prioritizes the need to categorize other beings as worthy or not and does little to address the root disease of human exceptionalism. In short, as Gruen writes, 'being perceptive about dignity-enhancing or dignity-diminishing activities or conditions is a central part of our ethical capacity to treat others as they should be treated'.

Beginning with dignity also changes the questions we ask and thus the discoveries we can make about and with the world. Martha Nussbaum reasons that embracing animal dignity brings us to prioritize questions about how other animals (and other organisms) flourish and reach their many and diverse capacities (Nussbaum, 2005) – areas of research ripe for exploration. Elsewhere we have written about how empathic science changes science – altering the hypotheses we form, how we ask them, what we are then able to see, and ultimately, how we conceptualize ourselves and the world around us (Webb *et al.*, 2023). Dignity has the same potential – presuming the inherent worthiness of our study subjects will close some avenues of inquiry, but it will open others. For example, research has shown that when animals are given decision-making power over their own lives, their health and well-being improves (Franks and Higgins, 2012; Špinka and Wemelsfelder, 2011). Within conservation biology, new conversations are developing regarding the ways in which recognizing the autonomy and inherent wisdom of individual animal actors can reveal how they can be partners in their own survival rather than passive subjects of our (often sadly futile) efforts (Edelblutte *et al.*, 2022).

Fish dignity undoubtedly involves a dramatic shift in perspective, but there is reason to think it may be a useful, even necessary, shift. Seeking fish dignity will change us, our understandings and our concepts of ourselves, echoing Barbara Smuts's (1999) essay on personhood:

> Thus, while we normally think of personhood as an essential quality that we can 'discover' or 'fail to find' in another, in the view espoused here, personhood connotes a way of being in relation to others, and thus no one other than the subject can give it or take it away. In other

words, when a human being relates to an individual non-human being as an anonymous object, rather than as a being with its own subjectivity, it is the human, and not the other animal, who relinquishes personhood.

(Coetzee *et al.*, 1999: 118)

The modicum of humility that is required from us to see the dignity of fishes may help us reclaim some dignity of our own. And so, we wonder, what if you were so lucky as to come across a koi-fish waving their radiant pectoral fins at you from their water-lily pond? How would you respond?

Notes

1. http://fishcount.org.uk/.
2. Abri du Poisson: http://www.visual-arts-cork.com/prehistoric/abri-poisson.htm.
3. Fisher-peoples, attentive anglers, dedicated field researchers, avid snorkelers, and SCUBA enthusiasts aside.

References

Baum, D., S. Smith, and S. Donovan. (2005), 'The tree-thinking challenge', *Science* 310(5750), 979–980.

Coetzee, J. M., M. Garber, P. Singer, W. Doniger, and B. Smuts. (1999). 'Barbara Smuts', in A. Gutmann (ed.), *The Lives of Animals*, Princeton, NJ: Princeton University Press, 107–120. http://www.jstor.org/stable/j.ctt7s37f.9.

Edelblutte É., R. Krithivasan and M. Hayek. (2022), 'Animal agency in wildlife conservation and management', *Conservation Biology* Mar 9:e13853.

Franks, B., C. Ewell, and J. Jacquet (2021), 'Animal welfare risks of global aquaculture', *Science Advances* 7(14), 1–8.

Franks, B. and E. T. Higgins. (2012), 'Effectiveness in humans and other animals: A common basis for well-being and welfare', in M. Olson and M. P. Zanna (eds.), *Advances in Experimental Social Psychology* 46, 285–346.

Gruen, L. (2014), 'Dignity, captivity, and an ethics of sight', in L. Gruen (ed.), *The Ethics of Captivity*, Oxford: Oxford University Press.

Harland, J. (2019), 'The origins of aquaculture', *Nature Ecology and Evolution* 3: 1378–1379.

Kolbert, E. (2021), *Under a White Sky: The Nature of the Future*, London: Bodley Head.
Miller, L. (2020), *Why Fish Don't Exist: A Story of Loss, Love, and the Hidden Order of Life*, New York: Simon & Schuster.
Morton, T. and D. Boyer. (2021), *hyposubjects: on becoming human*, London: Open Humanities Press.
Nussbaum, M. (2005), 'Beyond "compassion and humanity": Justice for non-human animals', in C. R. Sunstein and M. C. Nussbaum (eds.), *Animal Rights: Current Debates and New Directions*. Oxford: Oxford University Press.
Penn, J. and C. Deutsch. (2022), 'Avoiding ocean mass extinction from climate warming', *Science* Apr 29:376(6592).
Špinka, M. and F. Wemelsfelder. (2011), 'Environmental Challenge and Animal Agency', in M. C. Appleby, J. A. Mench, A. Olsson, B. O. Hughes (eds.), *Animal Welfare*, 2nd edn, Wallingford, UK: CAB International, 27–43.
Webb, C., B. Franks, M. Gagliano, and B. Smuts. (2023), 'Un-tabooing empathy: The benefits of empathic science with non-human research participants', in F. Mezzenzana and D. Peluso (eds.), *Conversations on Empathy: Interdisciplinary Perspectives on Imagination and Radical Othering*, London: Routledge, 216–234.

Chapter 19
Dignity, Respect, and the Education of Biologists

David George Haskell

Lesson one, in primary school

To avoid slicing internal organs, keep the scissors pointed up as you cut the skin. Hold your earthworm gently in one hand as you work along the body from the midpoint to the head. Cut into the flatter side of the animal, the ventral side. Once opened, lay the worm onto dissecting pan, and pin the skin to each side. You'll see the internal organs. Can you see the heart and gizzard? Look closely to see the ventral nerve cord.

What do I, the young child, sense? The surprisingly tough rubbery texture of the skin. The difficulty of holding the deflated body to make the incision. The sharp and sweet aroma of formaldehyde, mixed with wet earthiness from the earthworm's innards. The slight resistance of the wax as the pins enter. Slack organs corded down the opened belly.

And what do I learn? That to be affirmed by the teacher, 'we must not be squeamish'. To progress, we must find a way past a sense of disgust or wrongness. The task is made easier, perhaps, by the fact that we cut a worm, not a mammal. But still, that childhood affection for the writhing, animated beings I found in the garden soil as my family dug potatoes must be suppressed. The link I feel to the worms populating the pages of storybooks must be severed, too.

I take a first step in letting go of a sense of dignity in other animals.

Lesson two, in secondary school

Using your probe and forceps, find the frog's sciatic nerve. It runs under the thigh muscles and looks like a thick cotton thread parallel to a blood vessel. You'll need to remove the skin from the leg and work down through the muscles and fascia. Remember to keep the skin moist. Although the frog has been pithed by your teacher, it is still breathing through the skin and the heart is still pumping. Attach the double-pronged transducer to the nerve. You will observe the response of the gastrocnemius muscle in the leg.

What do I, the boy, sense? The flaccid frog in my hands, its pumping heart sending little pulses into the chest. An animal in a dual state: unresponsive and uncommunicative, yet alive and breathing. My own heart rate surges and acid rises in my stomach as I see the leg muscle twitch, marionette-like as we shoot the nerve with little zaps of electricity. On the teacher's desk at the front of the room, a thin silver probe gleams. After we file out of the room, I wonder what happens to the frogs now we're done with them.

What is the lesson? Nominally, a classroom demonstration of the structure and function of nerves. But the verb 'to pith' is the strongest memory. The procedure happened out of sight. But we learn that to pith a frog, you grasp it firmly, press its head forward, then use a probe to find the soft spot at the base of the head. Pushed forward then jiggled, the probe enters the cranial cavity and scrambles the brain. The frog is now ready for class, its physiological functions intact and amenable to human curiosity. We receive no instruction about what species the frogs are, how they live in the wild, or where these individuals were sourced. The pithing process is presented as a matter so commonplace and self-evidently appropriate that it merits no questioning or conversation. We offered no dignifying words of thanks to the frog. The frog is a machine. We are here to learn its mechanisms. We are merciful because we pith our 'subject' first.

Lesson three, undergraduate

An unplanned lesson. Look up from your notetaking in the teaching lab and see a rat die.

What do I, the undergraduate, sense? The pencil moves scratchily on my page, copying a diagram. The echoey lab room magnifies the amiable laughter of the lab technician chatting with his colleague as he walks into the room with a rat in a box, plucks the animal by its tail, then lowers it into a columnar glass container. The rat bucks and scrabbles for half a minute, then goes still. Gassed by chloroform vapours? The human banter does not pause and the technicians' eyes do not linger. Routine matters can be done while conversing about other things.

The lesson: my work as a biology student exists in a different world than life at home. My girlfriend and I share our one-room apartment with a companion rat. He is curious and affectionate. He has a rodent's caution about open spaces and a gourmand's discerning palate. We will mourn him when he dies. No doubt living away from other rats impoverishes his life, but he has personhood in our family. No such regard is given to the rat in the lab. The technician is not cruel. He follows all protocols. The rat died swiftly and with seemingly only momentary distress. But this rat is not family, kin, or a being with agency worth noting. The rat's death seems of the same order as filing papers or putting away glassware. No one intends this lesson, but I learn that the everyday practice of biology requires a cut inside ourselves. Non-human animals must live across a chasm that we create, with dignity on one side and lack of regard on the other.

Lesson four, graduate student working as teaching assistant

To start our exam, please retrieve your rat from its shelf in the cabinet. Now, I'd like you to use your probe to point out the aorta and vena cava on your specimen. Please show me the direction of the blood flow and explain the difference between arteries and veins. The specimen's vessels are injected with red and blue latex. How do these colours relate to the function of the circulatory system? Next week, please study the urogenital system.

What do the student and I sense? The tang of mammalian fur marinated in formaldehyde, methanol, and propylene glycol. When we lean in to poke at the vessels, a slight whiff of latex. The arteries are cobalt blue, the veins pinkish red, contrasting with the brown-grey flesh of the pickled animal. As we move the animal on its tray, the limbs are stiff as thick leather. What we do not sense is the outdoors or any living beings. The entire two-semester sequence of Introductory Biology is conducted in lecture halls and 'learning labs'. Every week I give the students their exams about the latest stage of their dissections. At the end of the semester, the rats are slung into hazardous-waste bags, destined for an unknown processing plant or incinerator. In between my scheduled times as a teaching assistant I wander the other rooms in the biology education building. In one, I unscrew the lid of a barrel and find a gorilla submerged in preservation fluid. Thirty years later, I remember how the hair on its scalp floated in the stinking fluid.

What is the lesson? A strange paradox: anatomical kinship and ethical otherness. We dissect the rat because it is a mammal and has organ systems similar to our own. The rat is a cousin that instructs us about ourselves. Yet we also learn that physical homology has not

Figure 20 Turtle hearts, credit David George Haskell.

produced homology in how the 'other' is treated. Every weekly dissection reinforces the lesson. We do not grant the rat or other 'specimens' the dignity of having their origins or destinations known, let alone honoured.

Lesson five, first-year professor

'Er, Dr Haskell? Could I interrupt you for a moment? I don't know who to talk to about this and I know you're not the teacher for BIO [X] class, but in lab this week we're meant to break open the shells of snails to study their hearts and other organs. I don't know if I can do this. Dr [Y] said there is no alternative lab and that I have to do the work. This is so horrible. The snails will be alive. But I need to do well in this class.'

What do we sense? A choice that settles heavily in the stomach. Dark anxiety under the hallway's fluorescent lights.

What is the lesson? A filter. A gate. The snail-breaking professor is senior. Curricular decisions and hiring decisions are entirely in their hands. Get used to it or get out? Or find ways to change the system from within?

§

Formal education in biology is too often a stepwise initiation into the removal of dignity from non-humans. Starting young, we learn to distance ourselves from other animals. We train our bodies not to puke during dissections. We dissociate emotionally and think about non-humans differently. We also learn the social cues demanded of us by other professional scientists, speaking of other living beings as 'subjects' and 'study systems'. All these learned ways of being, feeling, thinking, and acting remove dignity.

For some animals, we deny dignity by removing agency. We cause pain and prematurely terminate their lives in service of human curiosity and education. We do the same every time we eat meat, too; we are heterotrophs and so we kill to live. But in the classroom, few say thank you. Not once in my education or career as a college biology professor have I heard of a teacher giving thanks for the lives of the animals about to be dissected or experimented upon. Dignified education, then, might pause and acknowledge what we do. If the use of animals in classroom is justified, as many teachers believe it is, then surely it is also worthy of reflection and an expression of gratitude?

When we present a 'specimen' unrooted from any ecological context, we also remove its dignity. Every species lives enmeshed in relationships that define its home. To present students with an animal with all such stories stripped away is to deny that we are in the presence of a storied living being. But to bring a non-human animal's stories and relationships into human consciousness and conversation is to honour that other being and acknowledge its dignity.

When we teach wholly indoors, we quite literally turn inward. The lives and voices of other species appear in these enclosed spaces only through the filters of human interpretation. Outside, our senses and thus minds and emotions are open to connection to non-human animals in ways that transcend our control. This dignifies them.

This training in indignity matters for three reasons.

First, if dignity is an inherent property of all living beings, then our training ought to increase our awareness of this dignity. Instead, we too often erode awareness through our pedagogical practices. Or, if dignity is not an inherent property but is instead ascribed (that is, created by social context), then the classroom is surely one of the primary places in which dignity emerges. Teachers transmit not only information, but cultural practices and values.

Second, this process of training changes how biologists think and feel, and thus reshapes our relationships with the living Earth and its creatures. Part of what the current crisis of extinction and injustice calls for is deeper senses of belonging, kinship, and responsibility, followed by actions that evince these values. But an education system that teaches us to objectify and to distance ourselves leads in the opposite direction. It is no accident that the scientific endeavour as practiced in the West is often seamlessly integrated with colonial processes of extraction and despoliation. A beloved cousin has dignity. A 'natural resource' does not.

Third, and perhaps most pernicious of all, this approach to education excludes from the professional field of biology the very people we need the most in this era of crisis and disconnection. For those with strong empathetic connections to other beings, the path that many biology degree programmes offer is often impossible to walk. And so, these people chose other educational and career options. For those who have had deep ecological, spiritual, or other communion with living beings, the curriculum is often unbearable. They turn away. For those who believe that the whole Earth has dignity and should be treated as such, our biology classrooms can be places of discouragement or disengagement. A science of life that excludes so many people fails not only to treat other species with dignity, it fails to treat our students with dignity.

How might we change course? Instead of reaching for preserved specimens, perhaps step outside with our students and allow the living world to teach us? When we do kill, invite students in solemnity and gratitude. If the anatomical study of dead beings is necessary, get a salvage permit and glean from roadsides. The dead lying there have much to teach us. In ecological experiments, use non-destructive methods. Instead of the pitfall trap, use the sweep net. Instead of electroshocking streams, use visual or net surveys. Ask students to know their homes, to honour other beings with their curiosity: what are the common trees and birds outside the lab building, and how did they come to be the way they are?

Respectful attention from a teacher is a powerful lesson. Respect can be built into the structure of how we enculturate future generations in our classes. Dignity can be taught.

Afterthoughts

PRELUDE VI
Characteristics of Life
Camille T. Dungy[*]

A fifth of animals without backbones could be at risk of extinction, say scientists.[**]

—Ella Davies

    Ask me if I speak for the snail and I will tell you
    I speak for the snail.
                    speak of underneathedness
    and the welcome of mosses,
                         of life that springs up,
    little lives that pull back and wait for a moment.

    I speak for the damselfly, water skeet, mollusk,
    the caterpillar, the beetle, the spider, the ant.
                                  I speak
    from the time before spinelessness was frowned upon.

    Ask me if I speak for the moon jelly. I will tell you
               one thing today and another tomorrow
          and I will be as consistent as anything alive
    on this earth.

---

[*] 'Characteristics of Life' by Camille T. Dungy from *Trophic Cascade*, © 2017 Camille T. Dungy. Published by Wesleyan University Press, Middletown, CT. Used by permission.
[**] Reproduced with permission.

I move as the currents move, with the breezes.
What part of your nature drives you? You, in your cubicle
ought to understand me. I filter and filter and filter all day.

Ask me if I speak for the nautilus and I will be silent
as the nautilus shell on a shelf. I can be beautiful
and useless if that's all you know to ask of me.

Ask me what I know of longing and I will speak of distances
between meadows of night-blooming flowers.
I will speak
the impossible hope of the firefly.

You with the candle
burning and only one chair at your table must understand
such wordless desire.

To say it is mindless is missing the point.

Figure 21 Hawaiian tree snail, credit Hawaii DLNR.

Ways Forward

Melanie Challenger

Philosopher Tomasz Pietrzykowski suggests that evolutionary history has given us 'two important moral divides that should be recognized and reflected in the law.' The first, he says, is sentience, as 'it begets subjective interests emerging from the capability of experiencing one's existence as composed of positive and negative stimuli.' The second is moral agency, as it 'underpins moral duties and responsibilities' (Pietrzykowski, 2021).

Sentience, he argues, is better suited than dignity to generating a 'third category' before the law, between persons and objects. Sentience could reduce the risks of certain animal harms, without expecting other animals to have any moral duties or responsibilities; and sentience offers us a compromise when human interests conflict with another animal's subjective interests. In this way, sentience claims could extend current welfare approaches by increasing the traits under consideration (more positive mental or physical states) and by extending moral considerability out to other taxa (cephalopods and crustaceans, for instance).

This third legal category of sentient, non-human animals would rely on scientific measures for sentience, much as proofs of the capacity for pain feature in welfare legislation. Indeed, science-based sentience studies are well underway (see, for instance, Jonathan Birch *et al*. at LSE), and the importance of animal sentience has recently been acknowledged by the UK government. These are positive moves, although it is worth noting that the moral relevance of sentience isn't new (see Bentham, 1789; Singer, [1975] 1977; Regan, 1983). But would formal recognition of sentience really do away with the need to also recognize dignity? One reason for caution is that the current focus on animal sentience is not a moral development that is necessarily invested in affording any fundamental status to another animal. Sentience claims don't require us to respect other animals or to listen to them. Rather, the science-based recognition of sentience is a *mitigatory* approach. It might reduce some dignity violations but it cannot resolve the harms that follow from fundamental and systematic disrespect, denigration, or objectification.

§

The most significant argument against animal dignity comes from the belief that dignity is inherently about being human. More than this, it is about the human difference from other animals. And even more provocatively, in its current guise, it is about *protecting* us from being perceived as animals. How then can dignity apply to non-human animals?

Speaking on BBC radio in 1981, Mary Midgley spoke of the 'colossal confidence' that the majority of eighteenth and nineteenth century thinkers had about human exceptionalism and dominion. 'To their minds,' she said, 'human dignity justified and depended on a total separation of man from all the rest of creation. That's why they got such a shock when the *Origin of Species* came out. Someone who has buttressed his sense of his own dignity by allowing no dignity at all to anybody else, naturally feels any suggestion of a relationship with those others as intolerably degrading.'

In my book *How to Be Animal: What It Means to Be Human* (2021), which I discussed on several occasions with Midgley in the years before she died, I spent a good deal of time on the subject of dehumanization. Dehumanization is crucial to our modern concept of dignity in several ways. First, dehumanization is intimately associated with dignity violations. These violations are understood as originating in perceiving and treating a human as if they are a 'lower' animal, thereby justifying negligent, cruel, or even violent treatment. Dehumanization is a shortcut to lowering or removing another person's moral considerability. As such, intuitively, it feels as if something *specific* to humans (i.e., dignity) is required to counter dehumanization. Indeed, this something specific should – in clean, absolute terms – separate us from other animals to *prevent* animalistic dehumanization. By this logic, dignity cannot, therefore, be associated with other animals.

As already noted, dignity assumed its global, moralized sense after the atrocities of the Second World War. Animalistic dehumanization played a considerable role in the propaganda campaigns between enemy forces, and against Jewish, Roma and Sinti peoples, along with individuals with disabilities, with utterly devastating consequences. In the testimonies of survivors, it is common for individuals to report feeling as if they had been 'stripped' of their humanity or treated as 'animals'. In the light of the dehumanizing events of the Second World War, politicians, dignitarians and legislators cast around for a moral mechanism to prevent such appalling denigrations from happening again. The concept of dignity seemed well suited as a formal and informal obstacle to dehumanization because many of its theoretical antecedents conceptualized dignity in such a way as to morally separate humanity from the rest of nature or by singling out uniquely human capacities to describe the contents of dignity.

As highlighted by Remy Debes in his opening contribution to this volume, the seventeenth-century natural law theorist, Samuel Pufendorf, offered the world its earliest predecessor to the modern concept of dignity. 'There seems to him to be somewhat of Dignity (*Dignatio*) in the appellation of Man,' Pufendorf wrote, 'so that the last and most efficacious Argument to curb the Arrogance of insulting Men, is usually, I am not a Dog, but a Man as well as yourself.'

For Pufendorf, then, to designate oneself as distinctly human is to summon dignity. Kant, too, tied his notions of *Würde* and of dignity (as *Dignatio*) to the salvation of humanity from a degrading association with animality. But for Kant, dignity emerges not simply by dint of the capacity to be a moral agent but by the proper, rational relationship to one's moral gift (for full discussion of the forms of this relationship see Alan Wood, 1999). In Kant's words, 'morality is the condition under which alone a rational being can be an end in itself'. As such, while the earlier forms of dignity as social rank excluded vast swathes of humans from the benefits of respect, Kant also limited who came under dignity's radiant shield.

Yet the animal, more broadly, has always lurked in the background of any non-spiritual approach to species-based/kind-based claims (Challenger, 2021). From Aristotle to Aquinas and from Locke to Kateb, we can see a long line of head-scratching thinkers trying to puzzle out ethical certainty by means of exceptionalism.

Treating another human as a commodity, or objectifying them, is also intimately bound up with dehumanization. 'Whatever has a price', Kant said, 'can be replaced by something else as its equivalent; on the other hand, whatever is above all price, and therefore admits of no equivalent has a *Würde*.' Other animals, he once declared, are 'only means to an end'. In this way, Kant intuited what many studies today have since confirmed, that relationships of exploitation arise from and amplify denigration.

Today it feels breathtaking that so few Western thought-leaders at the time recognized or spoke up against the obvious abuses of the slave trade, given the insights into objectification. Still, dehumanization played a role here too. Many slave owners dehumanized those they had enslaved to justify an abhorrent crime. People at the time described African slaves as 'beasts of burden'. And the Linnean *Systema naturae* further inculcated an entirely scientifically false race-based hierarchy. Linnaeus distinguished humans as the highest among animals for our ability to 'know ourselves' (*Nosce te ipsum*). Yet humans were separated into types based on skin colour and region. So, we have 'white' Europeans, 'red' Americans, 'tawny' Asians, and 'black' Africans. Predictably, given prevailing attitudes, Africans were lowest on this human scale, furthest from the angels and nearest to the beasts. And, while racialized slavery in the context of imperialism was a new and shocking manifestation of violence, as long ago as Aristotle (and one should presume, still earlier), slaves and servants were associated with non-human animals, particularly livestock (see Bradley, 2000: 110–25).

Hardly surprising, then, that American abolitionist Frederick Douglass made sure to highlight the human characteristics that were shared among *all* humans, regardless of rank. For Douglass, every human of every ethnicity possessed dignity by virtue of their specific capacities to reason, to will their actions, and to retain their identity across the course of their lives.

After the Second World War, most dignitarians looked to apply dignity to all people without limits. One of the challenges of this conceptual shift was that to transform dignity from social rank, or even from the constraints of Kant's conception, into a measureless form of value, an *invaluable* value, if you will, dignity was conceived as the unqualified state of *being* human.

'When we talk about human dignity as such (as opposed to the dignity of humans belonging to this or that class) we may be saying something about rank, but not about the rank of some humans over others,' Jeremy Waldron notes. 'We may be talking about the rank of humans generally in the great chain of being' (Waldron, 2007). In recent years, Waldron has suggested that we reverse the dominance structures that flow from high rank or status so that we can universalize them in a way that makes us all equals both inside a democracy and in accordance with the rights we are owed. This is dignity as 'universalized rank'.

In a 2021 analysis of dignity, philosopher Lennart Nordenfelt concluded: 'Human dignity, as understood by most debaters (including me), is a quality possessed by everybody *simply through the fact of being human*' (Nordenfelt, 2021: 55, emphasis mine). This goes some way to explaining why this modern, moralized concept of dignity was tolerable to Christian leaders without recourse, necessarily, to *imago Dei*, because, implicit in this species/kind-based approach was a sacralization of the human form and way of being.

But is dignity as human exceptionalism a good candidate to counter violations like dehumanization? To answer that question adequately, we need to understand dehumanization better.

§

There is a flourishing scientific and humanities literature on dehumanization, with the work of scholars like Albert Bandura, Emile Bruneau, Kristof Dhont, Nour Kteily, David Livingstone Smith, Nick Haslam, Jeroen Vaes, Lasana T. Harris, and Susan Fiske as excellent first resources for those who wish to get an overview of the field (see, e.g., Bandura, 2016; Dhont *et al.*, 2020; Kteily and Bruneau, 2017; Livingstone Smith, 2020; Haslam, 2006; Vaes and Paladino, 2010; Harris and Fiske, 2006).

There's scant room for a full analysis here, but it's useful to know that scholars in the field often separate the concept into different parts, both in the mechanism of dehumanization (e.g., in the use of dehumanizing metaphors like animals or machines, etc.) and also in the forms (e.g., 'blatant' or 'subtle', etc.). In other words, not all dehumanization relates to perceiving humans as animals. Animalistic dehumanization is a special form within a broader phenomenon.

Current work in dehumanization, especially from neuroscience, suggests animalistic dehumanization exploits animal metaphors to manipulate aspects of our social cognition. Such manipulation can take the form of suppressing aspects of our social cognition or, by contrast, readying aggressive responses. The work of unpicking such pathways in the brain and endocrine system of humans, as well as tracking the effects in behavioural outcomes, is difficult and incomplete at this stage. Nonetheless, the widespread nature of dehumanization both across time and cultures suggests it has a significant role in human affairs.

The animal metaphors used in dehumanization both exploit and distort natural facts about our world. Two of the commonest animal types recruited by us to dehumanize one another are pigs and rats. As mammals that often live in proximity to us, these animals act as hosts for pathogens that have spilled into human populations, from H1N1 swine flu to bubonic plague. It is this adaptive response to diseases and pathogens that we tap into to provoke fear or disgust towards a fellow human.

There has been some preliminary work that suggests positive framings like dignity can disrupt such psychological pathways to neglect or even violence. Lasana T. Harris and Susan Fiske (2006) have contributed important work in this area, particularly in terms of the aspects of our social cognition that come into play. This kind of evidence from neuroscience and psychology suggests that the invocation of dignity may be intuitively sensible. The error has been in the assertion of dignity as a hierarchically based determinant of our humanness and as a source of moral superiority. Indeed, there are good reasons to suggest that this kind of exceptionalism is unhelpful at best, and sometimes dangerous.

In experiments designed by Kimberley Costello and her colleague Graham Hodson (2010), university students convinced of strong human uniqueness were found to be more prejudiced towards immigrants, while those who subscribed to the 'animals are similar' category exhibited the least immigrant dehumanization and highest measures of empathy. Strikingly, Costello and Hodson discovered that it was possible to reduce or temporarily eliminate someone's dehumanizing beliefs about other people not by manipulating their insights into their fellow humans but by prompting these individuals to reconsider other animals. Such a reappraisal failed if someone was asked to drag humans down to a perceived 'lowly' level of animals. But it worked if someone was called on to see both humans and other animals as precious entities sharing valuable needs and feelings. In other words, perceiving animals as having significantly lower status than humans is neither inevitable nor necessary to protect us from our own cruelties.

To make sense of this, we must recognize that humans are group-living primates, whose adaptive social environment was hierarchical. Humans are physically and psychologically affected both by competition within the group and by competition between groups. Group living also affects humans in affording social buffering opportunities – i.e., the ability to confer positive psychological and physiological effects from positive relationships with one another. Social buffering is common across social animals, particularly mammals. But what is remarkable about our species is that we don't just rely on being physically close and supportive of one another; we experience buffering effects from *psychological* experiences of togetherness. In other words, belief systems of belonging – the group or ideology we associate with, for instance, including the belief in human exceptionalism – provide physical benefits. The flipside is that we can also exploit certain mechanisms – like operationalizing metaphorical uses of animals we fear – to disrupt the affiliative bonds between us.

Groupishness can also manifest as a belief that those within our group are more intelligent or experience more complex emotions than those on the outside. Psychologist Jeroen Vaes (Vaes and Paladino, 2010) believes that fears or perceived threats may also prompt people to see ingroup members as more distinctly human. As social bonds provide both buffering and real survival opportunities, an affiliative mindset comes at a premium in times of stress or danger. But this can leave outsiders to be perceived as if they have fewer of the human capacities that warrant a moral response. 'In particularly ghastly cases,' psychologist Matt Motyl writes, 'people will support or participate in the killing of those who threaten their system of meaning' (Motyl *et al.*, 2013).

Some experimental work suggests that identifying with our animality is threatening in and of itself, as animality includes the risks of disease and death. Using the ideas of Ernest Becker (e.g., 1973), psychologists Tom Pyszczynski, Jeff Greenberg and Sheldon Solomon hypothesized that subconscious fears of death generate feelings of meaninglessness and insecurity about our place in the world (Pyszczynski et al., 1999; see also Solomon et al., 2015). When fears are high, people favour the idea of human uniqueness as a way of protecting us (e.g., see Goldenberg, 2001; Rodríguez-Ferreiro et al., 2019).

The work is yet to be done, but it is an interesting hypothesis that dignity as a concept might confer social buffering benefits on us as members of the 'human' group by encouraging both reassuring and affiliative tendencies, just as it might once have offered solace to those whose special status derived from their higher social rank.

There's considerable wariness within philosophy about any recourse to the science of our moral psychology. At least since G. E. Moore's scrutiny of the concept of goodness in his *Principia Ethica* (1903), 'non-naturalism' in ethics has prevailed, such that moral philosophy and the natural sciences shouldn't be reconciled with one another. I believe that is a mistake, most especially when we come to make sense of our actions towards other species. One does not commit the naturalistic fallacy to acknowledge we are continually subject to biological processes. Dignity shines through the prism of biology, through the minds and actions of a biological being. Only when we cleave philosophy from our animal reality and interpret moral concepts and axioms as if they float in some pure aether of logic, do we miss the obvious. A failure to understand that moral impulses can be deeply rooted in psychological and physiological processes that alter our cognition and behaviour is a failure to confront the human condition.

Today, dignity, in its latest guise, is a kind of apotropaic concept, a philosophical amulet to protect us from the degradation of being an animal. To say this is not to belittle dignity. But the realities of life on Earth range, as Darwin noted, from parasitism to pandemics, from the killing and consumption of others as food sources to sexual aggression and the monopolizing of resources. It has long been the dream of many to salvage human morality from the amorality of nature. Yet much that we formalize in moral axioms and concepts are harvested from particular facets of mammalian sociality. Human moralists, whether they know it or not, are in the business of attempting to bias biological affiliative processes (including mental states and levels of hormones in one's bloodstream) for *good*.

§

If one takes from the history of ideas that dignity is *only* about being human, then the notion of the dignity of non-human animals would seem to be a nonstarter. But no philosophical or legal construct arrives fully formed. Concepts evolve. The history of dignity is one of a slow widening of moral visibility, as if a beam of light has steadily spread out from a point. The first stages of this expanding radiance were precipitated by the efficacy of exploiting sensitivities to rank to increase respect-recognition to a larger number of humans in society. In this collection of essays, we argue that there's good reason to allow that light to outspread towards non-human animals too.

Yet dignity isn't being *expanded* to include other animals (or ordinary people or people of colour or women, for that matter); rather we have grasped human dignity, only to realize we have the tail of a larger concept. As such, as the concept has come under scrutiny over time, we have realized that all dignities are species of *animal* dignity. As Nussbaum puts it, human dignity is 'an animal sort of dignity, and that very sort of dignity could not be possessed by a being who was not mortal and vulnerable, just as the beauty of a cherry tree in bloom could not be possessed by a diamond' (Nussbaum, 2006: 132). Hence, if *all* dignity is animal dignity, then respecting non-human animals doesn't violate the logic of dignity because humans are animals too.

But if all dignity is animal dignity and animals are so profoundly different, not only as individuals but across taxa, what can dignity consist of that isn't so general as to be meaningless? In his critique of animal dignity, philosopher Federico Zuolo notes his concern that 'all animal species differ from one another. Hence, the theoretical problem of this approach is to find out on what basis a single moral notion may be employed given species diversity' (Zuolo, 2016). But, in fact, dignity in its commonest modern conception seeks to overcome those problems by moving away from the content of supremacy. By responding to how our social cognition functions, the great strength of dignity is in attending to another being's particularity.

Looking across the work in this volume, our authors suggest that dignity is grounded, primarily, in animal agency, the ability to flourish on one's own terms, the autonomy embedded in one's nature, and the remarkable reality of one's biological distinctiveness. For non-human animals or for humans, the most important work of dignity is to release us from arbitrary measures or, as the late philosopher Tom Regan noted in his formulation of 'Subjects of a Life', those harms that follow from denying 'the dynamic and diverse nature of biological life'.

For Killmister, we should not see other animals as having a species-fixed, essentialist nature. Rather, she says, we should follow Chris Cuomo's idea of 'dynamic charm' as a way of capturing the 'presentational and evocative aspects of dignity'.

Here is a key Cuomo passage in full:

> It is an entity's dynamic charm – its diffuse, 'internal' ability to adapt to or resist change, and its unique causal and motivational patterns and character – that renders it morally considerable, and that serves as a primary site for determining what is good for that being or thing. In common use 'charm' refers to a quality that attracts and delights . . . Whatever it is that living things and systems have – what evokes our awe, respect, and what draws us into relationship, and what enables us to change and adapt . . . And although something's charm is real, we might not be able to grasp or identify the boundaries of that charm. Yet we might say that charm is evident when something is thriving, in terms of its own capacities or physical requirements, in terms of its 'charms'.
>
> (Cuomo, 1998: 71)

Nussbaum conjures the importance of this kind of dynamic charm:

> We see that dignity intuitively when we watch dolphins swimming freely through the water in social groupings, echolocating their way around obstacles and leaping for joy; when we see a group of elephants caring communally for their young and attempting to rear them in safety despite the ubiquity of man-made threats. Our sense of wonder is an epistemic faculty oriented to dignity: it says to us 'this is not just some rubbish, something I can use any way I like. This is a being who must be treated as an end.'
>
> (Nussbaum, 2023: 93)

She argues further that an animal's agency is fundamental to their being able to pursue their own capabilities. For Nussbaum, freedom to pursue capabilities is a key to dignity. It is a life-based capacity to flourish on one's own terms. Her approach, she writes, 'is animated by the Aristotelian sense that there is something wonderful and worthy of awe in any complex natural organism' (Nussbaum, 2023: 93–4).

For Gruen, animals can be denied dignity when 'de-animalized', which is to strip the individual animal of their specific capacities and interests. Invoking dignity brings the details and value of another being into our direct attention from which positive action follows. This recalls the counsel from Suzanne Cataldi to see the vital sense or basis of dignity as relating 'to being who or what one is' (Cataldi, 2002: 112).

'A better, more holistic approach might be to start by paying close attention to others in their own right,' Celermajer writes, 'noticing how they are in the world and how their ways of being might constitute them as beings with dignity.' For Eisenberg and Nelson, dignity is a gift of seeing. 'Beyond direct moral standing, to be granted dignity is to be worthy of a place of honour.'

One of the most consistent elements is that dignity violations involve an aberration from a state of autonomous flourishing. This draws in terms like humiliation, shame, degradation, and denigration, some of which seem to originate inside the subject and others as conditions to which another is subjected by an outside violator. One can even see this in the human sense of violating one's own dignity. We see echoes of this in Baindur's description of *prana*-wringing as our sensitivity to the thriving of an animal within 'its own capacities'.

Crucially, dignity violations are not only distressing, but they can also be the mechanism by which greater harms become rationalized or facilitated. Killmister argues that 'dignity violations are any impediment to the species-relevant capacities of the individual'. She goes on to clarify that 'not all setbacks to welfare, or violations of rights, will constitute dignity violations – there needs to be an element of *denigration*'.

We can't understand this dimension of dignity studies unless we naturalize the issue. Dignity actions actively *exploit* our social cognition. Active denigration as a dignity violation alters the aspects of our brain that are recruited and the hormone levels in our body that result in behavioural outcomes. In this way, we can reasonably conclude that there are different kinds of dignity violations, from passive dignity violations (e.g., that emerge as incidental to degrading contexts) to active dignity violations, such as ridicule, that actively encourage the lowering or removal of the respect-status of another.

And so, how the recognition of dignity matters is that it is a special kind of moralized attention that facilitates a relationship founded on respect, with a particular function of *preventing* harmful denigrations. That moralized attention is an attention *to* the formal properties of dignity, which (this is contestable, of course) by most definitions include agency, autonomy, and biological distinctiveness.

As noted in the Introduction, it helps to understand that what we call 'dignity' is both a psychological and physical intervention. To recognize dignity is to generate a state of mind that will facilitate a positive relationship and prevent particular kinds of degrading ones; and, especially, degradations that result in the treatment of another being as if they are a *thing*. Holding dignity in mind is a mental intervention to prevent any individual with a world of their own from being objectified as if they have no intrinsic value. Recognizing dignity prevents a subject becoming an object.

Our aims in this book have been to clarify the following: that the nature of dignity is such that the concept can include other animals *and* the function of dignity is such that acknowledging dignity can assist other animals. To do this, we have, in the words of Wai Chee Dimock, looked at 'the multiple habitats of dignity' (Waldron, 2012: 120).

Dignity is perceived by a moral agent through a form of attention; it is a mechanism of non-instrumental value-conferring recognition. And the honour is a kind of promise, to respect another in their integral state of worth – that their life has value purely on its own terms. It is a reverential term, by some measures. It can't be reduced to any one ingredient over another, nor can it just be called 'life' to properly capture the importance of denigration.

Dignity doesn't ground human rights in our distinction but in our *distinctiveness*, a property we share with other animals. From the perspective of dignity, our moral autonomy as humans doesn't afford us *special respect*, so much as generate *special harms*. As the frequent subjects of those harms, animals are excellent candidates for the radiance of dignity.

Gruen also signposts the importance of the context in which animal dignity might become relevant – especially the instrumentalization of other species. Today, if accepted, animal dignity concerns not only some of the ways we currently treat non-human animals – the denial of any moral or legal status beyond that of an object or possession – but the ways we are currently approaching the uses of radical new instruments of exploitation, such as CRISPR-Cas9, xenotransplants, chimerical study animals, and so forth. Animal dignity may well have much to offer the ethicists of the future as they grapple with applications of gene drives, gene-editing, along with the cloning of pets or research subjects. Scientists and bioethicists may panic at the possibility that animal dignity might emerge as a threat to ambitions to exploit new technologies to advance human medicine. But well-grounded moral incumbrances, if they are fair and reasonable, will not stand in the way of science.

And dignity may have a particular role to play in generating better relations with non-human animals during the demanding environmental challenges we face, from climate change to biodiversity loss. For Kurki, animal dignity in law would be welfarism+, with the 'plus' being the recognition of a value beyond measure. That fundamental respect cannot be captured by welfarism based on sentience, for example, which would only extend the duties we might owe to other species a limited distance beyond negative affective states like pain. Animal dignity in law, by contrast, is a respect command based on the distinctive qualities of both species and individuals.

There is a lingering question of how far into the biotic community we apply the concept of dignity. As this is a volume about animal dignity, we will leave it to others to consider whether the criteria only comfortably map to animals or could reach elsewhere in the living world, to plants, for instance. My own inclination is that the less formal notions of respect and honour might be better suited to life *per se* and to the vegetal kingdom, reserving dignity for a special kind of respectful attentiveness that emerges between animal agents.

References

Bandura, A. (2016), *Moral Disengagement: How People Do Harm and Live With Themselves*, New York: Worth Publishers.
Becker, E. (1973), *The Denial of Death*, New York: Free Press.

Bentham, J. (1789), *An Introduction to the Principles of Morals and Legislation. Printed in the year 1780, and now first published. By Jeremy Bentham.* printed for T. Payne, and Son.

Bradley, K. (2000), 'Animalizing the slave: The truth of fiction', *The Journal of Roman Studies* 90, 110–125.

Cataldi, S. (2002), 'Animals and the concept of dignity: Critical reflections on a circus performance', *Ethics and the Environment* 7(2): 104–126.

Challenger, M. (2021), *How to Be Animal: What It Means to Be Human*, London: Canongate Books.

Costello, K. and G. Hodson. (2010), 'Exploring the roots of dehumanization: The role of animal-human similarity in promoting immigrant humanization', *Group Processes and Intergroup Relations* 13(1), 3–22.

Cuomo, C. (1998), *Feminism and Ecological Communities: An Ethic of Flourishing*, New York: Routledge.

Dhont K., G. Hodson, A. C. Leite, and A. Salmen. (2020), 'The psychology of speciesism', in K. Dhont and G. Hodson (eds.), *Why We Love and Exploit Animals: Bridging Insights from Academia and Advocacy*, London: Routledge, 29–49.

Goldenberg, J. L., T. Pyszczynski, J. Greenberg, S. Solomon, B. Kluck, and R. Cornwell. (2001), 'I am *not* an animal: Mortality salience, disgust, and the denial of human creatureliness', *Journal of Experimental Psychology: General* 130, 427–435.

Harris, L. and S. Fiske. (2006), 'Dehumanizing the lowest of the low: Neuroimaging responses to extreme out-groups', *Psychological Science* 17(10), 847–853.

Haslam, N. (2006), 'Dehumanization: An Integrative Review', *Personality and Social Psychology Review* 10(3), 252–264.

Kant, I. (1996), *Groundwork for the Metaphysics of Morals*, in M. Gregor (trans. and ed.), *Practical Philosophy: The Cambridge Edition of the Works of Immanuel Kant*, New York: Cambridge University Press.

Kteily, N. and E. Bruneau. (2017), 'Darker demons of our nature: The need to (re)focus attention on blatant forms of dehumanization', *Current Directions in Psychological Science* 26(6), 487–494.

Livingstone Smith, D. (2020), *On Inhumanity: Dehumanization and How to Resist It*, Oxford: Oxford University Press.

Moore, G. E. (1993 [1903]), *Principia Ethica*, Cambridge: Cambridge University Press.

Motyl, M., J. Hart, D. P. Cooper, N. Heflick, J. Goldenberg, and T. Pyszczynski. (2013), 'Creatureliness priming reduces aggression and support for war', *British Journal of Social Psychology* 52(4), 648–666.

Nordenfelt, L. (2021), 'The concepts of dignity: An analysis', *Ersta Sköndal Bräcke Högskola Arbetsrapportserie*, 99. Available from https://philpapers.org/rec/NORTCO-27.

Nussbaum, M. (2006), *Frontiers of Justice: Disability, Nationality, Species Membership*, Cambridge, MA: Belknap Press.

Nussbaum, M. (2023), *Justice for Animals: Our Collective Responsibility*, New York: Simon & Schuster.

Pietrzykowski, T. (2021), 'Against dignity: An argument for a non-metaphysical foundation of animal law', *Archiwum Filozofii Prawa i Filozofii Społecznej* 27(2): 69–82

Pyszczynski, T., J. Greenberg and S. Solomon. (1999), 'A dual process model of defense against conscious and unconscious death-related thoughts: An extension of Terror Management Theory', *Psychological Review* 106(4), 835–845.

Regan, T. (1983), *The Case for Animal Rights*, Berkeley: University of California Press.

Rodríguez-Ferreiro J., I. Barberia, J. González-Guerra, and M. A. Vadillo. (2019), 'Are we truly special and unique? A replication of Goldenberg *et al* (2001)', *Royal Society Open Science* 27;6(11):191114.

Singer, P. ([1975] 1977), *Animal Liberation*, New York: Avon Books.

Solomon, S., J. Greenberg. and T. Pyszczynski. (2015), *The Worm at the Core: On the Role of Death in Life*, New York: Penguin.

Vaes, J. and M. Paladino. (2010), 'The uniquely human content of stereotypes', *Group Processes & Intergroup Relations* 13(1), 23–39.

Waldron, J. (2007), 'Dignity and rank: In memory of Gregory Vlastos (1907–1991)', *European Journal of Sociology / Archives Européennes De Sociologie* 48(2), 201–237.

Waldron, J. (2012), *Dignity, Rank, and Rights*. New York: Oxford University Press.

Wood, A. (1999), *Kant's Ethical Thought*, Cambridge: Cambridge University Press.

Zuolo, F. (2016). 'Dignity and animals: Does it make sense to apply the concept of dignity to all sentient beings?', *Ethical Theory and Moral Practice* 19 (5): 1117–1130.

Index

abortion 204–205
Abraham 136
Abram, David 173
Acampora, Ralph 214
Actinopterygii lineage 232
'ag-gag' laws 188
ahimsa (non-violence) 169
A'ho 163, 163n.1
air-chilling 30
Alex (African grey parrot) 71
Alzheimer's disease 165
Ambros, B. 169
American Civil Rights Movement 36
Anderson, Elizabeth 87
Anderson, Roland 73
Animal Farm (Orwell) 170–171
Animal Intelligence (Romanes) 80
Animal Protection Act 2008 (Switzerland) 191, 202–204
animism 173
Animism: Respecting the Living World (Harvey) 173
Antares 99
Anthony, Susan B. 38
Anthropocene era 234–235
anthropocentrism 51, 85, 136–137, 160, 193–194, 197
Antigone (Sophocles) 43
antivivisectionism 81
apes 80
    see also baboons; bonobos; chimpanzees; gorillas; orangutans
Aquinas, Thomas 254

Aristotle 34, 103, 254, 261
Artemis 99
arthropods 80
Atharva Veda 167
atheism 181
Athena (octopus) 68–71, 73–77
Attenborough, Sir David 98–99
ATVs 110
Australia 76, 117
Axial Age 173

baboons 186
    see also apes; bonobos; chimpanzees; gorillas; orangutans
Baindur, Meera 126–127, 261
Baraga, F. 158
Barclay, Linda 56, 58
Barstow, G. 168
bats 72–73
bears 110–112
Beattie, Tina 38
Becker, Ernest 258
Becoming Animal (Abram) 173
Beebe, William 70
bees 113
Belmont Report 211
Bembas (ethnic grouping) 139
Benthamism 184
Berrill, N. J. 75
Big Dipper 99–100
biodiversity loss 263
biology 12, 93, 116, 126, 178, 234, 236, 241–245

Birch, Jonathan 251
Bird, Colin 9–10, 54
birds 71, 167, 182–183, 196, 209, 220, 232
Black Lives Matter movement 36, 45n.2
bonobos 129, 186
  see also apes; baboons; chimpanzees; gorillas; orangutans
Boyer, Dominic 234
Bradshaw, G. A. 110, 112, 114n.1
Brahman 147–148, 170
Bronstein, Scott 29
Brownell, Phil 98–101
bubonic plague 256
Buddhism 167–169, 186
Budongo forest 132
Buitendag, J. 166
Bukamba, Nelson 125–126
bushmeat 134, 136

CA (Capabilities Approach) 24, 181–186
cabbage loopers 113
The Cambridge Handbook of Human Dignity (Düwell et al) 10
campylobacter 27
Canis familiaris see dogs
Canticle of Brother Sun and Sister Moon (St Francis of Assisi) 170
Capabilities Approach (Nussbaum) 194
cara 152–153
Cataldi, Suzanne 7, 9, 84, 261
Catholic Church 38, 181
cats 80–82, 172
cattle *see* cows
Celermajer, Danielle 16, 64, 261
cephalopods 68, 72
'Characteristics of Life' (Dungy) 249–250

Charlotte's Web (White) 5
Chibvongodze, Danford 139
chickens 25–31, 188
  see also birds
chimerical study animals 263
chimpanzees 69, 125–126, 129, 132, 186, 193
  see also apes; baboons; bonobos; gorillas; orangutans
China/Chinese 134
chlorine baths 27–30
Christianity 103, 136, 166, 170
Cicero 42–44
Ciceronian platitude 42–44
clams 69
climate change 177, 263
cluster concepts 11
collaborators 183, 189n.3
The Collins Dictionary 10
'Come into Animal Presence'(Levertov) 109
Compendious Dictionary (Webster) 36
conferralist position (Waldron) 24
consciousness 170, 173
Consumer Reports 27
Control of Dogs Act (Zambia) 135
Cophenaver, Brian 41
Cornwall 113
cosmos 170
Costello, Kimberley 256–257
COVID-19 pandemic 165
cows 145, 151, 167–168
CRISPR-Cas9 263
Critical Review 40
Cuomo, Chris 260
cuttlefish 72, 76

Darfur war 36
Darwall, Stephan 12, 40
Darwin, Charles 79, 231, 258
Dawkins, Marian Stamp 220
de Castro, Vivieros 224

de Waal, Frans 186
Death Valley 97–98, 102
Debes, Remy 8, 12, 23–24, 253
Declaration of Independence (US) 37
degenerative myelopathy 92
dehumanization 252–257
Devine, Tom 30
Dharma 151
Dictionary (Johnson) 36
A Dictionary of the Ojibwa Language (Baraga) 158
dignitas/dignité 36, 42
Dignitatis humanae (1965 decree) 38, 45n.4
Dignity: A History (Debes) 8
Dignity Funeral Directors 165
'Dignity Is a Useless Concept' (Macklin) 8
Dignity of Man (Pico della Mirandola) 41
'Dignity Project' (Wein) 11
Dignity, Rank and Rights (Waldron) 54
Dimock, Wai Chee 262
dinosaurs 71, 233
disability 225–226
distinctiveness 126, 262
dogs 80–82, 85, 91–95, 101–103, 134–140, 151, 153
dolphins 72, 84, 178, 182, 186, 213–214
Douglass, Frederick 38, 254
Dowd, Scott 69, 71, 74, 76–78
du Motier, Gilbert 37
ducks 196
    see also birds
Duke (slug) 67–68
Dungy, Camille T. 249–250
Düwell, Marcus 10
Dworkin, Ronald 204–205
'dynamic charm' (Cuomo) 260

E. coli 27
ecocide 162, 163n.1

ecofeminism 15
Ecuador 162
egalitarianism 203–205
Eisenberg, Cristina 127, 261
Elasmobranchii lineage 232
elephant Ethogram 187, 189n.4
elephants 80, 84, 86, 182, 186–187, 189, 193, 214
empathy 34–35
English Bill of Rights (1689) 37
equine Cushing's disease 220
Erickson, Nancy 114
Ethics and Animals (Gruen) 84
Ethiopian famine (1983–85) 36
Etieyibo, Edwin 136
Etinson, Adam 56
European Union Agency for Fundamental Rights 9
euthanasia 92–93, 135, 140, 204–205, 220
euthasol 135
evil eye 168

F-89 Scorpion 102
factory farming 188, 214–215
farming 25–27
Finnegan (dog) 91–92, 94–95
fish 178, 229–237
Fiske, Susan 256
fleabane 113
'Flight Ways: Life and Loss at the Edge of Extinction' (Van Dooren) 180
Foster, Charles 9, 11
fox hunting 81
Franks, Becca 178
freedom 9
'freedom of association' 188
'freedom of the press' 188
'freedom of speech'188
French Revolution 37
frogs 3–6, 12, 14–15, 240
Fuh, Divine 6–7
'fur babies' *see* dogs

Gagliano, Monica 178
gazelles 2121
Geneva Convention 211
George (octopus) 74, 77
Gilabert, Pablo 53
Gliese 103
God 41, 43, 103, 166
Godfrey-Smith, Peter 71, 75–76, 186
golden moles 100
the Good 114
Goodall, Jane 131
Gopashtami festival 167
gorillas 129–130, 242
  see also apes; baboons; bonobos; chimpanzees; orangutans
Government Accountability Project 30
GPS collars 162
Grandi, Francesca 10
'Great Binding Law of Peace' 177
'Great Chain of Being' 103, 233–234
Great Spirit 157
great white sharks 232
Greenberg, Jeff 258
grief 117–120
Griffin, Miriam 42
Groundwork for the Metaphysics of Morals (Kant) 39–40
group-living 257
Gruen, Lori 33, 64, 210, 214, 224–225, 230, 236, 261–263
Guite, Malcolm 172
Gwenevere (octopus) 74

H1N1 swine flu 256
Hamilton, Alexander 37
hamsters 232
Harris, Lasana T. 256
Harvey, G. 173
Haskell, David George 178, 243

Haudenosaunee confederacy 177
Hauskeller, M. 223
hawks 232
  see also birds
Hehemann, Lena 203–204
Helsinki Declaration 211
Hinduism 167–170
Hobbes, Thomas 36
Hodson, Graham 256–257
Hollenbach, David 38
Holloway, Kerri 10
Holocaust 13–14
Holy Cross churchyard 172
Homo sapiens 15
Hopkins, Gerald Manley 171
hornworms 113
Horowitz, Alexandra 64, 85
horsemint 113
horses 107–110, 151, 196, 219–222, 224–225
Horsthemke, Kai 136–137
How to Be Animal: What It Means to Be Human (Challenger) 252
Human Dignity (Kateb) 6
Humane Methods of Slaughter Act 28
humans
  distinctiveness 43
  equality 36
  exceptionalism 43, 137, 162, 234, 236
  nature relationships 161
  rights 51
  uniqueness 234
Hunt, Tom 107
hunting 76, 81, 97, 110, 133, 150, 153, 162
Hurn, Samantha 178
Hymenoptera world 113
hyposubjects on becoming human (Morton/Boyer) 234

Iglesias, Teresa 44
imago Dei 41–43, 166, 255

'indefinite morality' (Romanes) 80
India 145–152, 153–154nn.1–2
Ingold, Tim 223–224
'inscape' (Hopkins) 171
International Whaling Commission (IWC) 185
invertebrates 67, 69
Isa Upanishad 148
Isle Royale 162

Jagger, Mick 113
Jainism 167, 169
Japan 169
Jefferson, Thomas 37
Jewish people 253
Jimmy (pig) 117–121
Jiva (consciousness) 169
Jiva-himse 150
Johnson, Samuel 36
Journal of Comparative Psychology 73
Judaism 166
Justice for Animals: Our Collective Responsibility (Nussbaum) 177

Kabbalah mysteries 41
Kankan may basa Ram! 148
Kant, Immanuel
  approach to dignity 43, 50–53, 55, 58n.2, 86–87
  capacity for agency 34
  and Christine Korsgaard 109
  dignity contingent on rational acting 194
  introduction 7, 15–16
  moral exceptionalism of humans 23–24
  and non-instrumentalization 203
  notions of *Würde* 253–255
  platitude 39–41, 46nn.5–6
Kapembwa, Julius 126
karma 167
Kateb, George 6, 44, 52, 254

Katy (pig) 118–121
Kempers, Eva 177–178
Kent, Bonnie 41, 46n.10
Kibale National Park 129–130
Killmister, Suzy 24, 260–261
Kinomaagan (great teacher) 157
Kohn, Eduardo 224
koi-fish 229–230, 237
Kolbert, Elizabeth 235
Kootenai Nation 111
Korsgaard, Christine 109, 182
Krishna (Hindu deity) 167
Kurki, Visa 177–178, 263
Kymlicka, Will 49–50, 52, 84

labradors 101–102
  see also dogs
Lafayette, Marquis de 37
'Land Ethic' (Leopold) 160
'The Last Safe Habitat' (Perez) 179–180
Lawrence, D. H. 112
Lecture on Ethics (Kant) 7
Leo 99
leopards 153
Leopold, Aldo 103, 160, 162
Levertov, Denise 109, 112, 114
Leviathan (Hobbes) 36
Linnaeus, Carl 254
lions 108, 212
Lobb, Richard L. 29
Locke, John 254
Lu (horse) 107–109
Lusaka Animal Welfare Society (LAWS) 139–140

McCrudden, Christopher 42
McDonald Peak, Montana 111
Macklin, Ruth 8, 222–223
Magna Carta (1215) 37
magpies 182–183
  see also birds
Mahabharata 151
Ma'iingan 157

Malamud, Randy 214
Manaaji'idiwin (go easy on) 158–159
Mann, Janet 186
manta rays 232
'Maria' (example) 28
marine parks 213, 215
Marino, Lori 178
masturbation 7
Mather, Jennifer 73, 75–76
medical ethics 51
Menashi, Wilson 73–74
Mental Evolution in Man (Romanes) 79
metates 101
methylated spirit 135
Metz, Thaddeus 137–139
Mexican Constitution (1917) 37
Meyer, E. 222
Midgley, Mary 252
Milky Way 100
Mill, John Stuart 188
Miller, Lulu 233
Mission Mountains (Montana) 110–111
molluscs 69, 73, 80
Mongolia 162
Montgomery, Sy 63
Moon (horse) 219–222, 224
Moore, G. E. 258
moral agency 15–16
moral status 137–138
Morton, Timothy 234
Moscow Circus 84
Moss, Cynthia 186
moths 101
Motyl, Matt 257
multivariate statistical analysis methods 162
Mumme, P. Y. 151
Murdoch, Iris 64, 109–110
Murphy, Bill 74, 77
Mweshi, John 139

Nagel, Thomas 72, 172
Namib desert 100
Narayaniya 151
National Chicken Council 25, 29
Natural Horsemanship school 108
nature 149, 157
Nelson, Michael 127, 261
neurons 71, 75
'new dignitarians' (Kymlicka) 52
New England Aquarium 68, 73
Nike child labour factories 36
Noah (horse) 109–110
Non-human Rights Project 193
non-instrumentalization 203–204
Nordenfelt, Lennart 255
normativity 6, 23
North American Residential School system 161
North American Tribal Nations 158
Nuremburg Code 211
Nussbaum, Martha 24, 52–53, 177, 194–197, 204, 212, 224, 236, 259–261

Octavia (octopus) 78
Octopus Enrichment Handbook 73
Octopus: The Ocean's Intelligent Invertebrate (Mather/Anderson) 73
octopuses 68–77, 186
Ojibwa people 156–159, 162
Ojibwe philosophy 127
Olivelle, P. 148–149
On Liberty (Mill) 188
orangutans 129
  see also apes; baboons; bonobos; chimpanzees; gorillas
orcas 84, 213
Origin of Species (Darwin) 252
Orion 99
Orwell, George 170

Palaeozoic Era 232
Palsson, Gili 223–224
panentheism 148
panpsychism 169–170

Parelli, Pat 108
penguins 209
Perez, Craig Santos 177
Perpetual Peace (Kant) 39
personhood 194, 210
Pico della Mirandola, Giovanni 41
Pierce, Jessica 93
Pietrzykowski, Tomasz 251
pigs 117–120, 170–171, 188
Pinker, Steven 8
Pituitary Pars Intermedia Dysfunction (PPID) *see* equine Cushing's disease
poachers 152
'political participation' 188
Poole, Joyce 186–187
'Position Paper on the Control of Stray Dogs' (Zambia) 135
Poverty and Famines (Sen) 188
prana (prayer) 126–127, 147–153, 261
Prevention of Cruelty to Animals Act 1994 (Zambia) 135
Principia Ethica (Moore) 258
Pufendorf, Samuel 40, 46n.9, 253
Pyszczynski, Tom 258

quantum theory 170

Rabie-Boshoff, A. C. 166
rabies 135–136, 140
Rachels, James 7
Rapier, James 38
rats 240–242
ravens 167
   see also birds
Rayleigh waves 100
Redford, J. A. C. 172
Regan, Tom 135, 260
reincarnation 168
Reiss, Michael 127
religious bioconservatism 8
Rendell, Luke 186
Rich, Simon 5–6, 12
Rig Veda 167

Ritvo, Harriet 63
robins 209
   see also birds
Rodriguez, Philippe-Andre 11
Rolston, H. 151
Roma people 253
Romanes, George 79–81
Roschian concepts 209–210
Rosen, Michael 42
Rossello, Diego 54–55
Rousseau, Jean-Jacques 39, 46n.5
Rwanda war 36

Sahacara (co-foraging/moving) 152–153
St Francis of Assisi 170
Salish Nation 110–111
same-sex marriage rights 36
sanctuaries 215–216
sand-swimming snakes 100
scala naturae see 'Great Chain of Being'
Schachter, Oscar 43–44
Schweitzer, Albert 103
scorpions 97–104
Scorpius 99, 101
Seattle Aquarium 73
Second Vatican Council 38
Second World War 13, 36, 44, 252, 254
Semple, J. W. 40, 46n.7
Sen, Amartya 188
sentience 159–160, 183, 189n.2, 251–252
Sepia officinalis (cuttlefish) 72
sharks 233
   see also fish
Simba (dog) 129
similarity-argument 194
Sinti people 253
Sites of Special Scientific Interest (SSSI's) 220
slavery 193, 254
Slicer, Deborah 64
slugs 67–68

Smuts, Barbara 178, 186, 236–237
'The Snake' (Lawrence) 112
social buffering 257
Solomon, Sheldon 258
Sophocles 43
SPCA 81
speciesism 132
squid 72
sraddha 148
Stanton, Lucy 38
Stuart Little (White) 5
'The Stupidity of Dignity' (Pinker) 8
'Subjects of a Life' (Regan) 260
Sufism 166
sweat bees 98
Switzerland 191, 202, 204–205
Systema naturae (Linnaeus) 254

Tanzania–Zambia railway 134
Tasioulas, John 52
Taylor, Ross 93
Taylor, S. 225
Thompson, William 38
Tiananmen Square massacre (1989) 36
tigers 152, 214
Tracie (dog) 101
Traditional Ecological Knowledge (TEK) 162
Truman (octopus) 70, 74
Truth, Sojouner 38
Two-Eyed Seeing 163

ubuntu (humanness) 126, 137, 139–140
Ukuteeka imbwa 139
umwelts 16
Under a White Sky: The Nature of the Future (Kolbert) 235
United Nations 36
Universal Declaration of Human Rights 36, 45n.1, 86–87

Upanishads 147, 170
Upper Great Lakes, United States 156
USDA 28–30
'Uyu muuntu!' 139

Vaes, Jeroen 257
Vaisnavas 151
Vedic beliefs 148, 169–170
Veterinary Association of Zambia 135
virtual constitution 185–186
Visions of Caliban (Goodall) 131
Vlastos, Gregory 204
Vrindaban, Uttar Pradesh 167

Waldron, Jeremy 24, 54–55, 58n.3, 204, 255
Walker, David 38
Warburton, Alexa 71
Washington University 72
wasps 112–114
Webb, Christine 178
'The weight of Glory' (Lewis) 172
Weil, Simone 44
Weimer Constitution (1919) 37
Wein, Tom 11
welfare 201–203, 206, 212, 220–221
Wells, Ida B. 38
whale sharks 232
whales 178, 185–186, 213
'What Is It Like to Be a Bat?' (Nagel) 72, 172
Wheeler, Anna 38
white colobus monkeys 131
White, E. B. 5
White, Thomas 186
Whitehead, Hal 186
Why Fish Don't Exist (Miller) 233
'wild dignity' (Gruen) 33, 64
Williams, Charles 172–173
Wise, Steven 193
wolves 157, 162

Wood, Alan 253
Woods Hole Marine Biological
    Laboratory 72
World Health Organisation 140
worldviews 161, 163

xenotransplants 263

Yellowstone National Park 162

Zambia 134–136, 139–140
Zeus 99
Zimmerman, F. 152
zoos 212–213, 215
Zuolo, Federico 50, 55–56, 259